JAPANESE AMERICANS

ETHNIC GROUPS IN AMERICAN LIFE SERIES

Milton M. Gordon, *editor*

JAPANESE

HARRY H. L. KITANO

University of California, Los Angeles

Second Edition

AMERICANS

The

Evolution

of a

Subculture

PRENTICE-HALL, INC., ENGLEWOOD CLIFFS, NEW JERSEY

Library of Congress Cataloging in Publication Data

KITANO, HARRY H. L. (date)
　　Japanese Americans.

　　(Prentice-Hall ethnic groups in American life
series)
　　Bibliography:　p. 215
　　Includes index.
　　1. Japanese Americans.　I. Title.
E184.J3K5　　　1976　　　301.45′19′56073　　　75–34034
ISBN　0–13–509430–5
ISBN　0–13–509422–4 pbk.

10　9　8　7　6　5　4　3　2　1

Printed in the United States of America

PRENTICE-HALL INTERNATIONAL, INC., *London*
PRENTICE-HALL OF AUSTRALIA, PTY. LTD., *Sydney*
PRENTICE-HALL OF CANADA, LTD., *Toronto*
PRENTICE-HALL OF INDIA PRIVATE LTD., *New Delhi*
PRENTICE-HALL OF JAPAN, INC., *Tokyo*
PRENTICE-HALL OF SOUTHEAST ASIA (PTE.) LTD., *Singapore*

*This book is dedicated
to the Japanese and Asians in America,
as well as to all others of whatever ancestry
who have shared similar experiences.
May we all participate in a better future.*

Contents

CHAPTER EIGHT

The Culture   *120*

CHAPTER NINE

Social Deviance   *143*

CHAPTER TEN

The Japanese in Hawaii   *164*

CHAPTER ELEVEN

Foreword

As the United States, with its racially and ethnically variegated population, moves through the 1970s, the myths of the melting pot and complete
assimilation recede farther and farther into the distance both in this
country and abroad. Contrary to the expectations and pronouncements
of many social scientists, industrialization and urbanization have not
reduced the salience of ethnicity in the modern world, nor is there sub-
stantial evidence that ethnicity as a critical issue subsides because it happens to exist within the borders of a particular social system: capitalist,
socialist, communist, or some mixture in between. The stubborn persis-
tence of the racial and ethnic factor as a source of ethnic communality,
and the conflict of ethnic collectivities as interest groups seeking by various means their (frequently previously withheld) fair share of material
and status rewards make it all the more imperative that the resources of
the sociologist, the political scientist, the historian, the psychologist, the
anthropologist, and other practitioners of the art and science of understanding human behavior be brought to bear on the problem. Such appli-
cation should produce both the theoretical knowledge and the practical
measures that would help create a state of affairs where the positive potentialities of ethnic pluralism can be effectively realized while the negative results of unlimited ethnic conflict can be minimized and kept within
tolerable bounds.

Thus, the ethnic problem before the American people today is what
shape the new pluralism shall take. Is it to be cultural pluralism, with
its emphasis on a broad kaleidoscope of ethnic patterns and peoples
reaching to the point of conscious promotion of sustained bilingualism?
Or is structural pluralism, with its social separation in primary group
relationships, to be the dominant mode, with differing cultural heritages
to be recognized and maintained by symbolic appropriations and reinterpretations of one's ethnic past? What form and resolution will the
political contests take brought on by the black revolt and newly-empha-
sized ethnic consciousness and sense of pride among Mexican Americans,
Puerto Rican Americans, American Indians, and Oriental Americans, together with the probably consequent revival of collective consciousness

among the traditional white ethnic groups of European ancestral origin?

The issues around which this new pluralism will form have such names as affirmative action, de jure and de facto segregation, school busing to achieve racial integration, cultural nationalism, community control of local institutions, and breakdown of racial and ethnic barriers to housing, ethnic voting, and confrontation politics; and they are all intimately related to the overriding question of how present-day America deals with the problems of inflation, unemployment, and recession, which fall with particularly heavy impact on its racial minorities.

In order to make the best decisions on these issues, the American of the 1970s needs to be well informed on the history, contributions, and current problems of the racial and ethnic groups that make up the American people, and how the issues highlighted above are affected by, and in turn affect, the nature of the emerging pluralism. The books in this series are designed to provide this information in a scholarly, yet highly accessible, manner. Each book on a particular ethnic group (and we include the white Protestants as such a sociologically definable entity) is written by an expert in the field of intergroup relations and the social life of the group about which he writes. In many cases the author derives ethnically himself or herself from that group. I hope that the publication of this series will aid substantially in the process of enabling Americans to understand more fully what it means to live in a multiethnic society and, concomitantly, what we must do in the future to eliminate the corrosive and devastating phenomena of prejudice and discrimination and to ensure that a pluralistic society can at the same time fulfill its promised destiny of being truly "one nation indivisible."

MILTON M. GORDON

Preface

In the preface to the first edition of *Japanese Americans* I wrote:

> America likes success stories—the bigger, the better. Therefore, America should enjoy the story of the Japanese in the United States, unfinished as it is, for it is a story of success Japanese-American style. It has all of the elements of a melodrama: the Japanese (the hero) is faced with initial suspicion, mistrust, and hatred by the United States (the heroine). Starting from this background of hostility and discrimination, the hero begins the excruciating process of winning the hand of the heroine. He pulls himself up by the bootstraps, suffers rebuffs and rejection, and finally gains the grudging respect and admiration of the heroine. Acceptance, romance, and marriage may be in the offing.

We now have a chance to look back and see if the hypothesized process has continued. Has there been increasing acceptance, and has the pattern of acculturation been a smooth one? Has a newer, younger generation changed some of the goals and introduced different behavioral styles? What have been the consequences of a steady stream of new Japanese immigrants and of the continuing racial ferment of the 1970s? Have the twists and turns of United States policy toward Japan "shocked" the lives of Japanese Americans? For the Japanese in America do not live in isolation, and events beyond their ability to predict or control are critical in their adaptation.

We believe that Japanese-American accomplishments are a logical outcome of Japanese-American culture and institutions, but, more importantly, of the energy and spirit of the hundreds of thousands of Japanese, some prominent figures now, and many more unsung, who have made places for themselves in the American society.

Nevertheless, the Japanese American, like any American, is faced with ever-changing problems and with ever-changing conditions in an ever-changing world. For measures of success not only are temporary, but ultimately are based on value judgments, so that what is success, based on one criterion, may not be so, based on another. As I have indicated, the label "good" or "successful" is relative: what is viewed as positive from a majority group perspective may be negative if taken from a minority position. For example, the majority group position at one time defined a "good" Indian as a "dead one," and there is little doubt that the Indian perspective differed. Or, as we say,[1] in the area of race relations one is constantly challenged by value references—"a good adaptation, a successful ethnic group, a healthy personality, a functional culture and a conflict-free interaction."

Of even greater importance than the adaptation of a single group like the Japanese American are the questions raised by the problems of other ethnic groups as they attempt to participate in the American society. Conflict, violence, and chaos may be a legacy of man's interaction with other men, but, hopefully, such processes may be replaced by more humane and civilized types of interaction. Perhaps the major importance of this book is to present the experiences of one specific ethnic group as an illustration of a means of adapting to interethnic contact and conflict with a minimum of bloodshed and chaos.

However, I would like to emphasize that the purpose of the presentation is not to "show other groups how it is done," nor to sit back smugly and prescribe to others to "do it the way the Japanese did." For variables that explain the adaptation of a group are monumentally complex, and our presentation must barely scratch the surface. Since the publication of the first edition in 1969, the number of volumes dealing with the Japanese American and other Asian Americans has visibly grown. I estimate that writings about the Japanese American in the last five years has surpassed the total number of such publications over the previous fifty years. I will refer to these new volumes at appropriate places in the manuscript.

Major thanks for editing the original manuscript belong to Diane Johnson and Professor Milton Gordon. Valuable research assistance was provided by George Kagiwada, Tetsu Sugi, Mildred Silbar, and Marcia Winchester. The Japanese-American Research Project and Joe Grant Masaoka at UCLA were most generous in sharing their material. Professors Scott Miyakawa (Boston University), Roger Daniels (Suny, Fredonia), Frank Miyamoto (University of Washington), Mas Iwata (Biola), Robert Wilson (UCLA), Richard Kalish (Graduate Theological Union), and Abe Arkoff (Hawaii) were invaluable in giving of their time and information. Professor Dennis Ogawa and the Department of American Studies at the University of Hawaii were extremely helpful in the preparation of the new chapter on Hawaii. The typing was done by Nancy Zeiger and Carol Hansen.

---

[1] Harry H. L. Kitano, *Race Relations* (Englewood Cliffs, N.J.: Prentice-Hall, 1974), p. 7.

My deepest thanks go to all of my friends and relatives who provided much of the anecdotal, background, and experiential material that is invaluable when describing any group. Portions of the manuscript were completed with financial assistance from the National Institute of Mental Health through grants OM-476 and MH-11112.

HARRY H. L. KITANO

JAPANESE AMERICANS

Urashima Taro is the Japanese Rip Van Winkle. As a young lad he leaves on a long journey, and when at length he returns, he finds that everything has changed. His old friends are gone, and no one remembers him, although a few remain who have heard legends about him. Japanese Americans are fond of the story of Urashima Taro, and they like to tell it in modern dress. The young man leaves for his journey from America in 1942, at a time when the United States of America is at war with Japan, and West Coast Japanese, whether alien or native-born American citizens, have been herded into "War Relocation Centers" to face an almost hopeless future. Urashima Taro expects, on his return twenty-five years later, to find that his fellow Japanese have been deported en masse or confined like Indians to reservations, or that they have returned to the larger society at the bottom of the socioeconomic ladder, with all the symptoms of a "problem minority."

The Japanese in the United States

Instead, he rubs his eyes in disbelief, for he finds quite another situation. The Japanese are back in California and are also scattered throughout the United States. They appear prosperous, accepted, and successful. He reads the words of a sociologist:

> Barely more than twenty years after the end of the war-time camps, this is a minority that has risen above even prejudiced criticism. By any criterion of good citizenship that we choose, the Japanese Americans are better than any other group in our society, including native-born whites. They have established this remarkable record moreover, by their own almost totally unaided effort. Every attempt to hamper their progress resulted only in enhancing their determination to succeed. Even in a country whose patron saint is the Horatio Alger hero, there is no parallel to this success story.[1]

Common measures of success find the Japanese on the "right" side of the ledger. Both their income and educational levels are high. For example, in California, Japanese income is higher than that of any other group (e.g., Chinese, Filipino, black, Spanish surname) except white, and

---

[1]William Peterson, "Success Story: Japanese American Style," *New York Times Magazine*, January 9, 1966, p. 20.

the Japanese are the best educated of any group, although it is probable that if the white group were further separated, certain groups within it, notably the Jews, would equal and perhaps surpass the median educational level of the Japanese. On the other hand, the Japanese have among the lowest rates of crime, delinquency, and mental illness.

What accounts for this record? Can the lessons learned from the Japanese be applied to other minorities? Peterson continues:

> The Japanese Americans, in short, ought to be a central focus of social studies. Their experience converts our best sociological generalizations into partial truths at best; this is a laboratory case of an exception to test a rule. Conceivably in such a more intensive analysis, we might find a means of isolating some of the elements of this remarkable culture and grafting it onto plants that manifestly need the pride, the persistence and the success of our model minority.[2]

Such is the purpose of the present study. Certain elements of Japanese-American culture—its history, its institutions, and its operation—are far from obscure and yield themselves both to description and to analysis. Generalizations derived therefrom—for instance, about the function of the stable family—seem to confirm established sociopsychological premises. A study of the Japanese further documents the importance of group identity and community cohesion, and may provide possible rays of hope for other minority groups who are currently facing major problems in American society. However, it would go far beyond the purpose of this presentation to translate the experiences of the Japanese into rigid prescriptions for other groups.

STRATEGY OF ADAPTATION

Different immigrant groups have employed different strategies of adaptation in the move toward acculturation. Sherman, for example, attributes Jewish survival in America to their techniques of accommodation.[3] The large-scale resistance with which they were faced precluded assimilation on the one hand, while other factors inherent in the group prevented dissolution and disintegration. Other groups, such as blacks, have at times chosen strategies of confrontation, while various white Protestant groups have simply integrated. And, although each of these strategies differs in effectiveness, depending on the time and place, the Japanese strategy has apparently been consistent from the start.

What is this strategy? The Japanese themselves like to compare it

---

[2]Ibid.

[3]Bezalel Sherman, *The Jew Within American Society* (Detroit: Wayne State University Press, 1961).

to a small stream; like a stream they have followed the contours of the land, followed the lines of least resistance, avoided direct confrontation, and developed at their own pace, always shaped by the external realities of the larger society. It is basically a strategy of accommodation.

What, then, are the characteristics of the Japanese group that have permitted this mode of development? It is easy to seize on the customary generalizations; one often believes, for example, that the Japanese have "an inherent capacity to adapt to host cultures." But if this were always so, it would be difficult to explain their behavior in the South Pacific, in the Philippines, and in Asia, where they imposed Japanese culture on the host culture in a manner similar to that of European colonial powers in other parts of the world. The variables affecting Japanese acculturative behavior are clearly complex and beyond any simple generalization. Moreover, one is led into the problem of defining successful acculturation, or integration, or assimilation. If one holds that a group is successful when it is fully integrated—that is, scattered throughout the country, and equally distributed at various levels of income, housing, employment, marriage, and education—then one can say that Japanese Americans are not completely successful. Or, if the criterion of success is total assimilation, where physical and cultural differences have largely disappeared, the Japanese Americans are certainly not successful.

If, however, successful adaptation to the larger society consists mainly in acculturation, measured by the ability of a group to share and follow the values, goals, and expected behaviors of the majority, then the Japanese-American group has been very successful. Japanese-American values, skills, attitudes, and behavior apparently do not differ markedly from those of the average American. "Scratch a Japanese American and find a white Anglo-Saxon Protestant" is a generally accurate statement.

This distinction among the three terms *acculturation, integration,* and *assimilation* is a common and useful one, but it suggests several further questions. Should the adaptation of any group emphasize only one, or a combination, of these processes? Which combinations work best for what groups? The history of our country shows that different groups have indeed employed different strategies at different times in the past, but social scientists have never agreed on an "ideal" sequence. And perhaps agreement is not possible until it becomes possible to agree on the real goals of adaptation. Is total assimilation necessary? Are certain forms of cultural pluralism perhaps more realistic and desirable?

It may be possible to agree, however, that the adaptive process that minimizes problem behavior is perhaps one important criterion determining desirability for any group. Although the sequence of the process may differ with different groups, the sequence that the Japanese-American group has employed has certainly avoided many undesirable social consequences. In general, the Japanese-American pattern has included acculturation and integration, and probably will finally include assimilation. This developmental pattern may be contrasted with attempts by other groups to initiate the adaptive process at the integration phase, a strategy that often results in violence and reaction, but that may also result in quicker assimilation.

It may well be, of course, that other sequences may be more rapid than that generally followed by Japanese Americans. But our impression of those Japanese subgroups that have deviated from the regular pattern has been that they have encountered many social problems. Japanese war brides are the most visible example of this. They have both integrated and assimilated before being acculturated, and many show symptoms of problem behavior. On the other hand, those war brides who have succeeded often seem more advanced in their "Americanization" than their American-born peers. Each path involves risks and consequences.

The Gordon Model of Acculturation and Assimilation

In an attempt to provide some order to questions of acculturation and assimilation, Gordon furnishes a model that analyzes some of the factors that influence this process.[4] The four principal variables are: ethnic group, social class, rural or urban residence, and geographical location. There are, in addition, two sets of stratification structures—social status gained largely through economic and/or political power, and the race-nationality-religion structures. From the interaction of these variables, one can attempt to predict such behavior as social participation, cultural behavior, and group identity.

For example, the subsociety developed from the interaction between ethnicity and social class (Gordon's term *ethclass*), is illustrated by the upper-class white Anglo-Saxon Protestant (WASP), or the lower-class white Irish Catholic, or the middle-class black Protestant, and so on. One can further analyze these groups in terms of geographical location—the New York City WASP as contrasted to the Des Moines, Iowa, WASP, and from such analysis one can often predict friendship, dating, and marital patterns, certain values and beliefs, and even broad styles of life. Gordon's model has relevance for the Japanese. To ethnicity and social class—the ethclass—we propose to add a third variable, generation, so that the basic framework for analyzing the Japanese group is *eth-gen-class*.

Generation is especially relevant when discussing the Japanese. Not only do they use the generational reference to provide a convenient term

---

[4]Milton M. Gordon, *Assimilation in American Life* (New York: Oxford University Press, 1964).

for classification—they also use it to refer to character types and behavior. For example, the Japanese have a special terminology for each genera-. tion: *Issei* refers to the first-generation immigrant born in Japan; *Nisei* refers to the second generation, born in the United States to Issei parents; and *Sansei* to the third generation, born in the United States to Nisei parents. Further, the phrase "Oh, he's an Issei" is supposed to convey to the listener an adequate explanation of certain types of behavior, although the broadness of its use may often seem confusing to the outsider.[5]

Today, however, the generational terms may be less meaningful as newer generations are born (the *Yonsei*, or fourth generation) and new *Issei* arrive from Japan. The term *Nikkei*, which includes all of the generations, may become more appropriate (the term *Nisei* has also been used in this fashion). Size and area of settlement, both important variables in affecting Japanese-American acculturation, will be considered independently.

Eth-gen-class terms have overlapping functions. Each refers to an identity: an ethnic identity—"I am Japanese"; a generational identity—"I am an Issei (first generation)"; and a social-class identity—"I am middle-class." And each refers to a particular social structure or network of social institutions: an ethnic structure—the Japanese community; a generational structure—the Sansei teen-age group; and a social-class structure —the country club set. Finally, each team relates to a "culture," or set of values and preferred behaviors: the ethnic or Japanese culture; the generational or age-related culture; and the social-class culture. Thus, the variables of identity, social structure, and culture interact with those of eth-gen-class.

Ethnicity, the most clearly defined, is structurally separate, since it is generally restricted to its own members of whatever class. Whether a person is a professional, a laborer, or a gardener, and whether he is Issei, Nisei, or Sansei, he is a Japanese.

The generation and class variables are horizontal in that they cut across ethnic lines and provide a theoretical link with similar segments of the larger American society. A Sansei teen-ager may have more values and feelings in common with WASP teen-agers than with older Japanese. A Nisei professional man may identify more closely with others in his professional group than with the Japanese gardener.

By looking at the interaction among these three variables, it may be possible to analyze Japanese behavior more precisely than would be possible by using these variables independently. The first-generation Bud-

---

[5]Stanford Lyman, "Higher Education and Cultural Diversity," workshop presentation given at the Annual Program of the Western College Association, San Diego, California, March 10, 1967.

dhist gardener with a sixth-grade education may be differentiated from a second-generation Protestant, college-educated professional in regard to ethnic identity, social participation, and cultural behavior. And these differences can in turn be related to acculturation, integration, and assimilation.

Where Other Groups Are

One way of understanding the Japanese stage of acculturation and assimilation is to compare the Japanese with selected groups. Gordon hypothetically charts the assimilation of four groups in the United States—the black, the Jew, the Catholic, and the Puerto Rican—along his model of assimilation variables. We have added the Japanese (see Table 1).

According to the schema, only the Puerto Rican has not been culturally assimilated (acculturation), that is, has not taken on the values,

TABLE 1

GORDON'S PARADIGM OF ASSIMILATION APPLIED TO SELECTED
GROUPS IN THE UNITED STATES (Reference Group: American Middle Class)

		Type of Assimilation				
Group	Cultural	Structural	Marital	Identifica-tional	Attitude Recep-tional	Behavior Recep-tional
Blacks	Variation by class	No	No	No	No	No
Jews	Substan-tially yes	No	Sub-stan-tially no	No	No	No
Catholics (Excluding Black & Spanish-speaking)	Substan-tially yes	Partly (by area)	Partly	No	Partly	Mostly
Puerto Ricans	Mostly no	No	No	No	No	No
Japanese	Variation by generation & social class; substantially yes	Partly	Partly	Partly	No	No

From *Assimilation in American Life: The Role of Race, Religion, and National Origins*, by Milton M. Gordon. Copyright © 1964 by Oxford University Press, Inc. Reprinted by permission.

skills, and behaviors of the host, middle-class American society. Certain segments of other groups, such as the lower-class black and the Japanese Issei (first generation) immigrant, are also in this position. In general, none of the groups has gone far beyond acculturation—that is, very few are found in the social cliques of the WASP society, and the majority of them still face varying degrees of discrimination and prejudice.

In the Gordon model, the critical variable for full-scale assimilation is structural assimilation, which means entrance into the clubs, cliques, and institutions of the host society. As Gordon says:

> If children of different ethnic backgrounds belong to the same play-group, later the same adolescent cliques, and at college the same fraternities and sororities; if the parents belong to the same country club and invite each other to their homes for dinner; it is completely unrealistic not to expect these children, now grown, to love and to marry each other, blithely oblivious to previous ethnic extraction. Communal leaders of religious and nationality groups that desire to maintain their ethnic identity are aware of this connection, which is one reason for the proliferation of youth groups, adult clubs, and communal institutions which tend to confine their members in their primary relationships safely within the ethnic fold.[6]

The almost inevitable byproduct of structural assimilation is marital assimilation, which, if complete, means that the minority group begins to lose its ethnic identity. We then have identificational assimilation. Prejudice (attitude receptional) and discrimination (behavior receptional) are no longer major problems, since all become members of the "in group." None of the groups listed has made complete progress in the assimilation areas, except in the area of acculturation.

From this point of view, Japanese assimilation is closest to that of the middle-class black and Jew. Structural separation has meant that structural assimilation has been minimal. However, within the structure of his own ethnic group, the Japanese is highly acculturated to American models, especially the newer generations, and he has achieved "success" in a number of previously mentioned areas. Unlike the American Indian, whose geographical isolation has largely prevented acculturation, and unlike the lower-class black, for whom the lack of educational and occupational opportunities has often meant a lower-class status, the majority of the Japanese have taken on the ways of the American middle class.

This, of course, inevitably raises a question of values. What is so desirable about becoming a middle-class American? Rather than attempt to answer this question fully, we will instead concentrate on what has

---

[6]Gordon, *Assimilation in American Life*, p. 80.

happened, what is happening, and what is likely to happen to the Japanese group.

GENERAL BACKGROUND
OF THE JAPANESE GROUP

It will be useful here to summarize briefly the general background of the group. Although there is evidence of Japanese in the United States prior to 1890, the significant Japanese immigration occurred after this date. Japanese male laborers began coming to the West Coast from Hawaii and Japan in the 1890s, and the flow continued until 1924 and the passage of a national immigration bill.[7]

At first this population was generally homogeneous in terms of age (young), education (four to six years of schooling), sex (male), and general background, having originated in what may be thought of as rural Japan. These males were soon joined by Japanese females, again of somewhat homogeneous background, who immigrated for marital purposes.

However, even though we mention their relatively homogeneous backgrounds, the individuals in the group encompassed the full range of differences that can generally be found in all populations. The entire group was termed the Issei, or first generation.

Most Issei found employment as agricultural laborers or in small businesses, either working for other Japanese or establishing small shops of their own. In both the agricultural and small-business population there was a general tendency toward self-employment and interdependency with the ethnic group. The original Issei are a rapidly disappearing group, so that by another decade they will be a vanished generation. Even today the average age of the surviving pioneers is above seventy.

The children of the Issei, or Nisei, were generally born between 1910 and 1940, and by the 1970s their ages ranged from the thirties to the sixties. This group, influenced by their parents' attitudes toward education, availed themselves fully of American educational facilities and became much more "American" than their Issei parents. But opportunities for this group were still greatly restricted by prejudice and hostility from the majority, especially up through World War II.

At the outbreak of World War II, all Japanese Americans on the West Coast were evacuated from their homes and businesses and interned in relocation centers for the duration of the war. This evacuation had incalculable consequences, such as the destruction of the economic posi-

---

[7]Approximately 200,000 Japanese aliens were admitted to the United States from 1891 through 1924. From 1925 through 1942, the number of Japanese aliens leaving the United States was always larger than those entering. The Japanese immigrants from 1924 through 1942 were primarily temporary aliens arriving for business and governmental reasons.

tion of the group, the disruption of families, and loss of homes and businesses. Ironically, from it came certain advantages as well, especially in terms of upward mobility. Patterns of employment and cultural expectations among Nisei became, after the war, more congruent with their American background and less dependent on the economic sanctions of their Issei fathers.

The Sansei, or third generation, have in general been born since World War II, and by the 1970s were providing the bulk of the college-age and young-married generation. This population is almost totally acculturated, subject to certain distinctions that will be discussed more fully later.

The background of the Japanese-American group thus provides the social scientist with two convenient sets of categories. The first is generational, yielding three distinct, relatively homogeneous groups: Issei, Nisei, and Sansei. The second is chronological: the history of the group divides into four broad and influential periods—the immigration period (1890–1924), the prewar period (1924–1941), the wartime evacuation period (1941–1945), and the postwar period (1945 to the present). Because environmental and behavioral patterns have differed widely between each generation and during each historical period, these divisions are meaningful as well as convenient to any analysis of the group.

Generalizations about Hawaii present certain problems. For example, although we will discuss the lack of political activity among Japanese Americans on the mainland, the State of Hawaii is represented in the U.S. Senate and the House of Representatives by Japanese Americans. One of the most obvious differences between the areas relates to majority–minority group proportions—in Hawaii, the Japanese are one of the largest minority groups. Therefore, they can and do support political candidates. The Japanese in Hawaii also retain more "Japanese ways" than their mainland counterparts because of a larger and more cohesive ethnic culture. Nevertheless, sociopsychological data (Chapters 7, 8, 9, and 11) indicate the essential similarity of the Japanese, whether in Hawaii or on the mainland. The Hawaiians will be discussed in Chapter 10.

It must be added, however, that the convenient division of the present Japanese population into relatively homogeneous Issei, Nisei, and Sansei groups is complicated by the presence of the Kibei (Japanese-educated Nisei);[8] the postwar influx of Japanese war brides; the arrival of many new Issei immigrants beginning in the 1950s; the entrance of

[8]The Kibei are technically Nisei—that is, born of Issei parents in the United States. The basic difference lies in their upbringing—these children were sent back to Japan at an early age for socialization and schooling. A fuller discussion of this group is presented in Chapter 9.

Japanese businessmen, tourists, and sojourning students; and a continuous stream of Japanese from Hawaii, who are not necessarily homogeneous in education, generation, or other characteristics.

At the time of the 1970 census, most of the population of 588,324 Japanese were living in the Western United States. Hawaii is the state with the largest number—217,175 (169,025 in the Honolulu metropolitan statistical area); California is a close second with 213,277 (104,994 in the Los Angeles-Long Beach statistical area; 33,587 in the San Francisco-Oakland statistical area); followed by Washington with 20,188 (14,079 in the Seattle-Everett statistical area); New York with 19,794 (16,630 in the New York statistical area); and Illinois with 17,645 (15,732 in the Chicago statistical area).[9]

There is still a paucity of empirical studies on the Japanese in the United States. The vast majority of studies are based on impressionistic and experiential evidence. Much of our empirical data will be drawn from studies of the Japanese in the Los Angeles area. The generalizations made from this sample will be generally applicable to Japanese groups elsewhere, subject to variations according to geography and community size.

[9]A more complete statistical picture of the Japanese is in the Appendix.

The early history of Japanese people in America was, as in the case of many immigrant groups, beset with hardship, poverty, and discrimination. The conditions with which they were faced were so adverse that one is led, first of all, to inquire into any special conditions in the Japanese background of these people, in the hope of seeing there some special advantages or characteristics that enabled them to remain in America, to endure, and ultimately to succeed here.

Although successful adaptation is always subject to individual variations in intelligence, energy, and luck, the Japanese group had relatively homogeneous origins. Lanman describes Japan in the late nineteenth century as divided into four relatively rigid social classes: the warrior, or samurai, upper class;[1] a middle agricultural class; a group composed of mechanics and artists; and finally, the merchant, or lowest class. Below these was a small group of untouchables—individuals who performed various undesirable tasks, such as animal slaughter. As in many other agricultural societies, the peasant or farm laborer was more likely to be considered in the productive middle agricultural class, rather than the lowest class. Each class had hereditary castelike characteristics, and it was difficult to move from one to another.

Up to
World
War II

The great majority of Japanese coming to America for the purpose of settlement were from the farming class; that is, although many came from individually poor families, they were from a respectable class of people who set much store by the ownership of land. Most of these immigrants came from the southern prefectures of Hiroshima, Kumamoto, Wakayama, Fukuoka, and Yamaguchi. Strong, in his study of the Nisei, reports that the majority of the Issei had the equivalent of an eighth-grade education and were drawn from an ambitious, intelligent middle class.[2] Although there are difficulties in translating both education and social class to the American model, it appears that, in Japanese terms,

[1]Charles Lanman, *The Japanese in America* (London: Longmans, Green, Reader and Dyer, 1872). Although Lanman mentions just the four classes, it is assumed that the nobility remained as a ruling class.

[2]Edward K. Strong, Jr., *The Second Generation Japanese Problem* (Stanford, Calif.: Stanford University Press, 1934).

these immigrants represented an educated, middle-class population. There was also a selective factor in their early migration, since the Japanese immigrant was thought of as a representative to the country abroad so that there was governmental concern about who was to leave.[3] Most significantly, they were all products of a culture that itself was undergoing vast social changes from a feudal system toward urbanization and industrialization. And, finally, Japan had certain national fiscal systems—banking, savings plans—as well as compulsory education, practices that matched those in America at the turn of the century.

EARLY RELATIONS

The earliest relations of America and Japan were based on mutual respect and an awareness of these similarities. A peace treaty concluded in 1854 read:

> There shall be a perfect, permanent and universal peace, and a sincere and cordial amity between the United States of America on one part, and the Empire of Japan on the other, and between their people respectively, without exception of persons and places.[4]

For several decades after the treaty, cordiality and friendship prevailed. When the first Japanese ambassadors arrived in San Francisco in 1872, they were greeted with enthusiasm and goodwill. Fashionable ladies flocked to admire the ceremonial robes of the visitors and entertained them endlessly at lavish dinners and dances. Newspapers praised the Japanese as products of an intelligent nation and prescribed that "no impediment nor difficulty, either social, moral, political or religious, be placed in the way of her progress." It was a period of respect, of curiosity, of kindness, and of little fear of the rising Asiatic power. Part of the reason for this may have been that America had opened the door to Japan. Admiral Perry's black gunboats on their visit to Japan in 1853 had permanently changed the Japanese way of life. It was therefore natural that many Japanese looked to the United States for the knowledge and technology that might help them to become a modern nation, and it was to the United States that many young Japanese came for early education and training.[5]

The majority of the first Japanese who came were from the nobility,

---

[3]Yuji Ichioka et al., *A Buried Past: Annotated Bibliography* (Berkeley and Los Angeles: University of California Press, 1974).

[4]Lanman, *The Japanese in America*, p. 24.

[5]Many nations have influenced the Japanese. China and Korea were the most important; influential European nations have included the Netherlands, Portugal, England, France, and Germany.

and most of them attended the schools and universities along the Eastern seaboard. These constituted an industrious, studious, and shy group. An excerpt of a letter from one of them to his father illustrates one attitude toward American life:

> I am over 21 years old, but mentally a boy. After I have studied for 5 or 6 years longer, I may be fitted for parties, for drinking and smoking and dancing. . . . I do not think these are the accomplishments in which my country is anxious to have me successful.[6]

Census figures placed the number of Japanese in the United States by 1880 at 148 (see Table E in the Appendix). However, most of these were students who would eventually be returning to Japan. Nevertheless, the initial contact of some Americans along the Eastern seaboard with Japanese who represented the nobility and upper classes may have been important in shaping the positive experiences of the Japanese who later settled in this area.

The Lost Colony

A few Japanese settled in California during this period. Of historical interest is the Lost Colony of Wakamatsu, poignantly evoked today by a grave on Gold Hill, north of Sacramento, California. Here one can still make out the words:

> In Memory of Okei.
> Died in 1871.
> Age 19 years.
> A Japanese girl.

As far as is known, Okei was the first Japanese woman to die in the United States. She was a member of the Wakamatsu Colony, one of the first Japanese pioneering parties that came here in 1869 for permanent settlement.[7] This group, about twenty-seven persons including samurai, was led by a European named Schnell, who had been a military advisor in Japan. The vast social changes beginning in the Meiji era had led to a changed role for the samurai as well as many other Japanese.[8] Schnell arrived in San Francisco in October, continued on past Sacra-

---

[6]Lanman, *The Japanese in America*, p. 71.

[7]Yasushi Inoue, "Wadatsumi," trans. Chizuko Lampman, *The East* 2, no. 4 (1966): 71–75. The story of Okei appears in this journal as a part of a serialized novel written about Japanese Americans. The facts about Okei and Schnell appear to be historically accurate as another account by Strong relates a similar story.

[8]The reign of Emperor Meiji from 1867 to 1912.

mento, and founded the ill-fated colony at Gold Hill.[9] The colonists hoped to plant mulberry (for possible silk worm production), tangerines, Koshu grapes, and tea, and therefore settled in an area where the climate appeared to be similar to that of Japan. However, they ran into a long drought, lost their crops, and eventually disbanded. There is little trace of this group after they scattered, except for reports that several remained in the United States, including Okei, who died a short time thereafter. Another note of historical interest was that one of the members of this colony, Masamizu Kuni, was perhaps the first Japanese to marry in California. He married a black woman, and although they reputedly had one child, little more is known about them.

The Wakamatsu Colony failed for some of the same reasons that the first English colonies in America failed. The colonists had done little preliminary investigation, they were unprepared, they were short of funds, there were internal disagreements, their crops failed, and they finally were threatened with starvation. In addition, there were no fellow countrymen to help them. If the colony had started twenty-five years later, when other Japanese and Japanese associations were established in other parts of California, it might have received necessary aid. Nevertheless, it was a notable venture. One can imagine the disbelief that the American pioneer, having struggled across the Sierras in his covered wagon, might have felt at seeing a samurai swagger down the main street of a little California town.

The lost colony had been an illegal emigration. In 1636 an edict was issued forbidding Japanese nationals to emigrate. Although the Japanese government discouraged emigration from that time on, by 1885 there was a general loosening of the restrictions. Soon after Japan abandoned major emigration restrictions, the United States, Great Britain, and South Africa instituted immigration restrictions.

From 1885 on, Japanese were allowed to leave their country. At about the same time, there was a great need for laborers in Hawaii. These and several other factors combined to expand the flow of Japanese emigration. Wages in Japan were low, the Japanese were familiar with seasonal work, and steamship lines could make large profits recruiting and transporting them to Hawaii and the mainland. In 1868 the Hawaiian monarchy had recruited plantation laborers through its representative in Tokyo. About 148 Japanese, 142 males and 6 females, believing Hawaii to be as far away as heaven, left Japan on this first organized emigration of Japanese labor. The venture was not entirely

[9]Further accounts of this party can be found in the *Sacramento Union*, December 30, 1870. The Japanese-American Research Project at UCLA has collected many of these early documents.

successful. Kimura describes the young men as "vagabonds, engaged in fighting, gambling or highway robbery," and few were accustomed to strenuous plantation labor.[10] But the United States was ultimately to profit from this early mistake, because the Japanese government, in recruiting subsequent immigrant labor, literally selected for size, strength, and willingness.

THE WRONG COUNTRY,
THE WRONG STATE, THE WRONG TIME

From 1885 on, thousands of young Japanese men came to the West Coast of the United States, from both Japan and Hawaii. The Japanese immigration could not have been more poorly timed. In the first place, these early migrants came to California just after the "Chinese problem" had been "successfully" solved. It should be recalled that the full-scale Chinese immigration occurred after the discovery of gold in California in 1849, and that as early as 1852 the governor of California advised that restrictions be placed against them. His reasons have a familiar ring—Chinese coolies lowered the standard of living, they were unassimilable, they were heathens, they came only to take American money, and, unless checked, they would eventually overrun the state.

Cases of violence against the Chinese were common. For example, there was a massacre in Los Angeles in 1871:

> The trouble originated when two police officers, seeking to break up a Tong war in the Chinese quarter, were seriously wounded, and a third member of the squad was killed outright by frenzied Chinamen. [sic] A mob of a thousand persons "armed with pistols, guns, knives and ropes," immediately marched into the Chinese section, seized victims without any attempt to discriminate between the innocent and guilty, overpowered the officers of the law who were seeking to disperse the crowd, and hanged at least 22 Chinamen [sic] before the evil business came to an end. Most of the lynchings took place on Commercial and New High Streets, in what was then the very heart of the business district; and though the mob was composed of the "scum and dregs" of the city, no serious attempt was ever made to bring the ring-leaders to justice.[11]

Another large-scale massacre was reported in Rock Springs, Wyoming, in 1885, when twenty-nine Chinese were murdered, their homes destroyed, and their belongings scattered. There were probably economic motives behind this riot, because the railroad-building had just been

[10]Yukio Kimura, "Psychological Aspects of Japanese Immigration," *Social Process in Hawaii* 6 (1940): 10–22.

[11]R. G. Cleland, *A History of California, The American Period* (New York: Macmillan, 1922), p. 48.

finished, and unemployed Chinese were now competing with whites for jobs.

At any rate, the cry of "the Chinaman must go" became a rallying point, particularly in California. In 1879, 154,638 Californians voted for Chinese exclusion, and only 883 voted against it.[12] Law after law had been passed to harass the Chinese, even though most of this legislation was later deemed unconstitutional. In addition, since exclusion was outside the province of any individual state, California led the fight for national legislation against the Chinese. In two ways, then, Californians united to drive the Chinese out. First, they employed techniques of local harassment, hoping to make life intolerable for the Chinese, and second, they used every legal means at their disposal. The former technique, although often more dramatic and emotional, was never as effective as the latter, as the Japanese were to discover when they came into this almost unanimously anti-Oriental atmosphere a few years later. By the time of the Japanese immigration in the 1890s, the effective combination of harassment, massacre, restrictions, and local and national legislation had in effect "solved" the "Chinese problem." No more Chinese were coming in, and many were leaving. But between 1890 and 1900, 22,000 Japanese came to the American mainland.

Early Employment Patterns

Those Japanese who came to the United States mainland toward the end of the nineteenth century found employment as laborers on the railroads, in the canneries, in logging, and in the mining, meatpacking, and salt industries. They were desirable workers, because they were industrious, willing to work for low wages, and uncomplaining about working conditions—factors that earned them as much unpopularity with unions and employee groups as popularity with employers. But although they found work with ease in outlying areas, the Japanese immigrants had difficulty finding work in urban centers. Iwata concludes from reports of the United States Immigration Commission that they were unable to break into such higher-paying occupations as cigar, shoe, and clothing manufacture.[13] This may have resulted partly from earlier agitation against the Chinese, and certainly resulted from the competition of European immigrant labor. At any rate, external conditions—inability

---

[12]Sidney L. Gulick, *The American Japanese Problem* (New York: Charles Scribner's Sons, 1914), p. 35. It is also noteworthy that this election was of such interest that only 4000 registered voters (out of about 156,000) failed to vote. What other election has achieved a turnout of over 95 percent?

[13]Masakazu Iwata, "The Japanese Immigrants in California Agriculture," *Agricultural History* 36, no. 1 (1962): 25–37.

to find employment in cities and consequent location in outlying areas—prepared the way for the logical move toward agriculture.

THE JAPANESE AND AGRICULTURE

Most of the early immigrants came from an agricultural background, and their gravitation toward farming could almost be predicted. Iwata reports that by 1909 approximately 30,000 Japanese were engaged in various forms of farm labor, particularly hand labor. The group was ideally suited to this kind of work. Most had experience in and respect for farming. The pay was better and the jobs more certain than anything they could hope to find in the cities. Labor was in short supply, and the population, being male and unmarried, was able to conform to the seasonal demands of this type of occupation. Moreover, because the men lived and worked together, they were able to form labor gangs, represented by agents, for convenient negotiations with employers. Finally, agriculture did not require of them any initial cash investment or technical skill.

Nevertheless, at first some Japanese did not want to turn to farming. Some may have emigrated in the hope of leaving this type of occupation. Many remembered back-breaking labor, hard times, and poverty in Japan. For example, a successful Issei who today owns income-producing property has told us a typical story:

> I grew up in a farm in Japan. My father owned a fairly large piece of land, but it was heavily mortgaged. I remember how hard we all had to work, and I also remember the hard times. I saw little future in farm work; my older brothers would later run the farm, so at my first good chance, I went to work in Osaka. Later I came to California and worked as a laborer in all kinds of jobs. However, for the first five years I had to work in the farms, picking fruit, vegetables, and I saved some money. Then I came to live in the city permanently.[14]

In this statement we see the one factor that made the Japanese, otherwise so ideal—single, mobile, industrious—ultimately not the ideal farm laborer. They expected upward mobility, and most had no intention of remaining laborers permanently. In this, of course, they were like the typical American, but it was their ambition that drew suspicion from the white farming community. Many Californians did not accept the idea that nonwhites should share in the American dream. The feelings of the American community toward Japanese upward mobility are summarized in an editorial in the *San Francisco Chronicle* in 1910:

[14]Harry H. L. Kitano, private interviews with members of the Japanese community, 1964.

Had the Japanese laborer throttled his ambition to progress along the lines of American citizenship and industrial development, he probably would have attracted small attention of the public mind. Japanese ambition is to progress beyond mere servility to the plane of the better class of American workman and to own a home with him. The moment that this position is exercised, the Japanese ceases to be an ideal laborer.[15]

The Japanese quickly progressed from the level of ambitious laborers to that of economic competitors. Many began to work their own land, either as tenants or purchasers. The unity and cohesion of the group enabled them to pool money and resources. Past experiences in intensive farming, and the eventual development of a business structure that could handle all aspects of agriculture from the farming and harvesting to the retailing and wholesaling, made for rapid success in this area. Some, forced to farm the least desirable land, failed, but more, applying intensive farming methods to such crops as potatoes and rice, succeeded well enough to provide a serious degree of competition to native farmers.

The Alien Land Law

For this, the Japanese paid the penalty. In 1913 a California Alien Land Bill, the Webb-Heney Bill, was passed to provide that Japanese aliens might lease agricultural land for a maximum of three years only, and that lands already owned or leased could not be bequeathed. The object of this bill was clearly to drive the Japanese out of agriculture, and perhaps out of California. For example, Attorney General Webb stated in a speech in 1913:

> The fundamental basis of all legislation . . . has been, and is, race undesirability. It seeks to limit their presence by curtailing their privileges which they may enjoy here, for they will not come in large numbers and long abide with us if they may not acquire land. And it seeks to limit the numbers who will come by limiting the opportunities for their activity here when they arrive.[16]

But the effects of this law were more covert than overt, since by this time many Japanese were married and could place farm ownership in the names of their children and Caucasian friends. Nevertheless, it was a clear warning to the Japanese in California to go slow.

With the outbreak of World War I, the need for agricultural labor and products became great, and, in spite of the Alien Land Law, Japanese participation in agriculture entered its golden era. More than

[15]*San Francisco Chronicle*, 1910, n.d., n.p.
[16]Gulick, *The American Japanese Problem*, p. 189.

70,000 Japanese aliens entered the country between 1910 and 1920, and many settled on farms (see Table 2). Farm income reached a peak in 1920, when the Japanese in California produced land crops valued at $67 million.

But after the war, the release of war workers from city factories, the return of soldiers, and the "increasing danger" from a rising nationalistic Japan reignited agitation against the Japanese. Although they had developed much of the marginal land of California, they were accused of having secured the richest and most desirable farm land. Anti-Japanese forces, such as various farmer's associations, were able to secure passage of an amended Alien Land Law in 1920. This amended law now deprived the Japanese of the right to lease agricultural land; the act was designed to prevent the Issei from acting as guardians for the property of a native-born minor if the property could not be held legally by the alien himself. Although there was a question as to the constitutionality of an act that discriminated against American citizens (the Nisei), the spirit behind it was increasingly clear: the white farmer did not want yellow competition.

Now the Alien Land Law was effective in reducing the number of Japanese in agriculture. The trend of agricultural expansion reversed itself; Iwata reports that although the Japanese produced 12.3 percent of California's total farm products in 1921, by 1925 the percentages had dropped to 9.3.[17] Although its specific legal implications could be avoided in various ways, the Alien Land Law was symbolic of threats that the sensible Japanese farmer could not ignore. An alien, denied the right to citizenship, denied the right to own or lease land, and finding himself under continuous harassment, would think twice before investing hard-earned money in land that might be taken away from him at any

TABLE 2

NUMBER OF JAPANESE FARMS† IN CALIFORNIA BY DECADE, 1900–1940

	Years				
	1900	1910	1920	1930	1940
No. of Japanese farmers	39‡	1,816	5,152	3,956	5,135
Acreage	4,698	194,809	361,276	191,427	220,094

Adapted from Masakazu Iwata, "The Japanese Immigrants in California Agriculture," *Agricultural History* 36, no. 1 (1962): 25–37.
†Includes owned, leased, shared, and contract farms.
‡Total U.S., 37 in California.

[17]Iwata, "The Japanese Immigrants in California Agriculture," p. 7.

time. And in a capitalistic system where property rights are highly valued, the inability to own land is a tremendous handicap.

This probably explains the prevalence of tenancy and lease arrangements and the development of modes of farming that required quick growth crops and a minimum of capital investment. Truck farming proved highly suitable. Many of the difficulties inherent in tenant farming emerged—intensive cultivation of the land, low investment in property maintenance, and little participation in the community as a whole. But in spite of these disadvantages, opportunities for the Japanese in farming were still greater than in any other occupation. By 1941 they raised 42 percent of California's truck crops. Iwata declares that

> [The Japanese] raised 90% of the snap beans . . . spring and summer celery, peppers and strawberries; 50 to 90% of such crops as artichokes, cauliflower, cucumbers, spinach and tomatoes; and 25–50% of the asparagus, cantaloupes, and carrots, lettuce, onions and watermelons.[18]

Needless to say, part of the pressure for the wartime evacuation of the Japanese came from Caucasian vegetable growers and shippers. The wartime evacuation temporarily took all of the Japanese out of farming. Their losses from the evacuation can never be fully recompensed or measured.

URBAN OCCUPATIONS

The sociologist Miyamoto conducted one of the earliest research studies on the Japanese in the Seattle area. An interview from his study gives the flavor of early urban life:

> These Japanese came here with nothing but a blanket on their backs—they had no money, they didn't know any English, they didn't know how to do any of the things that Americans know, nor how the Americans made their living, so they had to start from the bottom. But, of course, the restaurant cooking of the day was relatively simple; all one had to know was how to fry an egg, toast bread and fry a steak. It was known as "fry cook." Mr. T was the first to get started in that line of business, and then other Japanese worked in his place, learned the trade, and started businesses of their own. They catered to the many laborers who lived down near the lower end of the city at the time, and they did very well, for the white men found these lunch counter services cheap and convenient.[19]

[18]Ibid., p. 9.

[19]Frank S. Miyamoto, "Social Solidarity Among the Japanese in Seattle," *University of Washington Publications in Social Sciences* 11, no. 2 (December 1939: 74.

Similar frontier conditions along the entire West Coast meant that newcomers could often launch trial-and-error businesses and enjoy a reasonable probability of success. There was indeed freedom of opportunity in the cities of the new West for those who knew how to take advantage of it, so that by 1924, next to agriculture, the major occupation of the Japanese was in small shops and businesses. Eating places, shops, cafes, laundries, cleaning establishments, and barber shops were common.

The success of these ventures was due to several factors—the expanding economy of the West and the traditional expectation of many Japanese to run their own businesses. Most important, probably, was the cohesion within the Japanese group. A Japanese businessman starting out would always have at least a few Japanese customers. This form of cooperation eventually led to more sophisticated forms, such as the pooling of capital for investment. People from the same *ken*, or Japanese state, often cooperated in various ways, and this was noticeable in particular trades. For example, Miyamoto writes that the first Japanese barber in Seattle was from Yamaguchi-ken. After he became established, he helped his friends from the same ken with training and money, so that, eventually, most of the Japanese barbers in Seattle were from Yamaguchi-ken. Other businesses showed similar patterns. It can be seen that the likelihood of success in a given occupation to some degree depended on the ken one had come from. An insurance salesman, for example, would almost have to come from a large, well-represented ken, because his success would often depend on purchases from his ken members. Conversely, those Issei from smaller kens would likely have to initiate enterprises that were less ethnically dependent. Ken was an important factor in the initial differentiation of occupation, experiences, and eventual acculturation.

The Japanese *tanomoshi* (the word in Japanese literally means "to rely on, or to depend on") is an example of the type of ethnic organization that helped early business ventures. In essence it was a pool of money, with credit, and in some cases resembled small-scale banking facilities. Miyamoto reports that a large prewar Issei hotel enterprise in Seattle (which later failed) financed a $90,000 transaction from a tanomoshi.

Group solidarity also meant group strength under negative conditions. There were many movements along the entire West Coast to boycott Japanese businesses, but, even at the height of anti-Japanese agitation, not one of these ever succeeded, principally because the Japanese themselves were able to present a united counterthreat of boycott against any Caucasian who refused to sell to or trade with them. Miyamoto reports that all attempts to boycott Japanese business in the Seattle area failed.

A closer examination of representative Japanese occupations demonstrates more clearly the type of Japanese-run business. Take, for example, the San Francisco cleaning establishment of Mr. S., an Issei.[20] He started his business as a family operation, but efficiency and ambition led to expansion, so that by the time of the wartime evacuation he had fifteen full-time employees and an annual gross income of several hundred thousand dollars. However, he continued to retain many typical Japanese employment practices. Half his employees were Issei and half Nisei, mostly males. The single ones among them lived nearby in a hotel run by another Japanese, and took their meals in the cleaning shop itself. Although their wages were low—about $60.00 a month—the workers were provided with such fringe benefits as job security, the company-paid room and board, and an atmosphere in general typical of a family relationship. The shop also sponsored a baseball team and provided interpreters and other kinds of assistance when necessary. It was a family, with the advantages and disadvantages of a family. It could mean economic exploitation and long hours, but it could also mean a sense of identity, belonging, security, and comfort. This combination was typical of the prewar Japanese enterprise, and, in fact, even though discontent was common, this paternalistic form of employment was about all the Japanese urban worker could find.

Nevertheless, the availability of these small businesses of the Japanese (and Chinese) was important, not only for their economic opportunities but also as symptomatic of community cohesion and the transmission of values. The lack of such structures for other groups, such as the blacks, was the subject of a study by the sociologist Light.[21]

The Small Business Economy

The importance of the interdependence of the small prewar Japanese businessmen cannot be overstressed. It was a particular advantage during the depression. Glazer describes how it was for the Jews:

> In the depression, the network of Jewish businesses meant jobs for Jewish young men and women—poor paying, but still jobs. The impoverished businessmen still needed a delivery boy, the small manufacturer needed someone to help with the upholstery, the linoleum retailer needed someone to help lay it. These were not only jobs, they also taught skills. In addition, the small businessmen had patronage—for salesmen, truck drivers, other businessmen. In most cases, the patronage stayed within the ethnic group. The Chinese restaurant uses Chinese laundries, gets its pro-

[20]Kitano, private interviews.
[21]Ivan Light, *Ethnic Enterprise in America* (Berkeley and Los Angeles: University of California Press, 1972).

visions from Chinese food suppliers, provides orders for Chinese noodle makers. The Jewish store owner gives a break to his relative who is trying to work up a living as a salesman. The Jewish liquor-store owner has a natural link to the Jewish liquor salesman. These jobs as salesmen are often the best the society offers to people without special skills and special education.[22]

Similarly, there were always low-paying jobs for Japanese. Issei and Nisei growing up in San Francisco during the 1930s remember some of these—soliciting ads for and delivering Japanese newspapers, working for the many small Japanese grocery stores, service stations, and restaurants, or in one of the more prestigious jobs along Grant Avenue in the Japanese dry goods stores. And there were always jobs as laborers in Japanese nurseries and summer employment in Japanese farms.

The distribution of jobs and labor in the Japanese community was labor intensive. Many of the small businesses called on members of the family, the extended family, the family friendship network, or the regional associations for labor, and employees often worked excessively long but loyal hours for low wages. The firms could thereby cut costs and remain competitive, but the narrow base of the paternalistic enterprise made expansion difficult. Bonacich describes the ethnically based small business as one important factor that is characteristic of a middleman minority (to be discussed further in the final chapter).[23] The large number of interdependent small business enterprises provided the backbone of the prewar Japanese-American urban economy.

Gardening

Next to agriculture and small business, contract gardening came to assume primary importance among occupations available to the Japanese. It was in many ways an ideal job—it demanded little capital and yet was individual. It was congruent with both the values and the skills of the Japanese on the one hand, and coincided with the growing need of the majority on the other. As estates, particularly in Los Angeles, Berkeley, and Oakland, grew in size, the need for gardeners increased, and because the usual stereotype of the Japanese included agricultural skill, they found it easy to be hired in this capacity. The job was a fairly stable one. For a specified monthly fee, a gardener would water, cut lawns and hedges, plant and care for flowers, dispose of trimmings, and provide maintenance and clean-up work. And because a gardener needed mate-

---

22Nathan Glazer and D. P. Moynihan, *Beyond the Melting Pot* (Cambridge: MIT and Harvard University Press, 1963), p. 31.

23Edna Bonacich, "A Theory of Middleman Minorities," *American Sociological Review* 38 (October 1973) : 583–94.

rials, fertilizers and plants, trucks, and, if he had many contracts, assistants and apprentices to help him, the gardening business was interdependent with other businesses. Most important, gardening involved autonomy. Because it was skilled and necessary, the gardener enjoyed higher status than a servant and had a certain freedom for decisionmaking and creativity. Today, Caucasian newcomers to the West Coast are frequently surprised at the independence of their Japanese gardeners, whom they must please to retain.

In 1928, there were more than 1300 gardeners listed in the Japanese Southern California Telephone and Business Directory. By 1940 there were 1650, and another 200 working as caretakers on estates. However, the greatest expansion in gardening came after the end of World War II and the Japanese evacuation.

OCCUPATIONS
AND ACCULTURATION

Some Japanese occupations aided in direct acculturation, and others were much less direct. Small shops and businesses that were primarily dependent on the ethnic group clientele, and the Japanese-owned businesses (*Kai-sha*) maintaining headquarters in Japan, were primarily nonacculturative in a direct sense. Other occupations required frequent but ritualistic contact with the American majority. In housework and gardening, for instance, Japanese met the larger group, but on a servant–employer basis, which often led to acculturative incongruities. One might have heard his gardener in the 1930s talking about "that man in the White House," and exhibiting other attitudes gained from his upper-class employer.

Some occupations exposed the Japanese to other lower-class populations, such as the poorer blacks, Filipinos, and Mexicans. These were primarily small businesses, such as restaurants and cleaning and pressing establishments. But the Japanese in general did not assimilate or identify with lower-class attitudes or styles of life with the same ease that they did with the middle and upper classes. For example, Nisei growing up in lower-class settings were rarely influenced by the values they met there. It was fairly common to see the little Nisei boy leave his father's restaurant in the slums to attend his Boy Scout meeting, or the daughter running to change her waitress uniform in time to make her ten o'clock class at the University of California. And the upward mobility of the Nisei usually received tacit recognition from the populations they served. A group of tough bachelors hanging around a lunch counter would clean up their talk in front of the Nisei daughter, who, as a result of this kind of sheltering, often remained extremely naïve.

In any case, the majority of Japanese occupations during the prewar period did not provide any systematic contact with the middle-class world on an equal basis. Both the frequency and the quality of the characteristic contacts did little to further direct acculturation, and, in fact, most Japanese occupations were in an immediate sense nonacculturative, in that they depended on the ethnic community. Nevertheless, all of these occupations helped to bridge the gap between ethnic and American institutions. The immigrant press, for instance, helped to maintain the ethnic system but provided information about America.

EARLY EDUCATION

In Japan, during the late 1890s, at least four years of education was compulsory, and another four years was optional. Most Issei, therefore, came to America with the equivalent of eight years of schooling, and, in addition, had an understanding of, familiarity with, and respect for the educational process. It was with these attitudes that they devoted themselves to the educational preparation of the Nisei generation in America.

Most of what the Issei did for the Nisei was beneficial. A little of it was not so helpful. For example, they instilled and reinforced the notion in their children that the teacher was always right and that the perfect pupil was passive, conforming, unquestioning—but competitive. Most Nisei children can still remember the stern admonitions of their parents to "obey your teacher, she is always right," no matter what the circumstances. They also remember how their parents always asked how, let us say, their neighbor Mr. Watanabe's children were doing in school. They almost always did obey their teachers, and they were almost always highly rewarded, at least in primary and secondary school. Whether the attitude of conformity was of much value at the advanced graduate levels is debatable. But it is no wonder that Caucasian teachers and administrators discussing Nisei children in the 1930s found much to praise in the "ideal Japanese child and his wonderful, cooperative parents." Sansei children today tend to follow this prescribed Japanese model, but older teachers can be heard increasingly often to remark that "the Japanese youngsters are acting more like everybody else all the time." This means, essentially, that they are talking back more and conforming less.

Studies of academic achievement indicate a similar trend. Bell, in a monograph on the Nisei written in the 1930s, shows that the Japanese-American student was equal to the Caucasian on all levels including IQ and achievement.[24] This finding could be considered rather unusual, since the Nisei were from homes that today would be considered cultur-

24Richard Bell, *Public School Education of Second Generation Japanese in California*, Education-Psychology Series, vol. 1, no. 3 (Stanford, Calif.: Stanford University Press, 1935).

ally deprived. Their parents did not speak English, and they had little available to them in the way of books, art, and conversation. Nor did they have feasible long-term occupational goals to work for. We asked a Nisei why he got good grades in school. He replied:

> You know, I can't think of a good reason—that is, a reason based on a long term goal. When I was sent to school I was expected to try my best and to get good grades—there was no question about this in my or my parents' mind. I guess it's just like my mother and father—if Mom ironed a shirt, she had to do best; if my Dad dug a ditch he had to do it just right. So did all of the other Nisei kids. I guess that's why so many of us were on the Honor Roll.[25]

There was much reinforcement for conformity. As is often the case in primary and secondary school, conformity was rewarded by good grades. And with good grades came approval from teachers, parents, and peers—and from an entire ethnic community. Every element of the student's society sanctioned conforming behavior and school success. There were very few who reinforced deviant behavior. Children of some other lower-class ethnic groups often defy school and fail to profit from it because their reference groups place little value on education. The Nisei child knew no one who did not think he should do well in school. On top of this, he was always being compared with other Japanese children.

There is evidence, however, that the Japanese definition of a good student is changing with the new generation. Earlier, all he had to do was to get good grades. Now there is more emphasis on the American model of the all-around person. A Japanese student still tries to get good grades, but he also values participation in social and athletic activities. This writer, studying the changing achievement patterns of Japanese high-school students in Los Angeles from 1940 to 1960, found a gradual decrease in grade point average (even though at its lowest, Japanese achievement is still high: the mean grade level was B) and a corresponding increase in social participation.[26]

The Japanese-Language School

The Issei encouraged the Nisei to work hard and do well in the American schools, but there was more they wanted their children to learn. Many, if not most, Nisei were sent after regular school hours or on Saturdays to Japanese-language school to learn the Japanese language and Jap-

[25]Kitano, private interviews.
[26]Harry H. L. Kitano, "Changing Achievement Patterns of the Japanese in the United States," *The Journal of Social Psychology* 58 (1962): 257–64.

anese ethics and values. The one this author attended, typical of many, ran a summer program as well as educational trips and outings, and even a summer camp—structural pluralism perfectly exemplified.

The schools were sponsored by groups within the ethnic community. Parents paid a modest fee—several dollars a month, and adjustment for those with more than one child—and teachers were recruited primarily from Japan.

Most Nisei who attended these schools, some for as long as ten years, are still unable to speak Japanese with any degree of fluency, and have probably forgotten the moral lessons. But there was an undoubted social value; many Nisei look back with nostalgia on the friends they made there. For example, a Nisei, commenting about his life in 1940, stated:

> I was 17 years old then, and now that I think back I guess I was always busy. First it was regular high school—then into the Japanese school. We walked both ways to save money so that means we had school from about 6:30 in the morning to 6:00 at night.
>
> I sometimes wished I didn't have to go to Japanese school. I would have liked to try out for some of the regular after-school activities with some of the *ha-ku-jins* [white people], but I never could. I guess I enjoyed Japanese school though—I never really learned Japanese, but I made most of my close friends there. Some of my friends had it rougher—they would help in a grocery store, or deliver newspapers on top of all the other things.
>
> Even if I did go to school just to meet my friends and fool around, my parents never minded it just as long as they knew I was going to Japanese school.[27]

Another value of Japanese-language school, not often mentioned, was its baby-sitting function. Many of the Japanese families were large, and busy parents were much relieved to have the children spend time in such approved surroundings out of the house. Japanese-language school kept the children off the streets, it kept them busy, and it may have been one of the factors responsible for the low rates of crime and delinquency among this group during the pre-World War II decade.

These schools were most popular from 1930 until the wartime evacuation. In 1939 an estimated 10,000 Los Angeles children were enrolled in them. In the mid-1960s there were only 2000 children in the Los Angeles Japanese-language schools, but since Japanese is now considered a useful language to know, there may be a further rise in enrollment in the future.

[27]Kitano, private interviews.

ANTI-JAPANESE LEGISLATION

The Issei, during this prewar period, belonged to a particular class of immigrants, usually Oriental, who were ineligible for permanent citizenship. Certain basic civil rights were denied them. Throughout the immigration period, and through World War II, this group was the target of important and effective discriminatory legislation.

For example, Gulick mentions a sample of proposed anti-Japanese legislation emanating from the California legislature in the 1910s, and containing such items as: forbidding Japanese the use or ownership of power engines; forbidding Japanese to employ white girls; making Japanese inheritance of land illegal and raising the standard fishing license fee of $10.00 per year to $100.00 for Orientals.

Other attacks on them were primarily emotional. For example, the following interview appeared in the *Sacramento Bee*, an influential California Valley newspaper, on May 1, 1910:

> Now the Jap is a wily an' a crafty individual—more so than the Chink . . . they try to buy in the neighborhoods where there are nothing but white folks.
> The Jap will always be an undesirable. They are lower in the scale of civilization than the whites and will never become our equals. They have no morals. Why, I have seen one Jap woman sleepin' with half a dozen Jap men. . . . Nobody trusts a Jap. . . .[28]

These stories gained wide credence among many Californians. But in addition to the ever-present emotional outbursts, the California fight against the Japanese was also a calculated political and legal one.[29] Perhaps previous experience with the Chinese had developed more sophisticated techniques. Crucial battles took place in the courts, and the most visible Japanese scars were from legal decisions. Perhaps these battles are not as dramatic as lynchings and murders, but court cases do affect many more people in the long run. It is perhaps amazing that in spite of the continuous verbal and printed attacks on the Japanese, there never were any equivalents to the Chinese massacres, or the "zoot-suit" riots against the Mexicans during World War II, or to the many lynchings of blacks in the South.

Legislation like the Alien Land Laws, previously mentioned, was of paramount importance. In general, these laws prohibited the Issei

[28]Gulick, *The American Japanese Problem*, p. 188.
[29]Roger Daniels, *The Politics of Prejudice* (Berkeley: University of California Press, 1962). Daniels' important monograph covers anti-Oriental prejudice in Calfiornia through 1924.

from owning land. There were numerous proposals to add the same restrictions to their American-born Nisei children, but these attempts were never successful.

School Discrimination

Another issue was raised in regard to school segregation, which, in view of the fact that public education has been a primary technique of Japanese advancement, is perhaps somewhat surprising. On October 11, 1906, the San Francisco School Board passed a resolution requiring all Japanese in the public schools to attend a segregated Oriental school in Chinatown. School segregation was already in effect for Chinese children, as the *Argonaut*, an early San Francisco newspaper, explained:

> California has a law which makes it obligatory on her school board to provide schoolhouses for children of Indian, Chinese, or Mongolian blood. That law still stands on the statute books. It is a duty of the school board to enforce it. They are enforcing it. They will continue to do so.[30]

There were several problems in dealing with the Japanese. The "Mongolian blood" category was always a cloudy issue, since it was difficult to define exactly which Orientals belonged, but even more important was the fact that the Japanese were backed by a first-class military power. As Gulick mentions, Japan was the first "nonwhite" nation to defeat a "white power," Russia, in a war.[31] For the previous 400 years, Europeans had a string of unbroken conquests in North and South America, in Australia, New Zealand, Africa, and in large parts of Asia. Therefore, local moves toward racial segregation were related to international affairs.

Although the number of excluded Japanese was small, President Theodore Roosevelt eventually intervened, and the San Francisco School Board was obliged to rescind its order.[32] This incident was of particular importance because it was the first one to attract national attention to the Japanese problem, and, of course, because it involved international relations. For example, the *San Francisco Call* of February 2, 1907, stated that

> Officially, the President has not exposed the reason behind his urgent request that San Francisco and California back down in the matter of the segregation of Japanese and white children in the public schools of this city. In the usual left-handed manner, known as semi-official, it is made

[30]*San Francisco Argonaut*, December 1, 1906, editorial, n.p.
[31]Gulick, *The American Japanese Problem*, p. 232.
[32]Daniels, *The Politics of Prejudice*, pp. 31–42.

to appear, however, that if the present request be not heeded, Japan will be angered to the point of resort to arms.[33]

Immigration Restrictions

Not all Californians favored Japanese exclusion. Farmers of large tracts, merchants in need of efficient labor, and large businesses with interests in Japan opposed exclusion. Americans outside of California generally remained neutral. But the more articulate exclusionist interests were united and agitated for a series of acts to restrict the immigration of Japanese. Familiar arguments about unassimilability, about unfair economic competition, and about personally reprehensible habits were used to justify such legislation.

One result of the anti-Japanese agitation was the "Gentleman's Agreement" of 1908—a move on the part of the United States and Japanese governments voluntarily to cut back Japanese immigration.[34] Primary responsibility for implementing the agreement was left with the Japanese government, and from 1908 to 1913 the number of Japanese laborers entering the United States, either directly from Japan or by way of Hawaii, Mexico, or Canada, diminished by a third. But, after 1913, a large number of brides and wives swelled the figures again. Some 5000 more Japanese entered the United States between 1917 and 1924.

By 1924 agitation against any immigration was such that a national law was passed restricting numbers of immigrants from various nations to fixed quotas. Japan was given no allotted number at all. A major purpose of the bill was to exclude Asiatic peoples, but the Japanese felt the personal nature of the legislation, since Chinese immigration had already been banned. The clause, "excluding aliens ineligible for citizenship" meant that Japanese were now in a select group that was denied both citizenship and immigration privileges.

The 1924 immigration act was a major victory for racists, nativists, and exclusionists, and there is little doubt that it was resented by an insulted and bewildered Japan, which, having understood that it was to become an important member of the family of nations, did not now understand this slap in the face. Some of the feelings of Japan are sum-

[33]*San Francisco Call*, February 2, 1907, editorial page.

[34]The "Gentleman's Agreement" was not a formal document but more of a voluntary arrangement between Japan and the United States. President Roosevelt issued a proclamation on March 14, 1907, ordering that Japanese and Koreans who had been issued passports for Mexico, Canada, or Hawaii be refused admission to the continental United States. In 1908 the "agreement" was that the Japanese government would discourage immigration of Japanese laborers to the United States; the same agreement would also cover Japanese-Canadian and Japanese-Mexican immigration. (Gulick, *The American Japanese Problem*.)

marized by Ichihashi, a historian at Stanford University.[35] Japan felt that discrimination based on race violated all principles of justice and fairness; that the implication that Japanese could not be assimilated was based on false assumptions; and that, furthermore, the United States had violated the "Gentleman's Agreement," one part of which specified that the United States would not adopt discriminatory legislation against Japan.

The American bill of 1924 undoubtedly strengthened the hands of the militarists and nationalists in Japan. Mosley, in writing about the life of Emperor Hirohito, mentions this act as one important link in the chain that eventually led to the Japanese attack on Pearl Harbor in 1941.[36] In any event, from 1924 until the passage of the McCarran-Walters Bill in 1952, Japanese immigration was for all intents and purposes completely stopped.

From the point of view of the exclusionists in America, however, the 1924 bill was only a partial solution, because by 1940 there were still more than 126,000 Japanese in the United States, and 157,000 more in the territory of Hawaii (see Table E in the Appendix). Attacks against all Japanese—the Issei aliens, ineligible for citizenship, and their children, the American-born Nisei—continued. The attack was based on race (unassimilable), on nationality (land-hungry, imperialist, warlike Japan), on styles of life (mysterious, un-American), on personal habits (sly, greedy, dishonest), on economic competition (undercut labor standards), on sexual conduct (breed like rabbits), and on whatever other grounds appealed to the emotions. In 1927 a Stanford University professor surveyed the files of a California newspaper and found that the Japanese rated 20,453 inches of newspaper space during a short period. The general attitude reflected in these items was "irritation verging on hostility." He also found a correlation between newspaper attacks on the Japanese and periods of election years and economic depression.[37]

The Japanese group, in short, was a target for stereotyping and scapegoating. They had made enemies among labor, management, liberals, conservatives, and could be discriminated against on the basis of race, nationality, religion, or all three at once.

[35]Yamato Ichihashi, *Japanese in the United States* (Stanford, Calif.: Stanford University Press, 1932), p. 313.

[36]Leonard Mosley, *Hirohito* (Englewood Cliffs, N.J.: Prentice-Hall, Inc., 1966).

[37]C. W. Reynolds, "Oriental-White Race Relations in Santa Clara County" (Ph.D. diss., Stanford University, 1927).

CHAPTER THREE

All men may not be created equal, but it is hoped that eventually they may all have equal opportunity. It is useless to hope, however—even if it were desirable—that men will ever behave predictably alike. Anyone knows this from observing the children of a single family; one is never like another. What is true in a family is of course true of an ethnic group, within which the range of behavior may be even wider than variations between groups. Still, stereotypes about group behavior linger on. A Japanese-American Cub Scout leader told us:

> If it's an all-Japanese [Sansei] group, I'll volunteer to lead them. You tell them to cut out the horsing around and they'll stop. But the hakujin [white] kids—that's another story. They just won't obey. For gosh sakes, this is even when their parents are around. The fathers just ignore their kids even when they're throwing paper cups, popcorn, soda pop and even rocks.[1]

Up to World War II: The Family

Similar comments about the well-behaved Japanese come from teachers, policemen, and interested citizens, although it is significant that these observations are diminishing. Since World War II, people seem to find that Japanese children "are acting more like their American counterparts all the time."

Nonetheless, like many stereotypes, this one about the "goodness" of the Japanese probably contains a grain of truth. The Japanese have been a markedly well-behaved group, and it is widely believed that this is due in large part to the Japanese family—to its structure, to its techniques of socialization and social control, and to its role in mediating the congruent and conflicting demands of the Japanese and American styles of life.

Unfortunately, when one tries to generalize about this Japanese family, he finds himself in immediate trouble. For example, Japanese families are described as being vertical in structure, with the father in a position of absolute authority. We were recently talking to a Nisei family that certainly seemed to conform to this pattern. Mr. Watanabe, in re-

[1] Harry H. L. Kitano, private interviews with members of the Japanese community, 1964.

32

sponse to a direct question, confirmed our impression that he was the boss. He assured us that he made all of the major decisions, did what he wanted, and that what he said was final. "Ah, the typical vertically structured Japanese family, ruled by the father." Then the telephone rang. Mr. Watanabe's friends wanted him to go fishing the next day. It was plain that he wanted badly to go, and just as plain that he was afraid to mention it to his wife. His hemming, hawing, and hesitation raised some question as to who really made the major decisions in his household.

FAMILY LIFE IN JAPAN

Although there appears to be an infinite variety of family interaction, it is possible to point to discernible, fairly constant patterns in the traditional Japanese family. It was characterized by strong solidarity, mutual helpfulness, and a patriarchal structure. Family themes included filial piety, respect for age and seniority, and a preference for male children. There were clear-cut patterns of deference, including the use of special words for addressing elders. Cohesion and harmony were valued above individual achievement. Recognition of the relationship between generations was insisted on. Hard work, duty, obligation, and responsibility were emphasized.

One of the most important factors in Japanese family life was the ancestral clan, or house, and its name. In practice, the house was similar to an extended family. Amano, drawing from various Japanese writers, analyzes the difference between the house and the family:

> 1. A family could become an independent unit but could not discontinue its relationship with the house.
> 2. Because of the importance of the continuation of the house, and because the male was considered to be the only heir to the house, the father–son relationship took precedence over the husband–wife relationship.
> 3. The economic basis of the house was the total income and wealth of all its members.
> 4. The needs of the house preceded the right of any of its individual members.[2]

The house was itself a social entity and formed the basis for interaction with the larger social structure. Status, name, lineage, and customs were attached to the house, and this culture was passed from one generation to the next. The behavior of the families making up the house and the importance of generations to these structures can easily be seen.

---

[2]Matsukichi Amano, "A Study of Employment Patterns and a Measurement of Employee Attitudes in Japanese Firms in Los Angeles" (Ph.D. diss., University of California, Los Angeles, 1966), p. 10.

Marriage was a family affair, usually arranged through the offices of a "go-between." Blood, family, and ancestry were important enough so that surplus males representing one family name, when marrying into an all-female family, would often take on the female family name so that the latter name could be continued (*yoshi*). The go-between, in arranging a marriage, would be careful to analyze family lineages to be sure they were free of criminals, the tubercular, and those of inferior social status. Once established, a family and the house were nearly indissoluble units. The solidarity of the Japanese family and the house, and their ability to provide a stable environment for their members, is widely credited with having prevented widespread disruption of Japanese society when Japan abruptly shifted from a preindustrial to an industrialized urban economy.

Although there is little published data in English about the Japanese family during the period that the Issei were growing up in Japan, recent scholarship by Nakane[3] describes a Japanese social structure that is familiar to Japanese Americans. We have used her framework to make the following generalizations about the early social structure that was brought to America by the Issei.[4]

1. Japanese membership depends more on the situation than on individual qualifications. For example, in Japan an individual refers to the company that employs him ("I work for Mitsubishi") rather than to his position (secretary, engineer). Thus the Japanese system encourages a vertical orientation (identification with the family, the company) rather than a horizontal one (identification with a profession, a peer group).

The situational orientation can help to explain a relatively common prescription among the Issei—that the lives and future of their Nisei children be intimately related to the new situation and the new country, so that although the Issei themselves could remain Japanese, the Nisei should be encouraged to become Americans. However, other Issei maintained a "sojourner's orientation," so that retaining Japanese ways and returning home were high priorities. Then there were the realistic problems of racism and discrimination, which affected any long-range perception of the future. Issei reinforced the group membership of their children in terms of family ("I am a member of the Watanabe family") and their nationality ("I am a Japanese American"). The duality of nationality (in current usage it would be an ethnic identity) was a point of friction in the early days, and was often used by jingoists and nativists (who

[3]Chie Nakane, *Japanese Society* (Berkeley and Los Angeles: University of California Press, 1970).

[4]Harry H. L. Kitano and Akemi Kikumara, "The Japanese Family Life Style," in *American Minority Life Styles,* ed. Robert Havenstein and Charles Mindel (New York: Holt, Rinehart and Winston, Inc. [in press]).

never fully understood the issue) to question the loyalty of these hyphenated citizens.

2. The *ie*, or traditional household, is a community and social system that controls and manages the individuals comprising the unit. Even today, marriages in Japan are often between ies rather than between individuals. Since one of the main functions of the ie is socialization, a person marrying into an ie is reasonably certain of the type of "product" from that unit. A "good" ie will teach a certain style of life, values, and roles so that it serves as a "certifier" or "finishing school."

The ie remains one of the strongest reference groups in the Japanese social structure. An individual thinking of committing a deviant act may be discouraged from doing so when he thinks of the shame it might bring to the household. It also provides a ready reference group and is a central factor in traditional marriages by arranging for meetings between ies of proper rank, background, and status. Kin membership is not the only qualification; women marrying in become part of the structure, whereas males marrying out may soon be forgotten. The situation remains a powerful determinant of membership.

The ie unit survived in modified form in the early Issei era. There were no grandparents to serve as reminders of old traditions, and some of the immigrants felt relatively free from the strictures of the Japanese social structure. But the notion of "good" and "less desirable" families survived as a carry-over from the social-class structure of Japan. Certain groups, such as the *eta*, were pariahs in Japan, and Issei discouraged intimate social interaction with them.[5] There were prejudiced feelings about immigrants from Okinawa, especially in Hawaii.

"Good" Issei families provided an enriched cultural background for their children (Japanese-language schools, music lessons) and attempted to teach proper role behavior, homemaking, and other skills that would reflect their ability to socialize desirable Japanese-Americans. Issei parents set concrete goals for their children—including hard work and loyalty to the new country—so that they would become "good citizens." The more typically abstract American goals like "happiness" and "maturity" were less important than becoming good, obedient children.

Many Issei directed their major efforts toward Americanization, while others concentrated on the day-to-day tasks of sheer survival. In spite of these in-group differences, there was high ethnic solidarity when facing the majority group. Part of the solidarity came from the relatively homogeneous background of the Issei—although Japan was a highly stratified social system, the immigrant generally came from certain areas

5Hiroshi Ito, "Japan's Outcasts in the United States," in *Japan's Invisible Race*, ed. George DeVos and Hiroshi Wagatsuma (Berkeley and Los Angeles: University of California Press, 1967), pp. 200–21.

of Japan and from certain "class" groups. However, when the Japanese dealt with the dominant community, their reference group became the entire Japanese community. There were appeals to all individuals to behave in a manner that would reflect to the benefit of all Japanese, so that the family and the community became important reference groups, just as the ie served this purpose in Japan.

Opportunities in the United States have not been as dependent on the ie and family lineage as was and still is true in Japan. But the notion of the family as the primary socializing unit for manners and conduct was strong in Japanese-American families.

The Extended Family

The extended family played an important role in the Japanese-American system. Initially, it was horizontal (aunts, uncles), since the grandparents remained in Japan, but now some family units contain all three generations.

Large family gatherings, outings, and vacations often included numerous in-laws and other Japanese families. Discussions about the "successes and failures" of friends and acquaintances were told and retold so that they became a part of family folklore and possible models for the younger generations. Standards of behavior and acceptable norms were discussed in conjunction with everyday happenings, gossip, and jokes.

However, as children grew older, they tended to break away from the family. But family unity remained high during holidays and anniversaries; New Year's was a special occasion, when traditional Japanese foods were eaten and friends, relatives, and even the Japanese Consul General were visited. Many joined in the making of *mochi* (rice cakes); all joined in its eating.

3. The power of the group remains one of the strongest elements in the Japanese system. Group control of behavior extends into the shaping of ideas, etiquette, and the manner of behavior. In most cases the relationship is a unilateral one, and employees and family members have few alternatives, since their jobs and social life are interwoven with the organization. The unit feels responsible for its members, so conflicts are generally resolved within the group. Consequently, outside professionals who are not perceived as members of the unit usually are not brought in to help resolve the problems. This is one hypothesis to explain the low use of community resources by the Japanese as well as their low rates of deviant behavior as measured by official records. A group orientation meant that social controls could be exerted by asking "What will others think"? Individual needs and preferences were of less importance.

4. The Japanese social structure prepares an individual for a nar-

row range of living. There is a tendency to think in local and particularistic terms rather than in universals; thus there is little horizontal (cross-group) interaction in the Japanese system. Professional membership and unionization, which tends to achieve a horizontal integration, is new to the Japanese experience.

The need to adapt to a smaller, ethnic world was a part of the Japanese-American family and community experience. All Japanese athletic teams, community groups, and organizations were logical developments arising from the social structure of Japan. This model fostered high in-group understanding and cohesion, but it also meant that some Japanese had difficulty dealing with the "outside" world.

5. The Japanese system encourages loyalty to one system. Japanese stories often depict the loyal retainer who would never think of changing masters or who gives his life to save his lord. Job changing is minimal; for many Japanese, especially the older generation in the United States, loyalty may include such varied activities as the place where one shops and the doctor or dentist one visits, even if the service is less than satisfactory.

The Japanese system can be likened to a number of parallel structures in which loyalty and identification are within one parallel, rather than cutting across the structures. As a consequence, there is less likelihood of an open struggle between management and labor; rather, the competition is between company A and company B. The model is similar to that of American athletics where competition is between teams, and many familiar practices (for example, team songs, team spirit) are recognizable in Japanese companies. The Japanese sociologist Maeda further believes that the extent of these parallel structures in Japan (for example, village by village, neighborhood by neighborhood) still remains unappreciated and unresearched.[6] For example, the commonly held belief that Japan is a male-dominated society may be true for certain parts of the country (in Kyushu, there are areas where male and female clothing must be washed separately), but in other areas, such as northern Honshu, female domination, especially in the economic realm, is not uncommon. The stereotype of Japan as a homogeneous nation is difficult to fully accept given the perspective of parallel structures. Most generalizations about Japan are both accurate (there is a parallel system that usually fits) and inaccurate (there is another system that usually does not fit).

The parallel-structure system was brought to America. A member of one club, group, or organization often did not join others. This was especially true during the adolescence of the Nisei—if one were a member of the YMCA, one seldom crossed into the world of the Boy Scouts.

[6]Personal discussion in Tokyo, Japan, 1972.

High-school loyalties were especially strong, and even today such friendships often have priority, so that outsiders often complain of the difficulty of being accepted into Japanese-American social and recreational organizations.

6. Rank and status are determined primarily by age, sex, the order of entrance, and the period of service, as contrasted with a model that rewards competence, additional training, or efficiency. Leadership positions are important, but they appear localized into specific groups. A leader under this system comes from the group because recruiting from the outside is limited.

Nakane illustrated several examples of problems among the Japanese when a different system was introduced.[7] During World War II, captured Japanese officers in Burma went through a period of extreme discomfort when housed with fellow officers (horizontal) rather than with their units (vertical). Or, in Japan there remains difficulty in putting together a "team" of experts from different universities as a working unit, whereas an organization with a senior professor and a group of his own "underlings" can be molded quickly into a functioning organization.

The term that describes this relationship is *oyabun-kobun*, or, literally, or parent to child. It is similar to the master–apprentice or tutor–learner models, and appropriate reciprocal behavior is expected from the respective parties. Confusion and conflicts take place among many Japanese Americans over reciprocal behavior. For example, one of the most common complaints of the parental generation (oyabun) is that the younger generation (kobun) knows how to receive gifts, favors, and the like but shows little motivation or inclination to live up to their obligations in the relationship.

The Japanese social structure consists of a number of different umbrellas or frames. An individual is recruited and commits himself to one structure so that socialization and social control are developed within the unit. The relationship is idealized as a permanent one so that in return for loyalty, identification, and hard work, the structure feels obligated to provide for the total needs of its membership. Moving from under one umbrella to another is discouraged.

Individual competition in the Japanese structure is generally among those who are close to each other. The competition may lead to high, unresolved tension, since the competitors may often be close friends, and the resolution is left up to the individual. It is a difficult process, since the individual cannot share his problem with employees of other companies in similar situations, but must work on the solution with the members of his own group, who may be the cause of his problems.

This structure has been carried over into the Japanese-American

---

[7]Nakane, *Japanese Society*.

system. Japanese Americans feel that they are competing among themselves, especially in school. Many observers have noted how difficult it is for Japanese-Americans to work together unless they are following a formally appointed leader. Similarly, the Japanese family operated with ascribed roles flowing from the ranked status of father and male heir.

One of the strongest expectations that carried over from Japan was that of eventual upward mobility. As Nakane indicates, the Japanese feel that "because I could not go to college or university and I ended up at the bottom of the barrel, I wish to have my children succeed."[8] The story of Issei self-sacrifice to send their Nisei children to college is a common one in the Japanese-American community.

There have been changes in Japan since Nakane presented her framework, but her concepts remain helpful in explaining much of Japanese behavior that appears contradictory unless considered from such a perspective. For example, the rudeness of Japanese to strangers contrasted with their treatment of people within their own social circles; the loyalty to the company and the deference to those in authority; the emphasis on cleanliness in the home and the incredible filth one finds in public places can be understood within the model of parallel structures. Similarly, early Japanese-American behavior can be understood through a knowledge of the social structure transplanted from Japan.

THE FAMILY IN THE UNITED STATES:
THE EARLY PERIOD

Although one of the first American Issei families resulted from the marriage of an early immigrant to a Negro in the ill-fated Wakamatsu Colony (Chapter 2), marriage out of the Japanese group was an exception. The idea of marrying an American woman must have occurred to some, but this was made nearly impossible by factors of language, culture, race, and lack of social contact with eligible American families. Moreover, many Issei had emigrated with the idea of eventual return to Japan, and would have found themselves afoul of Japanese antimiscegenation feelings there had they undertaken out-group marriage. Most important, both Japanese and Americans retained strong preference for marriage within their respective groups.

It was therefore inevitable that when the young, vigorous Issei in America thought of marriage, he thought of Japan. He was used to arranged marriages and thought it quite natural to enlist the services of friends and relatives at home in choosing him a wife. The go-betweens set about matchmaking in a manner not unlike the computerized dating bureaus of today. Couples were matched in as many ways as possible—

8Nakane, *Japanese Society*, p. 111.

origin in the same ken, or prefecture, and often the same village, and similarity and suitability of family background. Women who were strong and could bear children were given high priority. The reputation of the matchmaker depended on the success of his efforts. Literally thousands of young Japanese women were betrothed in this way and sent off to America to join unknown bridegrooms.

These imported Japanese brides must have been extraordinarily adaptable or extraordinarily dutiful. They had usually been brought up in a large family and were not accustomed to intimate interpersonal relationships with men. Probably most received the news that they were being sent to a bridegroom in America with very little notice, and often knew little more of their future spouses than a photograph could provide. Unhappily, the photographs were often retouched at that. Marriage meant leaving Japan, familiar tasks, relatives and friends, home. It meant the prospect of a strange land and a strange and intimate new relationship—with a stranger.

Many Issei women still tell about the long sea voyage from Japan. Although the passage was "third class," it was for many the first experience of leisure. Food was abundant, and so was the opportunity to strike up new friendships with other "picture brides." Some were shocked at hearing overt sexual references relating to the impending marriages. Others felt grateful for the information. All felt for the first time a sense of independence and freedom from previous family ties.

Hawaii, then a territory, provided many of them with their first taste of America, primarily of its values of sanitation. They were herded into decontamination baths, underwent delousing procedures, and were exposed to strong-smelling shampoos and intimate physical examinations. Those with communicable diseases were detained. Those who passed breathed a sigh of relief and were shipped on, only to undergo similar ordeals on arriving at the mainland. Most of them even today still remember the disrobing, baths, fumigation, and physical examinations more vividly than they remember their first glimpses of the prospective groom.

The bridegrooms were waiting on the docks, pictures in hand. The debarkation scene must have been remarkable for its total confusion. There were many joyful meetings and, undoubtedly, many disappointing ones. We have heard several stories of last-minute swaps and even refusals. But for the most part, the new brides, having found their bridegrooms, were bundled off to begin their new lives in the strange land.

These early families continued in the traditional Japanese pattern, particularly in being interdependent with larger neighborhood and community units. They usually lived in rooming houses run and populated by members of the same ken. Community solidarity was quickly established, and the natural group cohesion, fostered by intimate social interaction and shared experience, was strengthened by hostility from the outside community. Not surprisingly, therefore, these initial enclaves played a conservative role in acculturation. Community and family life continued in the traditional Japanese pattern, with one important exception. There were no grandparents, no older generation to fulfill its traditional responsibility in teaching the young the roles and rituals of Japanese life. Japanese family patterns in rural America were similar and probably even more conservative, since contact with the outside community was even more limited, and since the Issei father-farmer role was so similar to that in Japan.

STRUCTURE OF
THE JAPANESE FAMILY

An understanding of the circumstances of the early Japanese family in America is essential in deriving generalizations about its present structure and function, its methods of problemsolving and decisionmaking, and its values and norms.

The Intact Family

The early Japanese family in the United States had many apparently unfavorable aspects to its makeup: the arranged marriage, the requisite adaptation both to a new spouse and to a new land, the crowded and inferior housing, poverty, continuous deprivation, and little expectation of immediate social change. Under the circumstances, it might be logical to predict early disillusionment and a high rate of divorce, desertion, or separation. For example, an Issei woman told us:

> Life was intolerable. Everything was different. My husband was not much help. Cooking, shopping, cleaning, washing dishes and washing clothes, taking care of the babies—many Issei women remember getting up after childbirth to go to work in the fields—these are some of the things I remember. *Hon-to ni ku-ro shi-ta* [We truly suffered].[9]

The disillusionment was there, but not the divorce. This was partly because there were few alternatives to staying together. More important, however, were the Japanese values and expectations. Much emphasis was placed on sticking things out (*ga-man*) and on the rearing of children. Expectations of marriage lay not in the traditional American reverence

[9]Kitano, private interviews.

for love and romance, but in a conception of duty and obligation, which, as has frequently been observed, may constitute a more realistic social attitude after all. The stability of the Japanese marriage is represented in Table A of the Appendix. Although these figures represent the divorce rate by age rather than generation, they do roughly approximate a description of the rate for each generation, and it will be seen that this rate of 1.6 percent does not radically change within any age or generational category. This lends support to the generalization that official divorce rates for the Japanese are exceedingly low and have not changed over time, although the Sansei rates are relatively meaningless because of their young age. There is current impressionistic evidence that divorce rates are rising (e.g., the rising number of divorces among one's own acquaintances), but it appears much too early to predict a trend. It is still possible to say that in this most important respect the Japanese have been consistent: there have been few broken families.

This does not, of course, take into account homes that have had an "emotional divorce." One younger Nisei told us:

> Sure, my parents are still together, but I don't see how they ever stuck it out. They don't really talk to each other. They're really worlds apart. He goes his way, she goes hers . . . they seldom have a kind word for each other, and I'm sure there never was love.

But also:

> She cooks, sews, cleans the house, washes the clothes, and raised all of us. He doesn't drink too much, doesn't smoke, doesn't gamble, never chased after women, always brought home a paycheck, worked hard and supported us through college.

Finally, when asked about his evaluation of this marriage, his own expectations were clear:

> I sure don't want to have a marriage like that. I want to marry a girl I really love.

And, as is typical of his group, he found it difficult to think in terms of much other than "love." Ironically, many Sansei perceive Nisei marriages as being similarly loveless and duty-bound, and hold that when they themselves marry, it will be for love. It would be interesting to know to what degree children of any ethnic group, viewing from the standpoint of adolescence the customary interaction of their long-married parents, find the love lives of their elders somewhat unexciting.

Vertical Structure

By vertical structure is meant a model of family interaction that places the father in a position of indisputable leadership, with other positions deriving from this authority and being clearly prescribed. Everybody knows his place. A true vertical structure is, of course, only hypothetical, and it is probable that few Japanese families ever functioned fully in this manner. There were certain factors that almost always modified it, the most important one being that, in America, the Issei father was at a cultural disadvantage—his Nisei son understood the American culture better than he did. The son was a citizen, while he was an alien, the son could own land, and the son was better educated.

Nevertheless, as a model, the Japanese-American family, even today, is more vertically structured and male dominated than comparable middle-class WASP families. The Japanese-American female obviously resents this position, and many marital conflicts arise from these differences in expectation.

The Traditional Family

Another way of describing the structure of the Japanese family is to liken it to a "traditional family," where interaction was based on clearly prescribed roles, duties, and responsibilities, rather than on personal affection. Love, although undoubtedly present in many families, was not the prime leverage for gaining social control; rather, rules and tradition had a higher valence. The more typical American model for obtaining social control through love and affection was secondary to an appeal to duty and obligation. Therefore, instead of the American prescription— "You'll obey Mother because you love her"—the Japanese child was more apt to hear—"You'll obey Mother because you have to." Perhaps this early training, emphasizing the more impersonal types of interaction, helped the Japanese to fit into such structures as bureaucracies with less difficulty than many Americans.

An important facet of family interaction was its emphasis on *oya-koko*, or filial piety. It was a reciprocal obligation from parent to child and child to parent and could be observed in simple, everyday decisions, such as the parent giving up the choicer cuts of meat to his child, or buying less expensive clothes for himself in order to better clothe his children. A major decision might include the parent sacrificing his own pleasures in order to send his son to college, so that the story of an aging parent living practically on bread and water in order that his children could gain a college education is not an unusual one in the Issei culture.

The idea of almost total parental responsibility for one's own children remains a strong one among the Issei, and many of this generation complain that the reciprocal obligation—that of the child to the parent—has been rapidly forgotten in the process of acculturation. The ungratefulness of children is a common topic among Issei.

TECHNIQUES OF SOCIAL CONTROL

It is not surprising that such a social system—intact family, prescribed roles, and a high degree of family and community reinforcement—was successful in controlling the behavior of its members, who in turn were characterized by conformity and little social deviance. Desired behavior was, of course, not accomplished merely by exposing children to the correct models. Behavior was constantly rewarded, punished, reinforced, and reshaped by such parental techniques as emphasis on dependence, appeals to obligation, duty, and responsibility, the use of shame, guilt, and gossip, and finally, emphasis on ethnic identity.

The most effective factor was economic dependence, but beyond this went a form of emotional dependence. For example, it is still not unusual to find unmarried children in their late twenties and early thirties living with their parents, and expecting to continue to live there, or, after marriage, nearby. Activities, friendships, perhaps even employment, are family oriented. The young Japanese, just out of high school or college, does not go east to Chicago or New York to look for job opportunities, even though this might be a sensible thing to do, because he expects and is expected to remain near his family.

These family ties were consolidated by family emphasis on duty, obligation, and responsibility. The Japanese word *giri* connotes a moral obligation toward others and is related to role position, involving an individual through his family with the ethnic community. He therefore has a responsibility not only to himself but to his family and to the community, both of which exert much inhibiting pressure on deviant behavior.

Much of this pressure is exerted through the fostering of feelings of shame and guilt. A good performance by a child reflects on the goodness of his family, but a bad performance shames the family and produces feelings of guilt in the member who has invited the disgrace. Parental disapproval and the admonition "shame, shame," may be used for anything from bedwetting to a bad report card.

The effectiveness of these sanctions was related to the degree of internalization, as the following comment by a forty-three-year-old housewife illustrates:

I don't know whether you would call it guilt or shame but I felt that my parents or others were looking over my shoulder all of the time. Whether

I went out on a date or whether I was studying at school I knew I couldn't let them down. I know it inhibited me in the sexual area and helped me study hard at school.[10]

More pressure comes from the community in the form of gossip. In a close-knit group, there is an effective "feedback" system, which ensures that if someone is being talked about, he and his family know about it. Thus, in the Japanese community, "good children," "bad children," "good families," and "bad families," are quickly identified through informal gossip channels and through the more formal networks of communication—the ethnic newspaper, radio station, organizational newsletters, and so on. Lind, in a study of delinquency in Hawaii, focused on the relationship between a cohesive Japanese community and one that was scattered and poorly organized.[11] He concluded that the organized ghetto, through such informal techniques as gossip, was able to control its members much more effectively. Deviants often found life so intolerable that they moved away.

The catch-all technique for reinforcing desired behavior in the Japanese individual was an appeal to ethnic identity. This was a combination of all the foregoing techniques and was often vague and contradictory. Many Nisei say it was only resorted to when an Issei parent did not know what else to say, and it took many forms—"Japanese boys don't cry," or "Good Japanese do it this way," or "Good Japanese don't even think about things like that."

These structures were amply reinforced by the Japanese community. For example, the consistency of attitudes is well illustrated by the history of a Nisei child who broke his arm playing basketball in the all-Nisei league while representing his Boy Scout pack. He was first told by his scoutmaster that Boy Scouts don't cry. This may be considered a reflection of the general American attitude about bravery. Next he was told that boys in a Japanese League don't cry, reflecting the values of the ethnic league. He was also told simply that Japanese boys don't cry. After he was taken home, his parents praised him for not crying by saying, "You were a brave boy, you didn't cry." This represented the values of the family. Later, the doctor (Japanese), said "That's a brave boy, you didn't cry, even though it hurt so much. You're a real Japanese." And the next day, his Japanese schoolteacher gave him public praise for his "brave" behavior. Soon the story of his ability to ga-man was known throughout the ethnic community. Perhaps, under these conditions, a Japanese boy who did cry should have received a medal for bravery!

[10] Ibid.
[11] Andrew Lind, "The Ghetto and the Slum," *Social Forces* (December 1930): 206–15.

Sexual Outlets

One of the basic functions of the family is to provide approved sexual outlets. In the Issei period, before the arrival of picture brides, prostitution provided the requisite sexual outlet for this population of young single men. There is some evidence that the Issei preferred Japanese women even as prostitutes; early documents refer specifically to Japanese brothels.

With the arrival of the Japanese brides, and with the establishment of family life, prostitution nearly disappeared. Gulick mentions that by 1914, the number of Japanese brothels in San Francisco had been reduced from twelve to three, and in Oakland from eight to one.[12] The ability of the Japanese-American male to repudiate so completely his former hedonistic bachelor life is quite remarkable. Even more unusual is the Puritanical orthodoxy, after marriage, of their sexual attitudes—attitudes that contrast sharply with those of the married man in Japan, where bars and baths and geishas are the time-honored province of the husband as well as the bachelor.

Communication between the Issei and Nisei was difficult on any subject, and the discussion of sex was nearly impossible. Many Nisei, therefore, were thoroughly misinformed on the subject. Some thought of sex in terms of the delicate, self-conscious lectures provided by the stereotypical unmarried physical education teachers, and others picked up what they could from street and gang groups. Older brothers and sisters provided the most balanced information.

Nisei boys, in general, tended to feel that there were two kinds of girls. The kind they would marry was usually another Nisei, of long acquaintance—either personal or through family contacts—and was "pure." She was not thought of as a sexual object. Then there was "that kind of girl," who might be non-Japanese. This way of looking at sex almost ensured that there were few "shotgun" marriages among the Nisei, despite the fact that many did not marry until their late twenties.

TYPICAL FAMILY PATTERNS

The Family Dinner

We have attempted to describe the Japanese family in terms of the dynamics of its interaction, but the reader may gain a more vivid impression of Japanese family life from an examination of daily behavior. For

---

[12]Sidney L. Gulick, *The American Japanese Problem* (New York: Charles Scribner's Sons, 1914), p. 57.

instance, a typical occasion, particularly before World War II, was family dinner.

All family members are present. The Issei mother announces that she has made a very simple dinner (*kan-tan no mo no*), but the children understand that she would say this even if she had been cooking for days beforehand. Her disclaimer is especially loud if there are visitors present, but there are seldom visitors, and almost never non-Japanese guests. The food is a mixture of Japanese and American dishes. The main dish is thinly sliced meat cooked with mixed vegetables, but yesterday's leftover spaghetti is also available as a filler. The parents drink tea or water, and the children drink milk. The food is simple but ample and includes large quantities of rice[13] and Japanese pickles. Purchased desserts are rare and reserved for special occasions.

Father is served first, then sons in descending order of age, sisters, and finally mother. Conversation is carried on quietly among the children, but rarely between the parents or between parents and children, except when direct questions are asked. The children attempt to ignore the slurping noise father makes when he drinks his soup, but they find it intolerably embarrassing on the rare occasions when non-Issei guests are present.

First words of praise come from the parents when the eldest son finishes his first bowl of rice and is given another. All family members are then urged to finish everything and ask for seconds. The girls, who are counting calories, suffer in silence or talk to each other about the dangers of overeating. The boys compete with each other and against father to see how many bowls of rice each can eat. Several Nisei have told us that the only words of praise they can remember ever receiving from their parents concerned their eating. It is no wonder that many of this generation grew up overweight.

Discipline is carried on throughout the meal—sister spills milk and is firmly warned against sloppy, lower-class behavior. Brother can't finish his vegetables and is told about the people in Japan who are starving and would like to have what he has. He finally manages to wash down his food with desperate gulps of water because the alternatives are another stern lecture or staying at the table until he finishes. Occasionally the good conduct of other Japanese children is introduced to serve as an example to follow.

Dinner ends (*o-go-chi-so-sa-ma*) as it has started (*i-ta-da-ki-ma-su*).

---

[13]The amount of rice consumed by certain Japanese families is truly awesome. We know of one family, parents and three teen-aged boys, who go through a 100-pound sack of rice per month with little difficulty.

Father makes unilateral decisions as to who is finished and when dinner is formally over, and at last everyone is excused.

Sunday Outing

Although family dinner was for most Japanese children not an unmixed pleasure, the Sunday outings were almost always happy occasions. These outings sometimes included friends and neighbors, and inevitably included dressing up in Sunday clothes. This usually meant, for boys, one good wool suit, worn whether the temperature was 40° or 100°. Sunday outings usually were public—going to the zoo or playground and using public transportation.

In these public appearances, discipline was even more important. Brother, if he fell and bruised himself, might find sympathy, but would be told firmly not to cry or make a public spectacle. Sister might be bumped by a Caucasian. She would be told in Japanese to watch where she was going and to apologize to the American. If the children started to run and shout, they would be told not to act up so much, and if verbal commands proved ineffective, a quick, hard slap from Father was a grim reminder. Mother, usually so sympathetic and lenient, also became different in public; her technique was a hard pinch, and it also worked well. Firm, disapproving looks were also clearly understood.

Sunday included a treat—an ice-cream cone or some other delicacy that had to be purchased, not homemade. Children soon learned that they had some freedom of choice, but only from among the five-cent, not the ten-cent, items. The limitations of the family budget were made quite clear. The children made every effort to conform to this and to all other strictures—to be polite, quiet, modest, and, most important, obedient. The whole family derived a great deal of pleasure from overhearing the harassed American parents of a shouting, demanding brood of children remark enviously about "the wonderful Japanese children over there."

Problemsolving

How to solve problems—whether to call on others or to handle them within the family—is an important item in family life. Here, the paternalistic structure of the Japanese family was often deceptive. In many cases, the father was simply unavailable except for major disciplinary issues, and many everyday problems were handled by the mother. In some families, both parents were unavailable, either because they worked, or because a language barrier made communication too difficult. Then, older brothers or sisters might function as arbitrators or confidants. In some families, certain kinds of problems were either repressed or referred. For example, financial problems might be brought up with parents, problems about sex and maturation might be discussed with older siblings and the peer group, occupational-educational matters were referred to the public-school teacher, while problems concerning self and identity were simply repressed.

The most distinctive characteristic of Japanese family interaction was, and still remains, the absence of prolonged verbal exchanges. Although some of the common strategies to gain support through manipulation or cajoling were present, very few problems were resolved through open discussion between parents and children. Instead, arguments were one-sided, and most Nisei can remember the phrase *da-mattre-ore* (Keep quiet) that concluded them. Verbalization, talking out, and mutual discussion were actively discouraged.

The pattern of nonverbalization was probably set very early and often arose from the characteristic use of "prescriptive" rather than "motivational" statements. By this we mean that an Issei would say, "Here are your eggs; eat them," in contrast to the more typical American motivational question that would set off a verbal exchange. The American mother says, "Johnny, do you want eggs? How do you want them? Oh, please, you know eggs are good for you. If you love me you'll eat eggs," and finally, with rising anger, "Here are your eggs; eat them." As exasperating as these exchanges might be at the level of the breakfast table, they provide a footing for future discussion of more serious problems. Such a foundation is not available in many Japanese families.

The more serious family problems—illness, delinquency, and so forth—often required help from outside sources. These sources were almost always—following the interdependent community structure—the extended family, fellow ken members, or professionals from within the ethnic community. The Issei family used outside specialists very seldom, and when obliged to, preferred a Japanese to a *ha-ku-jin* (white man). In general, the community was adequate to deal with most problems. A Nisei remembers how an instance of delinquency was handled in the 1930s:

> I knew these two brothers who were pretty wild. They would get drunk . . . were always fighting, always in trouble and were uncontrollable. Finally, their father came to talk to my father and other Japanese families in the neighborhood . . . all agreed that these boys would hurt the reputation of the other Japanese and provide poor models for the younger boys . . . so even though the brothers were already young adults and out of high school, they were sent back to Japan in 1937. As far as I know, they never came back to the United States.[14]

14Kitano, private interviews.

Obviously, this method of handling deviance helps to account partially for the reported low official rates of delinquent and other problem behavior among Japanese. The threat of being sent back to Japan was another source of family control, albeit more symbolic than real.

The current generation is more apt to consult experts. It reads Dr. Spock, or whoever else is in vogue, goes to lawyers and doctors, sometimes outside the ethnic group. Nevertheless, the pattern of in-group dependence is changing only slowly. Community agencies and family service facilities of the larger community still report almost no Japanese clientele. The retention of the ethnic model is, in fact, still much higher than one might expect from a population at their stage of acculturation.

Feeling of Shame about the Home

It was never possible to resolve satisfactorily the problem that came up when the Nisei started school and began to compare their own shabby homes, their non–English-speaking parents, and their Japanese family customs, with the picture-book American homes of their classmates. It was a rare Nisei who did not feel ashamed and unhappy about his background during some period of his school years. This is probably true of all immigrant groups, and must certainly provide some impetus toward acculturation. The important thing is that most people do handle these discrepancies without permanent psychological damage.

THE USE OF THE COMMUNITY

Not only in times of crisis did the Japanese community play an important part in the life of the family. Its function in sanctioning and reproving behavior has already been discussed. In addition, it assumed a positive role in the guidance of the young. Although the Japanese family exhibited a cohesive and controlling influence, in actual fact the relationship between Issei and Nisei was not apt to be close. Barriers of communication, while serving the function of avoiding overt culture conflict, also prevented much direct parental control. During early and late adolescence, Nisei generally were controlled by organizations within the community. These often took the form of leagues and clubs, which, although the Issei periodically attempted to control them, were usually guided by the Nisei themselves. The youngsters were left pretty much alone, to make mistakes, to try new things, and to translate their understanding of large community models in ways that could be of use to them. Erikson speaks of a "moratorium"—a stage of adolescent development during which an individual tries new roles without permanent commitment until a later stage.[15] The Nisei had such a moratorium, due

15Erik Erikson, *Childhood and Society* (New York: W. W. Norton & Co., 1950).

to loosening parental controls, and most explored their new identity and new experiences within ethnic community organizations.

ETH-GEN-CLASS INFLUENCES

The changes in the Japanese family illustrate the influence of acculturation, ethnicity, generational change, and social class. For example, much early Issei behavior appears to reflect behaviors commonly associated with a lower-class position in society. It was characterized by little power and few voluntary alternatives. Most families perceived few opportunities in the larger society, made few contacts outside of their own groups, and were generally ignorant of the larger world. Their existence apart from the mainstream of society meant that they lived in a narrow world in which alternatives were limited. Because they were poor, they often viewed their children as a source of possible income. This is unlike the more typical middle-class pattern of achievement orientation. Early employment of children and ignorance of the alternatives were characteristic features of early Issei family life.

Furthermore, Issei parents could not give informed and sympathetic advice about America to their children, so that the pattern was hard to break. Even the Nisei who went to college were often naïve and had little understanding of the purposes and demands of college education. Considerations of security prevailed over considerations of advancement, and, as is typical of lower-class life, chance rather than plan played an important part in their view of life. Another reflection of the lower-class view was Japanese hostility toward politics. This was partly because the Issei were not citizens. Also, their experiences with petty bureaucracies in Japan had given them the skepticism and mistrust of politicians that characterize lower-class attitudes everywhere.

But although many typical lower-class attitudes were present in early Issei family life, their cultural background introduced other patterns that were not typically lower-class. For instance, this was a "non-debt" group, which meant it was not entrapped in the cycle of high interest rates and continued poverty. Spending habits were middle-class, in that long-term goals had precedence over immediate gratification. The establishment of credit buying has been relatively new to the Japanese. Originally they were helped by their communities and extended families to handle financial crises and had a great respect for money and banking.

Furthermore, although they were not involved in American political life, the Japanese behaved with respect to those representing law and authority. Police were viewed not as enemies, as is typical in many ghettos, but as agents of justice and order. The influence of a single policeman was greatly extended by support from the family, the neighborhood, and the community.

All in all, Japanese reverence for hard work, achievement, self-control, dependability, manners, thrift, and diligence were entirely congruent with American middle-class perceptions. A Japanese was temperamentally unable to "loaf" and was uncomfortable on vacation. Children were not allowed to roam the streets and remained under the control of some community organization. Finally, the most important single intervening variable in explaining the rapid upward mobility of the Japanese was its use of the educational opportunities provided it by the larger society.[16]

However, to place Japanese family behavior in its correct context, one also has to take into account the marginal economic existence and even the poverty that were facts of life for many. The depression in the 1930s, the slow recovery, then the wartime evacuation meant that the Japanese faced several major external crises in terms of potential and real poverty. In spite of these external crises, poverty has not remained a typical problem for the Japanese family.

One plausible reason for the lack of a "hard-core" poverty population has been the ability of the ethnic community to handle their own problems through their own organizations. Although the objectives and purposes of federal, state, and local welfare programs are geared toward eventual independence, in practice they have often created semipermanent dependent populations.

It is difficult to pinpoint why the Japanese have seldom been "on relief."[17] It may have stemmed in part from "shame"; in part from ineligibility; in part from ignorance of such programs; and in part from alternatives available within the ethnic community. No matter what the reason, one explanation for eventual economic success has been the ability of Japanese families to avoid the development and maintenance of a hard-core poverty population.

---

[16]Possibly the most important variable to help explain high-school achievement was the reinforcements provided by schoolteachers. The writer remembers the constant rewards from this group in the form of praise, encouragement, and help. This variable appears to be much more realistic in explaining the educational achievement of the Japanese than variables like "a culture that places high value on education." Parental emphasis on discipline, respect for authority, obedience, and responsibility may be closer to explaining the positive interaction between Japanese student and teacher than "high values placed on education."

[17]It should be recalled that many Japanese began to use welfare assistance for the first time during the wartime evacuation. After their release from camps in 1945, groups of Japanese were dependent on public services for a short period of time.

Like a homing pigeon, a Japanese appears to possess an "instinct" that will guide him to the Japanese section of a strange town. A Japanese coming to Los Angeles for the first time will find himself at First and San Pedro almost without knowing how he got there. Perhaps he can smell the odors of soy sauce and *tsu-ke-mo-no* (pickled radishes). And whether he has come to the Little Tokyo of Los Angeles or the "Jap Town" of Walnut Grove or to any other Japanese community, he will find essentially the same things—a bar, often called "The Ginza" or "The Lotus Blossom," the poolhall, a sweet shop that carries both Japanese and American delicacies, a book and record shop, a shoe-repair shop, a cleaners and laundry (usually run by Chinese), a real estate office that may also handle legal and employment matters, the family grocery, the barber shop, and the churches, one Buddhist and one Christian. There will also be the inevitable Chinese restaurant. Larger Japanese communities may have a Japanese movie theater; smaller places show Japanese movies in the church or community hall on weekends. The Japanese community will usually be located in the center of a city, in an older and deteriorating area, contiguous with other ghettos subject to possible urban-renewal programs.

Up to World War II: The Community

The resemblance of one Japanese community to another does not lie only in the superficial similarities. All have similar underlying cohesive social structures. An understanding of this social structure is essential to an understanding of the resilience of the Japanese in adapting to life in the United States.

THE COMMUNITY IN JAPAN

The roots of the Japanese community organization lie, of course, in Japan. The Issei had been born into a social system that, although unlike the American system, peculiarly fitted them to adapt to the difficulties they found here. From birth a Japanese was accustomed to put the interests of his family, village, ken, nation, and emperor ahead of his personal interests. His behavior was dictated by clearly defined rules and obligations. A system of collectivism and ethical interaction pro-

53

vided mutual assistance for group members and proved effective in protecting the individual from the cultural shocks of both a rapidly changing Japan and, later, of a new land.

Community cohesion was fostered through what Dore describes as "honor":

> In Japan, where the local community has always been characterized by great solidarity and the existence of careful mechanisms for the smooth preservation of law and order, the fulfillment of one's duties to the wider community has always been considered as an essential condition for the maintenance of honour.[1]

COMING TO AMERICA

There can be few sights as dismal as the strange shores of an alien land. America, to the new immigrant from Japan, must have seemed from the deck of his vessel a bewildering welter of white faces and tall buildings. As he landed he was beset by immigration officials speaking to him in an unknown language. His future must have seemed precarious, but only for a little while, because he would soon hear someone shouting, *"Hiroshima no hito, ko-chi ni oide"* (All people from Hiroshima come over here). People from other kens were waiting to welcome their newcomers. They might be friends and relatives, or they might simply be people from the same Japanese county. In any case, the welcoming and socialization of the new immigrant began in the hands of other Issei. He was provided food and lodging, helped to find employment, and invited to share recreational and religious activities. Internal factors, such as similar language, food habits, and common experiences, and external pressure from a hostile American community served to strengthen the cohesiveness of the organized group into which he had been introduced.

The ethnic community was of great value in making life in America successful and comfortable for the Japanese immigrant. But there was a price: adaptation to a subculture often means limited participation and understanding of the larger community. It is a dilemma that is especially difficult for racially different groups—"Should we retain an ethnic identity since we can never be totally accepted?"[2] The questions of acculturation, integration, and pluralism are in the final analysis value questions and have to be answered from a value framework, although

[1] Ronald P. Dore, *City Life in Japan* (Berkeley: University of California Press, 1958), p. 22.

[2] Minako Kurokawa Maykovich, *Japanese American Identity Dilemma* (Tokyo: Waseda University Press, 1972).

empirical data on the difficulties of various adaptations may help to focus on problems.

The Issei ethnic community played a conservative role in acculturation. However, in the case of the Japanese, this circumstance did not lead to high conflict behavior. Many of the functions of the Japanese community were congruent with the values and life styles of the larger community. The general movement of Japanese community institutions was toward American models. Finally, expectations changed for each ethnic generation, so that adherence to the ethnic community has had different meanings for Issei, Nisei, and Sansei.

JAPANESE COMMUNITY INSTITUTIONS

We have already discussed the Japanese community and its structure for meeting occupational and economic needs. Perhaps closer analysis of several other Japanese community organizations will best illustrate the action of the community and the changes in community expectations from generation to generation. The Japanese Association is illustrative of an influential Issei organization, and the Japanese-American Citizen's League (JACL) of a Nisei-Sansei group. We will also examine the influences of acculturation on religious institutions, and of the community opportunity structure on Japanese youth programs.

The Japanese Association

The Japanese Association was the most important Issei group. Every community having a Japanese population would have a Japanese Association, so that a Japanese in Pocatello, Idaho, would be under the same kind of ethnic protection as a Japanese in San Francisco or Los Angeles.[3] Most of the associations were founded within a few years after Issei immigration; therefore they date well back to the start of the century. Although there was a loose coordinating structure, each of the associations operated somewhat independently.

A major portion of the activities of a Japanese Association was devoted to intracommunity affairs. It established and maintained graveyards, provided translators, placed people in contact with legal and other necessary services, and policed the activities of the Japanese community. For instance, the Japanese Association would try to curtail prostitution, gambling, and other activities that might "give a bad name" to the Japanese. They also sponsored picnics and gave backing to youth groups

3Kiyo Morimoto, "A Developmental Analysis of the Japanese Community in Pocatello, Idaho" (unpublished term paper, May 25, 1956). Harry H. L. Kitano, private collection.

and youth services. But these organizations had few contacts with the majority community, and those few contacts were limited to formal business or ritualistic occasions involving the leaders only. The Japanese Association might participate with the larger community to the extent of sponsoring a float in a local parade or helping to collect for the Community Chest.

The principal function of the Japanese Association, at least in the minds of its members, was protective. The following anecdote is illustrative. Mr. H. Takata, an Issei living in San Francisco, stated:

> I am a lodging house keeper. On August 28, 1906, about 9:00 P.M., my window was smashed by a person or persons unknown. Again on August 30, about 11:00 P.M., someone broke my large front window. I reported the incidents to the Japanese Association, but not to the police.[4]

The Japanese Association would then attempt to contact the police; they might also contact the Japanese consul, and even if there was very little that could be done formally, the Japanese individual felt somewhat better because he felt that his problems were being handled by people with his interests at heart.

Part of the protective power of the Japanese Association lay in its relationship with the Japanese consulate. The Issei were technically citizens of Japan, so that cases of discriminatory or wrongful treatment were often brought to the attention of the Japanese government rather than local officials. It was felt that most local police officers would ignore individual complaints by Japanese but might listen to the requests of the Japanese Association and the consulate.

Not surprisingly, the Japanese Associations played a conservative role in regard to acculturation. These organizations, modeled after Japanese groups, had in their prime (1920–1941) an important voice in keeping the ethnic community "Japanese." Many young Nisei groups chafed against the power of the elder statesmen of the Japanese Association, which reinforced the Issei motto, "Don't become too American too quickly."

The associations have gradually lost their former positions of power. The advanced age of the Issei, their loss of economic control, and the changing needs of the community have encouraged the development of differently oriented organizations in their stead.

The Japanese-American Citizen's League (JACL)

The JACL can be thought of as a second-generation counterpart to the Japanese Association. It, too, developed in response to the special prob-

---

[4]Herbert B. Johnson, *Discrimination Against Japanese in California* (Berkeley, Calif.: The Courier Publishing Co., 1907).

lems and interests of the Japanese, but primarily of the Nisei. Although its initial function was protective, it served, in a way that the Japanese Associations did not, to accelerate acculturation. It was first begun in the early 1920s by young Nisei, who felt that their interests were not served by the Japanese Association, and who therefore established local Nisei groups, called by various names, such as Loyalty League or Citizen's League. By 1930 these local groups had consolidated into a national organization (JACL), supported by local chapters that cut across religious, ken, political, and special-interest ties. The special plight of the Nisei was more than sufficient to override these previously divisive factors. There were problems of citizenship for their Issei parents, of the continuing discrimination and prejudice with which they themselves were faced, and of their own problems in the larger society. In addition, the Nisei group was relatively homogeneous in regard to age, interests, and goals, so that, as is often the case with groups formed in response to special social crises, the JACL developed quickly into an effective organization.

The gravest crisis with which the JACL had to deal was World War II and the evacuation. Because it was the only national Japanese-American organization, many Japanese looked to it for leadership. It decided to cooperate fully with evacuation orders. In this decision it actually had little choice, since there were few alternatives; the community was disorganized, many Issei leaders had been arrested by the FBI, and all ethnic organizations had been disbanded. Many Issei and Nisei had lost their jobs, and small businesses were in precarious condition. The might of the American government was paramount. For these reasons, it is not likely that JACL could have effected any other course. And it is probable that, whatever the JACL might have decided, the Japanese community would have cooperated with evacuation procedures as it did anyway.

However, because they had declared themselves willing to cooperate, many JACL leaders became scapegoats for feelings of resentment that later developed. Some had extremely harrowing experiences at the hands of fellow Japanese in the relocation camps, and the JACL is to this day resented by some for its cooperation during the World War II crisis.

The primary importance of the JACL was its role as a service and social organization for the Nisei. It broke away from the Issei and founded an organization modeled after American groups with an emphasis on Nisei needs. The early conventions, planned and financed by Nisei, concentrated on Nisei problems exclusively, but the debates and procedures followed American patterns. Most importantly, exposure to local and national issues widened the horizons of the Nisei. A possible measure of the general success and affluence of this group is perhaps provided by the sites of its present meetings. Early gatherings were held in local community halls or churches. Today they are held in expensive resorts, with all the external trappings of any middle-class American convention.

RELIGION

Religion, in the American sense of Sunday school attendance, belief in a single faith, and relative intolerance of other faiths, is alien to the Japanese. In general they are tolerant of all theologies and have not institutionalized religion to the extent that most Americans have. This was true in Japan at the time the Issei were growing up there, and appears to be true in Japan today. For example, while in Japan recently, we saw a pilgrim on his way to a Shinto shrine, carrying a Protestant Bible and wearing a Catholic crucifix. We were told that this was not uncommon, and that many people like to feel they were "touching all bases." The Issei brought with them to America a similarly flexible approach to religion. Most had gone through no baptismal or confirmation ritual and were not churchgoers, although most came from a broadly Buddhist background that influenced the ceremonial aspects of birth, weddings, and deaths. Otherwise, the focus of any religious training was ethical behavior—how one acted toward parents, friends, and strangers.

It is therefore not surprising to find certain discrepancies and inconsistencies in religious censuses even today. Many Japanese claim a Buddhist background but may attend an all-Japanese Christian church. A religious survey by Miyamoto of the Japanese in Seattle in 1936 showed that most were Protestants.[5] Data gathered at the time of the wartime evacuation show the same thing. Data gathered among Japanese in Brazil found most of them to be Catholic, suggesting that Japanese tend to adopt the religion of the country in which they find themselves.[6]

Initially, it was believed that religious preference was a good predictor of acculturation. Miyamoto indicated that the Buddhists were much more conservative and more "Japanese" than the members of Christian churches. There was rivalry between the groups, so as Hunter indicated, if the Buddhists started a language school that was successful, the Christians might launch a competing facility.[7] But this point of view, although historically correct, probably ignores the religious flexibility of the Japanese and of the Buddhist church itself in adapting to changing religious conditions.

[5]Frank S. Miyamoto, "Social Solidarity Among the Japanese in Seattle," *University of Washington Publications in Social Sciences* 11, no. 2 (December 1939): 99–104.

[6]"Japanese Immigrants in Brazil," *Population Index* 35, no. 2 (April 1965) (Princeton, N.J.: Princeton University Press, Office of Population Research), p. 136.

[7]Louise H. Hunter, *Buddhism In Hawaii* (Honolulu: University of Hawaii Press, 1971).

Early Christianity

Although early attempts to introduce Christianity into Japan were not successful, Japanese immigrants in the United States provided a fruitful missionary field. Their adoption of the Christian faith was strongly reinforced by practical considerations because Christian churches had much to offer the new immigrant in the way of employment and Americanization. Many found employment through their church, particularly as house boys. In fact, this was so common that at one time the Japanese house boy was referred to as a "mission boy." The churches also provided an opportunity to learn to speak and behave like Americans, and had therefore an important acculturative function. Several other factors contributed to the development of Christianity among the Japanese. The social-welfare functions of the church were congruent with Issei experience, and church attitudes of benevolence and helpfulness toward others were sympathetically received. Where the new immigrant was without family, the church served in a family role, supplying the feeling of group participation that the family had provided in Japan. Christianity was also less complicated and expensive than Buddhism when it came to such practical matters as weddings or funerals. Churches often provided mission schools, preschools, and kindergartens. The Christian concepts of ethical and moral training were congruent with those of Buddhism, and, finally, the churches played a strong part in defending the Japanese from legislative and political attacks.

Church activities were particularly important in the acculturation of Japanese women. Women's clubs provided for many a first exposure to American ways—food and fashions, democratic group procedures like voting, and an opportunity to serve in positions of leadership. Many Nisei remember the unexpected results of mother attending a cooking class—spaghetti, whipped cream desserts, Chinese chow mein, and Italian veal cutlets.

These early church activities were usually presided over, in a missionary spirit, by Caucasian ministers and interested congregations. However, as time went on, the Japanese tended to form all-Japanese congregations. This has by now produced an interesting reversal, in which the educational activities of the church provide not lessons in Americanization but lessons in Japanese culture—flower arranging and sukiyaki—and are for many Nisei and Sansei the sole contact with their Japanese heritage.

There was one potential source of conflict between Christianity and the Japanese culture. This was the Christian emphasis on individualism, which, on the surface of things, would seem to be incongruent with the group emphasis of Japanese social principles. But because within the cohesive Japanese community lay an inherent competitiveness, the apparent philosophical incongruence provided no real practical difficulties.

Although theoretical differences in the roles played by Buddhist and Christian churches in acculturation can be hypothesized, actual differences are difficult to detect. Both churches have Sunday school, Sunday services, bazaars, social services, and women's and youth programs. Buddhist weddings have been shortened and thereby resemble Christian ceremonies. Both churches provide services in English for Nisei and Sansei, and in Japanese for Issei. The ministers of both churches are usually Japanese, and both congregations are mostly segregated. In general, although there may have been initial differences in the direction of acculturation, both institutions have themselves changed to the point that they are remarkably similar and remarkably American. And Japanese parents of either religion usually agree that "it doesn't matter what church you go to, as long ts you go to church."

OTHER COMMUNITY ORGANIZATIONS

It would be difficult to overlook the vast network of services and opportunities available to the Japanese youth. Some are by definition acculturative—the Boy and Girl Scouts, the YM and YWCA's, and the Campfire Girls. Others, such as judo or kendo groups, are more ethnically enclosed, but all serve to function as agents of socialization and social control.[8]

Probably best known to the Nisei and least known to outsiders were the ambitious all-Japanese athletic leagues. These tended to concentrate on basketball, a sport that did not require expensive uniforms and facilities, and because of considerations like physical size, limited competition with non-Japanese groups. The all-Japanese leagues were organized into divisions according to age and locality and held regional and statewide playoffs. At one time there was a national Oriental championship. The golden age of Nisei basketball was in the late 1930s and again in the late 1940s and early 1950s. It offered the usual advantages of participation in a group activity—team and group identification, travel, competition, and rewards. Ironically, the Nisei basketball team was often the only group through which a youngster identified with his high school. For example, one Nisei relates:

[8]The popularity of the "martial arts" has spread to some non-Japanese. Aikido and karate clubs are examples where non-Japanese individuals can be seen in ever greater numbers. Many adherents feel that the discipline and training of these "arts" help to develop character.

> I used to wait for the All-Hi Tournaments. It was the time when all Nisei going to different high schools in San Francisco would get together and compete. We'd have rooting sections, championship playoffs, all-star teams, medals and trophies, and then a big victory dance.[9]

After the tournament, a Nisei, who might have been named the "most valuable player," and have been much-praised in the ethnic newspaper, would resume his anonymous role among the larger student body of his Caucasian high school.

The Nisei learned far more from these teams than the skills of athletic competition. It was an experience of independence, travel, social interaction, and role-playing. Here a boy could be a "big fish in a little pond"; his brothers, sisters, and girl friends would come to see him play; there would be dances, bazaars, and other fund-raising and supportive activities. The basketball teams therefore became primary reference groups for many, and a Nisei would often introduce himself by saying "I'm from the Cardinals," which meant that he was from Los Angeles, or as being from the Zebras of San Jose, or from the Greyhounds—a YMCA group in San Francisco.

The basketball teams served as vehicles for acculturation. The Issei remained aloof from them and considered them rather frivolous, so that the Nisei were free to develop in the American pattern. The play, the rules, the goals and values, were all American; only the players were Japanese. In spite of this, any integration attempts were firmly resisted. Big fights were apt to occur if a non-Japanese or part-Japanese played with one of the teams. In the 1930s a great crisis developed when a group called the San Francisco Mikados—perennial champions—left the league to play in a larger community league. "Do they think they're too good for us now?" stormed the other players, ethnic newspapers, and community sponsors. The offending group came back to play in the ethnic league again the following year.

The years have produced some changes in the Japanese athletic teams. Now the squads are much smaller and tend to be limited to those people with athletic ability. The play is probably better today, but its popularity has waned. Increased opportunities in other areas for individual and group participation and identification are reflected in a general lack of interest and support of these ethnic leagues.

The Little League has to some extent replaced basketball as the most important social-athletic institution in the ethnic community. The Japanese baseball Little Leagues in Los Angeles are extremely well organized and efficiently run and serve large numbers of Sansei. They still are predominantly all-Japanese, and there have been cases of reverse

[9]Kitano, private collection.

discrimination, in which Caucasian youngsters have been excluded when they have tried to join the impressive, well-run Sansei clubs. In the Little League, unlike the prewar basketball teams, there is a significant degree of father–son interaction, which may be a mixed blessing.

The Japanese continue to be interested in athletics. It is therefore somewhat curious that few Nisei have become professional athletes; this is an avenue often used by lower-class groups to earn money and status. It is partly accountable to the fact that the Nisei were apt to be physically smaller than other groups. Also important, perhaps, was their emphasis on team sports or on events like weightlifting, gymnastics, and swimming. Sports like tennis or boxing, through which some might have won recognition, have never been popular among the Japanese, although even this pattern is changing. Whatever the reason, the Japanese have never had the athletic heroes available to other groups—no Joe DiMaggio, no Hank Greenberg, no Joe Louis, no Henry Aaron.

The Family at the Japanese Community Picnic

On a day in early summer Japanese-American citizens gather for their most visible rite, the annual picnic. Here in microcosm may be seen the workings of the Japanese-American community as a whole and of the Japanese family through several generations. Thousands of families, congregating in larger groups related to the original ken or province of their forefathers, celebrate their Japaneseness, their sense of a heritage different from the white American culture of which they are a part in day-to-day life. The proportions of these picnics are staggering—ten thousand people are reported to attend the largest of them, in Elysian Park in Los Angeles. It is difficult to think of another American racial or national minority group, or indeed a group however categorized, that maintains a social event of such size and regularity, unless it would be displaced Iowans, whose immense annual picnic in Long Beach, California, provides a fair analogy.

The resemblance of the Japanese to the Iowa picnic will be apparent to anyone who has much knowledge of the traditional midwestern institution, and the resemblance should be borne in mind, for, developing as it does from two totally dissimilar backgrounds, the likeness of Japanese to Iowan enforces a critical point about the success of the Japanese in America. The essentially congruent values of Japanese and Caucasian middle-class American permit compatible coexistence without structural assimilation.

Picnic day, which is not dictated by tradition, has been settled on in advance by a committee of leaders of the Japanese community. Before the war, Japanese holidays were often designated, but now convenience and a hope of good weather are primary considerations. The day does not coincide with any other traditional Japanese festival, and opinion among Issei is divided about its origins. Some hold that there was never such a thing as a community picnic in Japan, while others maintain that they had them all the time.

At any rate, arrangements are made to use some available public park. Japanese merchants are canvassed for donations of merchandise to be used for prizes and favors. They are happy to comply and derive for their generosity the good will of their fellows, income tax advantages, and the removal from inventory of whatever has been superfluous anyway. Someone donates a loudspeaker system that, within a roped-off area, plays loud Japanese music, formerly of the traditional variety, but now betraying the Western beat that has crept into most popular music from Japan. In fact, this is all right with most of the picnic-goers, for none but the purest Issei ear really enjoys the old music. Similarly, none but the Issei can read with any assurance the large signs written in Japanese characters to guide the picnic-goers in the right direction. But the music and the signs and the gay lanterns have a Japanese feel, and feeling Japanese is what is wanted on this most festive of days.

Our typical family arrives at the picnic and spreads its blankets on the ground near relatives and friends. The littlest children immediately scamper off in the company of their fellows. Teen-age sons and daughters, at the age when they are likely to feel self-conscious and contemptuous of the whole affair, have usually not come at all, although a few can be seen holding hands and dancing rock-and-roll or the most current steps furtively at the perimeters of the gathering. They are generally disapproved of. But for the most part, teen-agers and young adults are absent. Most will reappear in a few years, when they have become young parents and find in themselves an awakened interest in Japanese pastimes and traditions.

The most conspicuous group at the picnic are not the young but the old—the Issei men—because many are "tipsy." The picnic is one of the few occasions during the year when workaday gravity, sobriety, and decorum are set aside. Now they gather in convivial groups on the grass, pass the whiskey (overtly if they are single, covertly if they are married), and indulge a license for "racy" talk. There is, in fact, a faintly Japanese formality to the talk; it is laden with stylized metaphor about sex through gardens and seed, but in any event it represents sufficient departure from the usual conversational conventions to be striking.

The Issei brand of loose talk probably sits unfamiliarly at first on the tongues of the younger Nisei men, who have learned the Western variety. But to the Nisei, it is a great satisfaction to be admitted to the Issei group; at least to be invited to drink with the Issei at the Japanese picnic is something akin to a *rite de passage*.

The young Nisei husband, now admitted to the company of men, nevertheless retains his role of son and is exhibited in this capacity far and wide, especially if he is successful, by his proud, inebriated, and garrulous father. The picnic is an occasion for boasting about one's offspring, introducing them to friends and acquaintances, and receiving praise and congratulations for one's good luck and fertility. Later in the afternoon there will be a prize for the Issei who has the most descendants and much public commendation of the efficacy of his seed. If he is able, the enviable patriarch will make a little modest speech about having been blessed with a fertile garden to plant. For children are a man's pride and blessing. During the races and competitive games that take place throughout the afternoon, much store is set on winning. It is important that a man's son be better than other men's sons, and the spirit of the games is more serious than one might find at an Iowa sack race. But there is also an interesting variation on the theme of winning because no one, not even the slowest, goes home without a prize. The winners receive the bigger and presumably more valuable packages, but all receive something for their efforts, even if it remains a symbolic pencil or eraser or lollipop.

Other forms of entertainment follow the games. These usually include a brief speech by the local consul from Japan, who is all dressed up in black coat and necktie, and is cheered enthusiastically by the rowdy crowd. Some attempt is made to arrange the picnic when the Japanese naval training ship is in port; the smartly dressed young naval cadets drill and demonstrate Japanese games and entertainment. In recent years most Issei have become too old to do their traditional dances as they used to, but there is increasing interest among Nisei groups in learning them, so it may be that these performances will not disappear. Something will be needed to combat the encroachment of the modern dances that are the favorite of the Sansei and Yonsei.

While the men are drinking, talking, visiting other groups of men, reveling, hoping to make a valuable business contact here, saying a few words to an old friend there, all—gardener and banker, Issei and Nisei, father and son—united in the splendid camaraderie of manhood and drink, the situation is somewhat different for the Japanese woman. As in all endeavors that require the family to eat out of doors, for her it is not such a picnic. For one thing, she is probably already tired and tense. If she is Issei, she probably has been cooking various delicacies for several days before. Visitors, coming to exchange a few words with her husband or her, will be offered a sample, and she will be covertly judged by the excellence of her cooking. Her daughter, of the Nisei generation, may have refused to be drawn into this subtle competition and will have brought potato salad instead of *o-su-shi*, but, as any woman knows (as far as female roles prior to World War II), it is not so easy to escape a practically inherent female tendency to become ego-involved when her cooking is on public display. Even the most advanced Nisei is likely to spend an extra, anxious moment over that potato salad. It is possible, too, that she has been in overt conflict with her mother or mother-in-law over the whole matter.

Add to this the fact that the wife has to sit more or less alone on the blanket, dishing up for strangers while husband and children disport themselves around the park, that critical eyes will be judging not only her cooking but her children, whose good deportment she is not very confident of, since they have escaped her direct intervention and are running around, and that her husband is making a fool of himself with the boys in a fashion more or less unprecedented since the picnic last year, and it will be understandable that the ladies get irritable and priggish. But this does little to mar the fun, and when the picnic is over at sundown, all, even the ladies, feel themselves to have had a wonderful time on this one day of vacation from the white man's world. They no longer leave the park with nationalistic cries of "Emperor Hirohito, Banzai," as they did before the war, but they do include one final, silent, reproach to white America. At a signal, at the end of the day, all, even the tiniest children, set about picking up every last scrap of litter—every wrapper, every plastic spoon, every paper plate and cigarette butt, every tiniest fragment of potato chip. They leave the park as clean as they found it—cleaner than they found it. In fact, it will not be so clean and tidy again for another year.

There have been several rather unpredictable developments arising from the Japanese community picnics. Those given in the city have not changed too much in ethnic composition, but those in the rural areas have served an unexpected integrative function. For example, a Japanese farmer may invite a Caucasian neighbor to the Japanese picnic. Year by year this practice may become more widespread. The Caucasian child, especially, has become fond of the organized games, races, and prizes, and his parents apparently enjoy the overall organization as a contrast to the usual informal small family outings that are his norm for the rest of the year. Therefore, in some instances, the Japanese community picnic has become the rural community picnic, given annually and looked forward to with anticipation. The role of the Japanese has become an ambivalent one—as hosts and instigators they find an enormous amount of work and responsibility. At one recent picnic, the Japanese hosts found themselves barbecuing 3000 chickens, *teriyaki* style, so that the picnic has become more work than pleasure.

The other observation, less surprising, concerns the takeover of the picnics by the Nisei from the Issei. People once believed that when the Issei were gone, the community picnics would die, but this prophecy has not come true. The Issei are no longer active, but their sons and daughters have taken over. The degree of similarity is startling—the mannerisms, the style, the talk, and the interaction have withstood the passage of time and generation at least on picnic day.

Other Groups

There are still many organizations within the Japanese community that are tied to the past. For example, in 1964, there were nineteen active *kenjinkais*, or prefectural organizations, listed in the Japanese telephone directory for Los Angeles, although the main present purpose for these groups appears related to asking for donations and assuming sponsorship for the annual picnics.[10]

The kenjinkais played an important social function in the past. Smith reports:

> The most important of the purely social organizations were the *kenjinkai*, the prefectural associations. The first contract laborers to arrive in 1885 had been so far as possible kept in groups according to the prefecture and even the town they came from. In a rural culture like Japan's, differences of habit and custom might vary considerably from one part of the country to another. It was natural enough that those who had come this far from home enjoyed the company of their own *ken* folk, with whom they shared the same dialect, the same birth and marriage customs, and often the same Buddhist sect. Doubtless the *kenjinkai* also served as a means of self-aggrandizement for those ... [with] qualities of leadership who could find no scope or acceptance in the larger community surrounding the Japanese. For the children the *kenjinkai* was chiefly useful as the sponsor of a summer picnic—a wonderful affair of games, soda pop, speeches, sweets, exhibitions of wrestling and fencing, and more soda water.[11]

COMMUNITY LEADERSHIP

Burma and Meredith have commented on the apparent lack of leadership among Japanese Americans.[12] Very few Japanese leaders ex-

---

[10]*Hokubei Mainichi Yearbook* (San Francisco: Hokubei Mainichi Shinbunsha, 1964).

[11]Bradford Smith, *Americans from Japan* (Philadelphia: Lippincott and Co., 1948), p. 57.

[12]John Burma, "Current Leadership Problems among Japanese Americans," *Sociological and Social Research* 37 (1953): 157–63; Gerald Meredith and C. G. W. Meredith, "Acculturation and Personality among Japanese-American College Students in Hawaii," *The Journal of Social Psychology* 68 (1966): 175–82.

hibit a charismatic, dynamic personality, a "hero" quality. This is possible because in the well-structured, interdependent system that is characteristic of Japanese communities a "dynamic" leader may not be too important and could even be a disaster. A better model for leadership among the Japanese is a man who knows the various organizations within the community, who can work together with them, and who possesses a thorough knowledge of how and when to act and yet avoids the spotlight. Any special gifts of individual talent would have to be secondary to his conciliatory abilities. The usual Japanese community leader, in fact, closely resembles the prototype of a corporation executive or bureaucratic manager. But it is a mistake to believe that leadership does not exist, especially if evidence for such a statement is based on an analysis of the personality characteristics of Japanese leaders, or if it ignores the nature of the community structure. The *genro*, or elder statesman, and the necessity of working through the ethnic power structure attest to the presence of much covert leadership and power.

In a summary of the importance of the Japanese ethnic community, and its development and structure, several generalizations appear appropriate. At the beginning, organizations were formed on the basis of immediate need. Long-range goals were not formulated with much clarity, but the hostility, discrimination, and prejudice with which the Japanese were faced did much to foster internal cohesion. Group structure was usually simple, role positions were explicit, and the community groups had considerable meaning for the members. The cohesion of the whole community was reinforced by the fact that most individuals belonged to several of the organizations within it. The primary leadership skill was therefore an ability to approach and handle different groups correctly.

In general, Issei groups played a conservative role in acculturation, although some have adapted to the American models to which they have been continuously exposed. The Buddhist church illustrates this change. Nisei groups are "American," but their membership remains ethnic, which greatly reinforces structural pluralism. And, even though they remain segregated, these American Nisei organizations do involve the Nisei with more and frequent social communication with larger community organizations. For instance, an annual convention of Lions, which groups attend from all over the world, provides the Nisei with a degree of exposure and interaction they would not otherwise have.

Nisei organizations from the very start were pointed toward acculturation. Although limited to ethnic membership, their models were clearly patterned after their interpretations of what they thought the American community offered. These organizations were important because they enabled Nisei to set up their own goals, to operate from power positions, and to retain an identity, so that a Japanese, blocked from active participation in the larger community, could respond to his situation without the high degree of alienation and anomie that appears to be characteristic of some other minority groups living under disadvantaged conditions.

All in all, the picture of the Japanese family and community prior to World War II was that of an immigrant group attempting to establish a foothold in the new country. Segregation into ethnic enclaves was a process encouraged by hostility, prejudice, and discrimination from the outside and ethnocentrism, nationality, and cultural similarities from the inside. But the Japanese were a small and powerless group (with the exception of Hawaii, see Chapter 10), so any attempt to seal themselves off and maintain a completely pluralistic system was bound to be ineffectual, especially for the Nisei.

One of the most difficult problems for an immigrant group is to acculturate, yet find that they are not accepted into the host society. It may lead to an identification with the majority culture through wishful thoughts or rhetoric, rather than on empirical reality. This was the general picture faced by the Japanese prior to World War II, and the attack on Pearl Harbor provided the impetus that marshaled the anti-Japanese forces in America toward a final solution to the Japanese "problem."

A member of a minority group has a tendency to feel that the experiences of his group are unique and that no one else can really understand them. He is apt to find himself playing a kind of game with members of other minority groups, much in the spirit of "can you top this," in which each recounts stories of prejudice and discrimination and contends that his own experiences have been worse than anyone else's. Presumably, the winner is he who can show the longest, deepest scars. In such a game, the Japanese provide stiff competition. The consistency and intensity of anti-Japanese hostility have had few parallels in American history, especially when the wartime evacuation is considered. This episode alone usually declares the Japanese to be somewhere near the top in any game of "Compare the Scars."

Many of the adverse conditions of Japanese immigration, however, appear no different from those facing other immigrant groups. In common with the others, most Japanese came to the United States during the great industrial and agricultural expansion that took place between the end of the Civil War and the beginning of World War I. Most were poor and had little capital to set up their own enterprises. Most were minimally educated, so that

The

Wartime

Evacuation

entrance into professions and fields of skilled labor was denied them. The majority could not communicate in English. Further, most Japanese had unrealistic ideas about America; many expected to make their fortunes and return to the old country in a short period of time. They were often attacked by nativist and racist groups and were forced to settle in the slums. Inevitably they started at the bottom of the occupational ladder and felt too socially inferior to seek much intercourse with the majority group. But as Daniels indicates, these were the conditions facing most newcomers to America.[1] A comparison of such scars is a standoff.

There are, however, several factors that make an "ideal" immigrant —ideal in that he epitomizes the expectations of influential segments of the core culture. In most cases, he should be white, Anglo-Saxon, Protestant, and come from a nation that has been friendly to the United States. It is presumed that such an immigrant adjusts, adapts, acculturates, and merges into the "melting pot" with a minimum of difficulty. From this

[1]Roger Daniels, *The Politics of Prejudice* (Berkeley: University of California Press, 1962).

perspective, the Japanese immigrant represented the opposite in every respect. He was nonwhite, Oriental, non-Christian, and was from a nation that would eventually be engaged in a full-scale war against the United States. It was no wonder that life in the United States was one of continuous hardship and discrimination. It can truly be said that he came to the wrong country and the wrong state (California) at the wrong time (immediately after the Chinese "problem"), with the wrong race and skin color, with the wrong religion, and from the wrong country.

MOUNTING ANTAGONISM

The Japanese attack on Pearl Harbor on December 7, 1941, provided impetus for the "final victory" for forces opposing the Japanese-American group. Nevertheless, plans for a final solution were never that clear. Instead, the months after the Japanese attack and the ensuing declaration of war were troubled and confusing ones. The question of what was to be done with the Japanese in the United States can probably be best understood in the context of this confusion, since even today it is difficult to ascertain accurately the roles of various individuals, officials, and institutions in relation to the decision to evacuate the Japanese from the West Coast.

Immediately after Pearl Harbor, selected enemy aliens, including 2192 Japanese, were arrested by the FBI. Curfew regulations and other precautions were also instituted. These steps might have been sufficient for protective purposes, except in light of the continued battle between Californians and the Japanese. The Hearst papers presented the issue vigorously; for example, the *Los Angeles Examiner* on December 16, 1941, led off with the headline, "Fifth Column Treachery Told," using a quotation from Secretary of the Navy Knox, but omitting the fact that Knox was discussing only rumors against the Japanese. The *San Francisco Examiner* picked up the cry, then the American Legion, then the Chambers of Commerce, then the farm groups, and finally the politicians —"all Japanese are traitors."

Evidence to the contrary was ignored. Bill Henry, conservative columnist for the *Los Angeles Times*, wrote on December 26, 1942:

> The FBI chief says the yarns about the dead Jap flyers with McKinley High School [Honolulu] rings on their fingers, the stories of the arrows in the cane fields pointing towards Pearl Harbor, and the yarns about Jap vegetable trucks blocking the roadway to Pearl Harbor that day are all unadulterated bunk.

But the rumors continued to fly and were picked up on a national level. On January 29, 1942, Henry McLemore, a syndicated Hearst columnist, wrote:

> I am for the immediate removal of every Japanese on the West Coast to a point deep in the interior . . . let 'em be pinched, hurt, hungry. Personally, I hate Japanese. And that goes for all of them.

Austin Anson of the Grower-Shippers Association in Salinas, writing in the *Saturday Evening Post* of May 9, 1942, said:

> If all the Japs were removed tomorrow, we'd never miss them . . . because the white farmer can take over and produce everything the Jap grows, and we don't want them back when the war ends either.

The Japanese handicaps of race and nationality, compounded by social and legal discrimination, isolated ghetto lives, and the outbreak of war, were even too much for the spirit of American democracy and fair play. Very few Caucasians really knew the Japanese Americans; their general ignorance about this group helped to foster and maintain negative stereotypes. The range of those attacking the Japanese was truly remarkable—the American Legion, the State Federation of Labor, the Native Sons of the Golden West, the California State Grange, the leftist parties, and individuals like then California Attorney General Earl Warren and "liberal" columnist Walter Lippmann, as well as the usual racists. The major newspapers in California kept up a constant attack and were joined by local and national magazines. Also as damaging to the future of the Japanese was the silence of the standard liberal organizations. Only some Quaker groups and the American Civil Liberties Union (ACLU) provided visible support.

Daniels[2] indicates that the planning steps leading to the evacuation could have been halted, delayed, or diverted if strong voices could have publicly questioned the wisdom and necessity of such a drastic decision. However, in the absence of such actions (it may have been that some of the top government officials privately were against the forced removal, but they never did speak out until years after the incident), the steps leading to the evacuation gathered momentum which culminated in the mass incarceration.

A SMOOTH EVACUATION

On January 29, 1942, the first of a series of orders by U.S. Attorney General Francis Biddle established security areas along the Pacific Coast that required the removal of all enemy aliens from these areas. On February 13, a West Coast Congressional delegation wrote to President Roosevelt urging immediate evacuation of all Japanese, whether citizens

[2]Roger Daniels, *The Decision to Relocate the Japanese Americans* (Philadelphia: J. B. Lippincott Co., 1975), p. 41.

or aliens, from California, Oregon, and Washington, and on February 19, 1942, President Roosevelt signed Executive Order 9066, which (1) designated military areas where military commanders could exclude persons, and (2) authorized the building of "relocation" camps to house those people excluded. This set the stage for the evacuation of more than 100,000 Japanese, both citizens and aliens, from the West Coast.

On March 2, 1942, General John De Witt, then commander in charge of the Western Defense Area, issued an order to evacuate all persons of Japanese ancestry (defined as children with as little as one-eighth Japanese blood) from the western half of the three Pacific Coast states and the southern third of Arizona. More than 110,000 of the 126,000 Japanese in the United States were affected by the order. Of this group, two-thirds were United States citizens.

On March 22, the first large contingent of Japanese, both aliens and citizens, were moved from Los Angeles to the Manzanar Assembly Center in California. Prior to this, there was initial governmental encouragement of voluntary movement away from the designated strategic areas, followed by an order on March 27 to halt voluntary emigration.

From then on, all evacuation procedures were controlled by the Army, and by August 7, 1942, the more than 110,000 West Coast Japanese had been removed from their homes. The evacuation proceeded in two stages—first into temporary Assembly Centers at such places as the Tanforan and Santa Anita racetracks in California (under control of the Army and the Wartime Civilian Control Agency), and then to more permanent camps under the jurisdiction of the War Relocation Authority (WRA). The permanent camps and their listed capacities were:

California:	Manzanar (10,000)
	Tule Lake (16,000)
Arizona:	Poston (20,000)
	Gila River (15,000)
Idaho:	Minidoka (10,000)
Wyoming:	Heart Mountain (10,000)
Colorado:	Granada (8,000)
Utah:	Topaz (10,000)
Arkansas:	Rohwer (10,000)
	Jerome (10,000)

By November 3, 1942, the transfer from Army to WRA jurisdiction and from the temporary assembly centers to the permanent camps was complete.

The evacuation was rapid, smooth, and efficient, primarily because of the cooperativeness of the Japanese population, who responded to the posted notices to register, to assemble voluntarily on time at designated points, and to follow all orders. The manner in which the Japanese obediently marched to the trains and buses hauling them to camp presaged a conflict-free camp life.

The Santa Anita Riot

But there was some conflict. The writer, then an evacuated high-school student, remembers one such incident. At the Santa Anita Assembly Center, a riot began in response to rumors that a group of evacuee policemen was illegally confiscating electrical appliances and other material for personal use. During this direct confrontation between those interned and those representing the United States Government, there were cries of *"Ko-ro-se!"* ("Kill them!") and *"Inu!"* ("Dog!"). A crowd of around 2000 Japanese, including large numbers of teen-agers, ran aimlessly and wildly about, rumors flew, property was destroyed, and finally an accused policeman was set upon during a routine inspection and badly beaten. The incident was controlled through the intervention of 200 Army MPs, installation of martial law, and stricter security. It was significant that the policeman was non-Caucasian (part Korean), since in most instances of conflict throughout the evacuation period Japanese turned on other Japanese (e.g., generation against generation, or pro-American against anti-American Japanese) rather than the Caucasian administrators.

A letter written by one of the evacuees, dated August 9, 1942, illustrates the significance of this riot to one observer:

> Although the censored version of the "rioting" in the newspapers gives a black eye to Center residents by not explaining the extenuating circumstances under which the uprising arose, it seems to have raised their spirits in anticipation of brighter prospects to come. The residents now feel that they shouldn't allow themselves to be imposed upon too much, that occasionally they should assert their rights and not to lie supinely on their backs when injustice is being done.[3]

CONCENTRATION CAMPS
AND THEIR EFFECTS

It is often asked if the war relocation camps were concentration camps. In most senses they were. The writer remembers when, on his second day in Topaz, he walked past the barbed-wire boundaries with a group of his high-school friends, in a typically adolescent attempt to test

[3]Harry H. L. Kitano, private interviews with members of the Japanese community, 1964.

established limits—despite the fact that the camp was located in the middle of a desert and there was virtually no place to go. After walking about fifty yards past a break in the wired fence, we were surrounded by military policemen with drawn guns, interrogated, our names recorded, warned, loaded on jeeps, and returned to camp. It was a frightening and sobering experience.

In other cases, Military Police actually shot evacuees who went beyond the fences, and the barbed wire and guard towers characteristic of concentration camps were always present.[4]

But there were important differences. One of the most important differences between these centers and concentration camps lay in the process of checking, clearing, and then releasing Japanese to areas of the United States away from the Western Defense Area. Some were students going to college, others were in search of employment. By the end of 1943, an estimated 35,000 evacuees, primarily Nisei, were attempting to establish themselves in the Midwest and East. It was the second voluntary emigration for the Japanese—in some ways resembling the first migration of the Issei from Japan. These immigrants, too, were a young, highly motivated group and were drawn primarily from those who could not stand the confines of barracks life. They characteristically held high expectations for upward mobility, either through further education or employment. Most of them presented a positive picture to those Americans who had never been in contact with the group before, and they carried on the pattern of selective migration that their Issei fathers had laid down a generation before.[5]

The benefits worked both ways. Most of the group had an opportunity to see themselves as Japanese in new situations; being a Japanese in Chicago was often different from being a Japanese in California, and the experience greatly broadened the horizons of a large group of Nisei.

Conversely, Americans from other parts of the country, coming into contact for the first time with Japanese Americans, generally found themselves impressed with and well disposed toward this intelligent, ambitious, and highly motivated group.

For those forced to remain in the camps, life was not so promising. Daily existence was desultory, monotonous, and self-defeating. Dillon Meyer, director of the camps wrote:

[4]Allan R. Bosworth, *America's Concentration Camps* (New York: W. W. Norton & Co., 1967).

[5]Robert O'Brien, "Selective Dispersion as a Factor in the Solution of the Nisei Problem," *Social Forces* (December 1944) : 140–47. O'Brien makes the point that these Nisei college students made "ideal ambassadors," since they entered into the American scene in the noncompetitive (in the economic sense) student role as contrasted to other immigrants who were economic competitors.

[Being] cut off from the main currents of American life does things to people. It saps the initiative, weakens the instincts of human dignity and freedom, creates doubts, misgivings and tensions. Even more important, the mere act of putting people in camps and keeping them there establishes precedents which are not healthy or hopeful for a democratic nation. Over the past three years, we have watched some of these formerly enterprising energetic people become steadily obsessed with feelings of hopelessness, personal insecurity and inertia.[6]

Obviously both positive and negative features of the evacuation must be evaluated.

There is little question about the economic and psychological damage brought about by the forced evacuation. For many Japanese it was the end of the line and a dramatic culmination of the racism that they had endured all of their lives. But the most relevant point for our purpose is that the wartime evacuation affected the acculturation of the Japanese, especially the Nisei. New exposure, new opportunities, the dissolution of old institutions and structures, and life away from the ghetto hastened change.

Some effects were felt immediately. The ghettos and "Jap Towns" in coastal cities were broken up, replaced by tar-paper barracks and community mess halls in the interiors of California, Arizona, Utah, Wyoming, Idaho, Colorado, and Arkansas. The invisible walls erected by housing discrimination had now become highly visible barbed-wire fences and guard towers.

Many Japanese families were ruined economically. Their property had been lost, stolen, sold, or confiscated. Camp jobs paid only sixteen to nineteen dollars a month, so there was no hope of savings or financial recovery at this time. Such a bleak outlook in turn caused unmeasurable damage to the self-respect of a proud, independent group of people.

Financial ruin, together with the camp policies of using American citizens (Nisei) in positions of camp responsibility, worked to shift power and influence away from the Issei and onto the shoulders of the Nisei. This exerted a definite influence on the structure of the Japanese family and operated to free the Nisei from Issei influence.

The family structure was reordered, too, by the physical conditions of camp life. Community mess halls and other facilities required certain basic changes in roles and expectations. A young father complained:

The worst part of it is not being able to bring up the baby right. He's just 18 months. . . . Naturally he cries some. If you were living alone in your own home, you could let him cry when he did it and not spoil him.

[6]Dillon S. Meyer, "The WRA Says 'Thirty,'" *The New Republic* (June 1945).

But here you've got to pay attention to it. You don't feel like letting him bother the people on the other side of the partition. They can hear everything that goes on. We've got to shut him up some way. So you have to fuss around with his crying and pay attention to him. That's not good for the baby.[7]

And in the mess halls, parental problems often became acute. One mother said:

My small daughter and I used to eat at a table where two little boys ate with their mothers. They had become so uncontrollable that the mothers had given up, and let them eat as they pleased. They behaved so badly that I stopped eating there . . . but my daughter was fascinated. They would come running into the mess hall and the first thing both of them did was to take off their shoes and stockings and jump up and down on the seat. Then they would start yelling for their food. . . . Now these little boys had older brothers and sisters, and if they had eaten at one table with both parents, things like that couldn't have happened, for the other children would have protested out of pride, and the father probably would have forbidden it.[8]

In general, under the influence of mess-hall conditions, eating ceased to be a family affair. Mothers and small children usually ate together, but the father often ate at separate tables with other men, and older children joined peers of their own age. Thus family control and the basic discipline of comportment while eating changed character rapidly, and different family standards became merged into a sort of common mess-hall behavior. Family groups ceased to encourage the enforcement of customary family rituals associated with the mealtime gathering of the group. The social control exerted by the family under more normal circumstances seemed to be loosening.

The changes also affected the roles of husband and wife. All husbands were no longer in the position of serving as the major breadwinner; in some families the wife and the children were drawing the same wage as the husband. There was an accompanying loss of prestige on the part of the husband and a gain in independence on the part of the wife and, in some cases, the children.

Immediate economic needs were not pressing; the provision of food, shelter, and minimum clothing was removed from the area of family responsibility and taken over entirely by the government. For some evacuees with higher economic aspirations, a way was open through departure

[7]U.S. Department of the Interior, War Relocation Authority, *Impounded People* (Washington, D.C.: Government Printing Office, n.d.), p. 68.
[8]Ibid.

from camp with government security clearance.[9] In general, the evacuation tended toward the destruction of established family patterns of behavior.

Other behavioral patterns were also changed. Riots, assaults, and other forms of violence "not typically Japanese" were now encountered for the first time in the Japanese-American group. The effects of the special situation can clearly be seen in the fact that such behavior ceased as soon as the camps were closed. For the first time, large numbers of older Japanese became recipients of formal social-welfare services. Dependence on the government, a concept heretofore rare among the Japanese, assumed a major role in camp life.

On the more positive side, Japanese Americans were exposed here for the first time to an American model of a small community, albeit of an extremely artificial nature. Block votes, community services, community decisions, and the like, provided a taste of "ideal" American community democracy, the likes of which few Americans have actually ever seen. But the important and final decisions were in white hands.

The camp schools were uneven in quality. For example, the writer's high school in Topaz, Utah, was oriented toward state standards of education, but some courses were taught by local evacuees who were not yet college graduates, and others were taught by Caucasian Ph.D.'s (among them conscientious objectors). All typical high-school activities—a yearbook, football and basketball teams, cheerleaders, student body organization, scholarship society—were available, and, for the first time, young Nisei were able to feel themselves in the majority and to run things. They became student body leaders, athletic, political, and social heroes— roles usually reserved for Caucasians in the everyday world.

Similarly, other community positions became available for the first time to adult Japanese. They became block leaders, firemen, policemen, foremen, supervisors, timekeepers, and almost every other type of non-administrative job was available to them. The variable of ethnicity was held constant so that competition rested primarily on qualifications and achievement.

The evacuation forced Japanese Americans to consider carefully their nationality and their ethnic identity. They now had choices to make, choices that previously had been delayed or repressed. Were they Japanese or American? The decision was difficult for many Issei and Kibei, and perhaps an easier choice for Nisei, who, as a group, remained completely loyal to the United States.

---

[9]A resettlement program to non-Pacific Coast areas was in effect from the early days of the evacuation. Wives of servicemen were usually the first to leave, followed by students, then by those seeking employment. Major cities for emigration included Chicago, Minneapolis, Cleveland, and New York.

The question of national identity was more easily resolved than the very personal question of ethnic identity. Fisher writes that only 2300 of the 110,000 evacuees asked to be sent back to Japan.[10] This was a surprisingly low figure from a group that might conceivably have seen little future for itself in the United States.

Ethnic identity had to be faced squarely for the first time by many of the group. Prior to the evacuation, one could dream of being an "American," perhaps at the 100 percent level, or deny that one was a hyphenated citizen. Now that they were behind barbed wire for simply having a common ancestry, many Japanese had to reevaluate their identity. The phrases "I'm a 'bootchie' " and "I'm a Buddhahead" became popular in camp and were used to refer to being Japanese. One could be a smart Buddhahead or a dumb one, or a good-looking one or an ugly one—all the definitions referred to a common element, the ethnic identity. Fortunately, the elements of the identity were not all negative, so that a reevaluation of their ancestry contained many healthy perceptions for the Japanese.

NOT ALL ACQUIESCED

The handful of Japanese who resisted the wartime evacuation by taking their cases to the courts eventually brought an end to the camps. In their quiet way, these Nisei were heroes—they faced the court decision almost alone, since many of the evacuated Japanese either did not know of their efforts or deplored the possible negative effects on the rest of the Japanese population.

Gordon Hirabayashi, a senior student at the University of Washington, and Minoru Yasui, a young attorney in Portland, Oregon, both challenged the evacuation orders. Hirabayashi wrote:

> The violation of human personality is the violation of the most sacred thing which man owns. This order for the mass evacuation of all persons of Japanese descent denies them the right to live. It forces thousands of energetic, law-abiding individuals to exist in miserable psychological conditions and a horrible physical atmosphere. This order limits to almost full extent the creative expressions of those subjected. It kills the desire for a higher life. Hope for the future is exterminated. Human personalities are poisoned. . . . If I were to register and cooperate under these circumstances, I would be giving helpless consent to the denial of practically all of the things which give me incentive to live. I must maintain my Christian principles. I consider it my duty to maintain the democratic standards for which this nation lives. Therefore, I must refuse this order of evacuation.[11]

10Anne R. Fisher, *Exile of a Race* (Seattle, Wash.: F and T Publishers, 1965), p. 103.

11Ibid.

Hirabayashi was arrested, convicted, and jailed for violating the evacuation orders. The government's treatment of Hirabayashi illustrated some of the incongruencies of the evacuation. Hirabayashi, after conviction, was sentenced to a federal prison in Arizona.[12] The presumably dangerous "enemy" was then given gas stamps and permitted to drive his car from Seattle to Arizona on his own and on arriving at the penitentiary, was denied entrance because the orders for his incarceration had still not arrived!

Yasui was also found guilty, fined $5000, and sentenced to one year in jail. Subsequent appeals led to a unanimous U.S. Supreme Court ruling of June 21, 1943, which said:

> We cannot close our eyes to the fact, demonstrated by experience, that in time of war, residents having ethnic affiliations with an invading enemy may be a greater source of danger than those of a different ancestry.[13]

These were words from the Supreme Court of the United States, and not from nativist or racist groups in California.

Daniels, in an analysis of the records at Heart Mountain, Wyoming, discovered that there were many young internees who refused induction into the armed forces of the United States and preferred to go to prison rather than to take up arms for the nation that placed them and their families in concentration camps.[14]

Finally, resistance does not have to be either overt or violent. As Kitano has written, dominated groups have historically adapted to their status through a variety of adaptations including ritualism and super-patriotism (e.g., interned Japanese purchased war bonds and held Fourth of July celebrations with pro-American speeches), internalization of stress, work slowdowns, inefficiency, strikes and tardiness, agression, displacement, ethnic humor, withdrawal, and intoxication.[15] All of these adaptations were part of camp life.

Fred Korematsu attempted a different tactic to avoid evacuation. He hoped to change his name and to alter his features.[16] But the FBI

12Private conversation with Gordon Hirabayashi, June 25, 1973, in Tokyo, Japan.

13Fisher, *Exile of a Race*, p. 114.

14Roger Daniels, *Concentration Camps, U.S.A.* (New York: Holt, Rinehart and Winston, 1971).

15Harry H. L. Kitano, *Race Relations* (Englewood Cliffs, N.J.: Prentice-Hall, Inc. 1974), pp. 99–115.

16It should be noted that, as a group, very few Japanese have lost their identity through deliberate name changes or face alterations. The only group to use name changes with some frequency is in the entertainment industry, where such changes are common.

caught up with him; he was found guilty of violating the exclusion order and was given a suspended sentence and probationary status. His was a potentially difficult case—his probation meant he was under court rather than Army authority, and therefore at large. But the Army immediately threw him into an assembly center, and his case was finally heard by the Supreme Court, which ruled that Korematsu was excluded not because of hostility to him or to his race but because of the war with the Japanese Empire and the military urgency of the situation. This decision was not unanimous: Justices Black, Rutledge, Reed, Douglas, Frankfurter, and Chief Justice Stone delivered the majority opinion, but Justices Murphy, Jackson, and Roberts dissented.

The most influential case in the cause of regaining Japanese-American liberty was that of Mitsuye Endo of Sacramento, California. In July 1942, she petitioned for a writ of habeas corpus, contending that her detention in camp was unlawful. She represented a test case for James Purcell, a young attorney who questioned that the War Relocation Authority had a right to detain a loyal American citizen for any of the various reasons used by the Army to justify the evacuation. Purcell carried the case to the Supreme Court, and finally, on December 18, 1944, the court ruled that she should be given her liberty. All nine of the justices agreed that the WRA had no right to detain loyal American citizens in camps. It was no accident that, after this ruling, the commander of the Western Defense Area announced that the West Coast mass exclusion orders would be revoked, effective January 2, 1945.[17]

The Endo case and the continued success of the Pacific war meant the close of the evacuation camps before the end of 1945, and the termination of the entire program by the middle of June 1946. Ironically, it turned out to be difficult to move some of the Japanese out of the camps. They had almost completely adapted to the close environment. Perhaps, along with the reservation Indian, the reservation Japanese might have come into existence as one result of World War II.

RETURN TO THE COAST

Part of the reluctance of many evacuees to leave the camps derived from their fear of returning to their former homes and hostile neighbors. Secretary of the Interior Ickes reported that by May 14, 1945, there had been twenty-four incidents of terrorism and violence—fifteen shooting

---

[17]Jacobus ten Broek, Edward Barnhart, and Floyd Matson, *Prejudice, War and the Constitution* (Berkeley, Calif.: University of California Press, 1954). See especially pp. 211–23, which cover the episodes in court, including the Hirabayashi, Endo, and Korematsu cases.

attacks, one attempted dynamiting, two arson cases, and five threatening visits.[18]

An especially notorious event occurred in Hood River, Oregon, about this time. The local American Legion attempted to exclude all Nisei soldiers' names from the "honor roll." They removed sixteen Japanese names—of these, fourteen had served overseas: two had been killed in action against the Nazis, ten had been awarded the Purple Heart, one was to die in Leyte, and another was the regimental interpreter in the Pacific, who volunteered for a dangerous mission and was killed in action. Yet, a headline advertisement in the *Hood River Sun* (February 2, 1945) read, "So sorry please, Japs are not wanted in Hood River."[19]

In such ways, toward the close of World War II, the outlook for West Coast Japanese was gloomy. Although some were returning to their homes in California, most were afraid, and others had simply resettled in other parts of the country. A final attempt was made in California, through a number of escheat cases, to seize property owned by the Nisei under clouded titles. (It should be recalled that since the Issei were ineligible to purchase land, many had put their property under the names of their American-born children.)

The two most critical events occurred in 1946. One was the Oyama case, which involved Kajiro Oyama, an alien "ineligible to citizenship" because of his race, who bought a tract of land for his citizen son, Fred. The California Supreme Court unanimously upheld the right of the state to escheat the Oyama property.

It looked as though the final solution to the "Japanese problem" was at hand. The state could claim much of their land, even that in the hands of the Nisei, and the losses the group had suffered during the evacuation would almost ensure a permanent inferior status. But the constitutionality of the California Alien Land Law was placed under scrutiny, and, although the Oyama case did not involve a direct ruling on this issue, the U.S. Supreme Court reversed the decision of the California Supreme Court on Oyama's citizenship rights. The tide appeared to be turning.

The second and possibly most influential event was the California vote on Proposition 15 in 1946. Proposition 15 was, in effect, an attempt to amend the State Constitution in order to incorporate the entire Alien Land Law of 1920 and to strengthen racist attacks on Nisei property. The voters of California overwhelmingly defeated the proposition.

---

[18]Bosworth, *America's Concentration Camps.* The exclusion order was lifted in December 1944. These incidents were noted along the Pacific Coast, primarily in California.

[19]Fisher, *Exile of a Race*, p. 199.

The Tide Turns

The sharp defeat of Proposition 15 marked the first retreat of the high tide of discrimination and the beginning of a series of acts designed to heal some of the scars of the last several decades. Politicians, instead of crying for more blood, now began to issue statesmanlike pronouncements about democracy, equality, and justice for all. It is difficult to pinpoint the elements that turned the tide. One was undoubtedly the record of Japanese-American soldiers, especially in the campaigns in Italy and France. The 442nd combat team and the 100th battalion, composed of Japanese Americans from the mainland and Hawaii, suffered more than 9000 casualties, had more than 600 killed in action, and became known as the most decorated unit in American military history. There was also a significant contribution by Nisei in the Pacific against Japanese of their own ancestry. Returning servicemen often told and retold the exploits of the Japanese Americans and were quick to rise to their defense. Part of the change may have been reaction-formation and may have come in part through a feeling of guilt. It is possible, too, that the evacuation and many other anti-Japanese acts were foisted on an apathetic majority by a small but active minority. And, unfortunately, part of the diminishing hostility against the Japanese may also be explained by the increased concern over the activities and problems presented by other ethnic and minority groups.

MOTIVATING FACTORS
IN THE EVACUATION

Two questions are involved in any explanation of the wartime evacuation. First, why did the American government intern the Japanese in violation of fundamental traditions? Second, why did the Japanese cooperate so willingly with the authorities during their evacuation and internment?

Plausible answers to the first question were covered earlier—racism, pressure from individuals and groups, the background of anti-Oriental prejudice, wartime conditions, the neutrality of many liberal organizations, and the general lack of knowledge about the Japanese held by most Americans.

White Racism

It is difficult to avoid the conclusion that the primary cause of the wartime evacuation was West Coast racism. Hawaii, the scene of the intial attack, was theoretically more vulnerable to a Japanese invasion and had a Japanese population of 150,000. Among them were 40,000 aliens, unable to read or write English, but there was no mass evacuation in Hawaii.

There were important differences between Hawaiian and mainland Japanese. The Japanese in Hawaii were a more integral part of the economy, while on the West Coast, Japanese had only a peripheral role or were viewed as an economic threat by some groups. Hawaii was more liberal toward nonwhites, and Hawaiian military leaders had an enlightened view of potential dangers from the Japanese population. Finally, it would have been difficult and expensive to move Hawaii's large Japanese population to mainland camps.

The decision to place the Japanese in camps, surrounded by armed guards and behind barbed wire, came about relatively late. Daniels reports that when the decision to move the Japanese into the interior was planned, the Army called a special meeting of governors of Western states in Salt Lake City on April 7, 1942.[20] Milton Eisenhower was asked to present information to the select group, and one of the basic questions was what would happen to the "Japs" after the war. Although the United States Government wanted to treat the evacuees with some degree of flexibility, including the possibility of homesteading and communal experiments, the hostility of the Western governors soon quelled any hope for a liberal solution. The emotional cry that no state should be a "dumping ground" for California's problems led to the policy of barbed-wire fences and armed guards.

Canada also treated its Japanese shamefully. Mass evacuations, incarceration, and the denial of constitutional privileges were their fate as well.[21] Japanese in Latin America were generally ignored, except in Peru and Mexico. Meanwhile, individuals of German and Italian extraction were generally left alone in the United States.

But on the U.S. mainland, anti-Japanese prejudice was not confined to the West Coast. Bloom and Riemer, comparing attitudes of Pacific Coast and Midwestern college samples, find general agreement concerning the wartime evacuation.[22] Of 2647 students of seventeen colleges and universities tested in 1943, 63 percent on the West Coast and 73 percent in the Midwest felt that the handling of the Japanese was correct. Conversely, only 6 percent of the Pacific Coast sample and 19 percent of the Midwesterners felt that American-born Japanese (Nisei) should be allowed complete freedom as in peacetime. Attitudes toward the Issei noncitizens were even more severe.

[20]Roger Daniels, *Concentration Camps, U.S.A.*

[21]Forest E. LaViolette, "Canada and Its Japanese," in E. Thompson and E. C. Hughes, eds., *Race* (Glencoe, Ill.: The Free Press, 1958), pp. 149–55.

[22]Leonard Bloom and Ruth Riemer, "Attitudes of College Students Toward Japanese Americans," *Sociometry* 8, no. 2 (May 1945): 166.

The authors also cite a National Opinion Research Center article reported in *Opinion News* on January 23, 1945, which classified responses to the following question: "After the war, do you think that Japanese living in the United States should have as good a chance as white people to get any kind of job?" Sixty-one percent of the respondents answered "No," that the whites should have the first chance!

It is difficult to single out a villain to take the blame for the evacuation. General John De Witt deserves his share of the opprobrium for his role as West Coast Theater Commander. He issued the evacuation orders and summed up his feelings at the time with the remark, "Once a Jap, always a Jap." However, Bosworth reports that the general regretted his actions before he died and felt that he had been the victim of bad advice.[23] Earl Warren, then California attorney general, played a role in the evacuation and may also have been the "victim" of poor advice. In any case, it does little good to point accusingly. Silence, denials, or the usual rejoinders about "doing one's duty" obscure the truth still, and perhaps it is not really important to affix guilt.

The shock of the wartime evacuation is that for the first time in its history the United States used the concept of collective guilt and initiated group incarceration, even though there was no evidence of prior wrongdoing. The important lesson of the evacuation was that it could and did happen in the United States, and to American citizens.

Japanese Nonresistance

Answers to the second question—why the Japanese did not resist—provide illuminating insights into norms of Japanese behavior. The explanations are both political and psychological.

Prewar Japanese on the U.S. mainland were politically powerless—the Issei were denied citizenship rights, and the Nisei were just reaching voting age. Further, there were no prominent Japanese public figures on the political front or on any other. Therefore, the American public was often only intellectually aware of the evacuation and felt rather detached from the process. It is not facetious to suggest that the Italians could never have been handled in the same manner because of baseball hero Joe DiMaggio. One can well imagine the publicity, the hue and cry for political scalps and investigations, if first- and second-generation Italians, including the famous baseball player, had been sent away.

Economic considerations also help to explain the behavior of the Japanese. There was a short period prior to the evacuation when the Japanese could have migrated to the Midwest and the East, but few did.

23Bosworth, *America's Concentration Camps.*

Most were poor, so that the financial risk of moving to other parts of the country was too overwhelming. Further, the economic structure of the Japanese community—low pay, small business, and high interdependence within the system—meant that very few Japanese could move out or into non-Japanese systems easily. The overall economic picture of the nation, too, was against any easy mobility.

Although there is an interdependence among all of the reasons, the social-psychological explanations of Japanese behavior appear to be the most relevant. Future chapters will describe the Japanese-American "culture," its norms, values, and personality, and Japanese behavior. Japanese reactions to the wartime evacuation provide an example of the working of the system.

For example, the community structure with its many small interdependent groups, the critical role of the Issei in terms of leadership, of understanding the system, of wielding power, and of providing for the social control and cohesion of the community, meant that when many Issei leaders were rounded up and incarcerated by the FBI, the system began to fall apart. Many Japanese families were affected by the incarceration, too, so that a group whose primary strength lay in the community and family structure found itself under extremely vulnerable conditions.

The emphasis on norms—the "how to behave in situations" direction of the Japanese culture—also contributed to their docility. Norms and values emphasizing conformity and obedience meant that those in power (e.g., the U.S. Army) were able to use this position to gain the cooperation of the evacuated population.

There were also some primary psychological reasons for Japanese behavior. Many Japanese held low expectations for any sort of "break" in America, so that a wartime evacuation was viewed as a validation of this point of view (e.g., "What else can a poor Japanese expect in America?"); others used the explanation of *shi-ka-ta-ga-nai* ("it can't be helped"), so that the fate of an individual was tied to forces beyond one's control. Other Japanese used a relatively common Japanese point of view —"I'll become an even better American. I'll cooperate more than 100 percent to prove it." The high need for love and acceptance among many Japanese often leads them to pattern their behavior according to their perception of the expectations of those in authority.

There is also a personality characteristic that is probably not peculiar to the ethnic group but is often found among individuals facing extreme stress. It is the denial of reality—the attitude that says, "It can't happen to me." It is a phenomenon that can be found among soldiers on the battle line and was observable among the Jews at Buchenwald and was present with the Japanese at the time of the evacuation. It was a naïve belief that nothing was really going to happen—that the notices to evacuate really meant something else; that the buses and trains were really not taking them anywhere; that the barbed-wire fences and guard towers were really not for them; and, finally, when in camp, that the situation was not real.

There were no models of resistance or of rebellion—some turned to Caucasian friends, who invariably counseled cooperation. Therefore, with no one to turn to, with their structures and institutions dismantled, with little political or economic power, with cultural norms and values emphasizing conformity and nonconflictual behavior, with a lack of feasible alternatives, and facing the awesome might and power of the United States government, the Japanese marched into camp. Could they really have done otherwise?

Can It Happen Again?

Melancholy traces of the evacuation remain today. Rumors that the evacuation camp at Tule Lake was ready for "enemies" were afloat during the McCarthy period and occasionally are heard today. Peterson mentions that Chinese citizens wonder if the same thing can happen to them if hostilities develop between China and the United States.[24] The Japanese evacuation set a precedent whereby a wartime emergency can justify the nullification of other constitutional guarantees. Justice Jackson, in his minority dissent on the Korematsu case, warned against the principle of sanctioning racial discrimination in criminal procedure.

> The principle then lies about like a loaded weapon ready for the hand of any authority that can bring forward a plausible claim of an urgent need. . . . I should hold that a civil court cannot be made to enforce an order which violates constitutional limitations even if it is a reasonable exercise of military authority. The courts can exercise only the judicial power, can only apply law, and must abide by the Constitution, or they cease to be civil courts and become instruments of military policy.[25]

Some of the external conditions leading to the evacuation appear to be ever present. There are pressure groups; there are targets; there is hate, discrimination, prejudice, and irrationality; and there is the noncommitted, fence-sitting majority. And periods in our history record what has happened to individuals and groups—the hanging of witches, the treatment of the Indians, and the guilt by association era during

---

[24]William Peterson, "Success Story: Japanese American Style," *The New York Times Magazine*, January 9, 1966.
[25]Fisher, *Exile of a Race*, p. 181.

the 1950s. But never was there such a mass evacuation of American citizens.

However, when the question of another possible evacuation is raised, we have to ask the question whether we can again find a visible, cooperative, and powerless population; a "popular cause" backed by the vast majority; emergency conditions so that the constitution can be suspended; and a mood whereby the very survival of the country is felt to be at stake. If there is massive resistance to an evacuation—tactics of confrontation, all-out court battles, countermobilization, and a sophisticated use of power and counterstrategies—then it is our hypothesis that something other than a mass evacuation will take place.

A RETROSPECTIVE GLANCE

The wartime evacuation has become the most prominent event in Japanese-American history. It has served as the focal point for hundreds of term papers, so that a new generation of students, especially those enrolled in Asian-American classes, have interviewed former evacuees, studied many of the past documents, and come forth with a variety of interpretations and reinterpretations of this incident. There is even available a published diary by a former resident.[26]

Earlier studies identified the "good" in terms of those evacuees who remained loyal to the United States, who cooperated with the war relocation authorities, who volunteered for the U.S. armed services, and who adapted to camp life with a minimum of overt stress. The primary impetus for this point of view came from the wartime evacuation officials and the journalists and writers (both ethnic and nonethnic) who covered this event.[27] Most of the authors wrote from a sympathetic and liberal perspective.

Recent writing has questioned some of the previous analyses. There is now a tendency to reverse some of the earlier labels, so that there is a more sympathetic portrayal of those who rioted and of those who were previously labeled as "troublemakers."[28] Perhaps the healthiest trend is the discarding of the simple moralistic labels and the attempt to understand evacuee behavior in the context of camp conditions, pressure groups, and the total war situation.

There can be no simple explanation of the events leading to the evacuation and of the reaction of the Japanese to their forced incarcera-

[26]John Modell, *The Kikuchi Diary* (Urbana, Ill.: University of Illinois Press, 1973). This book presents a day-by-day account from a "loyalist" (American) point of view.

[27]See Dillon Myers, *Uprooted Americans* (Tucson: The University of Arizona Press, 1971).

[28]Arthur A. Hansen and David Hacker, "The Manzanar Riot: An Ethnic Perspective," *Amerasia Journal 2* (Fall 1974): 112–57.

tion. Many of the incongruities remain to the present day. For example, the picture of former evacuees holding a reunion and inviting their former head "jailer"[29] to speak and presenting him with a scroll of honor (can one imagine the surviving Jews of the Nazi camps holding a reunion and presenting Eichmann with a scroll?) is as real as the memory of those evacuees who rioted, who were shot dead, and who were buried in the camps. Perhaps these disparate events remain as the best commentary of that period, which will continue to hold the interest of Americans for generations to come.

[29]Myers, *Uprooted Americans*, p. 342.

By 1946 the Japanese were again becoming part of the mainstream of American society. Some had relocated in the Midwest, notably Chicago, and on the Eastern seaboard, but most headed for California once more. Everywhere, they found themselves in a vastly changed country, and, although some wartime anti-Japanese feeling lingered, most of the changes were positive. The controversial McCarran-Walter Immigration Bill, passed in 1952 and opposed by liberal organizations, was favorable to the Japanese—it provided opportunity for naturalization and eventual citizenship for the Issei and a token quota for Japanese immigration. An evacuation claims bill attempted to repay some of the financial losses borne by the Japanese. The payments were meager, with the average rate of settlement estimated at ten cents per dollar. In 1942 the Federal Reserve Bank of San Francisco estimated the total loss for evacuees at $400,000,000, and when the last claim was adjudicated on October 1, 1964, the government had authorized payment of $38,000,000 to 26,560 claimants.[1] Although the average award per claimant was small and the losses per evacuee were great, the repayments were viewed by many Japanese as a symbolic gesture of sympathy and remorse from the government for its treatment

After World War II

of them. Popular feeling began to support rather than discriminate against them, and although most Japanese were still homeless, jobless, and bereft of whatever lands and business they had acquired before the war, they now devoted themselves to repairing their damaged lives in a tolerant emotional climate and as prosperous postwar economy. Most of them were successful.

Nowhere is this success so apparent as in a cursory examination of postwar patterns of occupation, income, and education. In 1940 more than a quarter of all Japanese males were laborers, while in the 1960s, the proportion had dwindled to about 5 percent. In 1960, 15 percent of Japanese males were classified as professional, the same proportion as in white groups, and a proportion that can be compared with a figure of 5 percent for Negroes. Yet in 1940, only 3.8 percent of Japanese had been professionals.[2] Income, too, has risen beyond that of other groups. A re-

[1]Allan R. Bosworth, *America's Concentration Camps* (New York: W. W. Norton & Co., 1967.

[2]U.S. Department of Commerce, Bureau of the Census, *U.S. Census of Population—Nonwhite Population by Race* (Washington, D.C.: Government Printing Office).

cent survey of employees in the California State Civil Service reported in a Japanese-American newspaper reveals that the modal civil service income for Oriental employees (primarily Japanese) was $7400 a year, nearly $3000 more than that of other minority groups in the Civil Service.[3] The Negro modal income, for example, was $4300, and that of all other minority groups was $4600. It is assumed that the civil service wage differences reflect advantages of education and training.

According to the 1970 census, the mean individual income of Japanese-American males sixteen years or older was $8049 ($3513 for females), and the mean family income was $13,511.[4]

In 1970 the median value of homes for the Japanese American was $27,900, and almost no members of the group thought of the problems of housing in racial terms. Rather, the problems of high prices and high interest rates were the main topics of discussion.[5] Thus one can comfortably generalize that economic progress and acculturation has taken place. It is of interest to ask how this has been accomplished in the face of the adverse conditions with which the group has been met.

These changing figures are mostly the result of the changed opportunity structure for the Nisei, and the changed expectations of this group. At the time the Nisei were becoming adult in the late 1930s and early 1940s, the occupational picture had been a bleak one. They were misfits in a depression economy, and their opportunities were not so great as their American ·expectations. Strong devotes a large section of his study to the occupational problems of the second-generation Japanese during the prewar years. Many of them were college educated but to little avail. Strong cites an interview, telling of the frustration and despair of many.

> I know of another American-born Japanese . . . graduated [from] the foremost university on the Pacific Coast. But no American firm would employ him. . . . Cases like these could be multiplied indefinitely.
> So, many of my friends are giving up the fight. "Why get an education?" they say. "Why try to do anything at all? Probably we were meant to be just a servile class."[6]

None of the possible alternatives to this bleak prospect was feasible. Nisei might have returned to Japan, and they might have gone East. But jobs were scarce in Japan, and the American-trained, English-speaking

---

[3]*Nichi-bei Times,* December 3, 1963 (English section), p. 1.

[4]U.S. Department of Commerce, Bureau of the Census, *Japanese, Chinese, and Filipinos in the United States.* 1970 Census of the Population, PC(2)-1G (Washington. D.C.: Government Printing Office, 1973), pp. 39, 42.

[5]Ibid., p. 46.

[6]Edward K. Strong, Jr., *The Second Generation Japanese Problem* (Stanford, Calif.: Stanford University Press, 1934), p. 12.

Nisei was a duck out of water in the country of his ancestors. Jobs were also scarce in the eastern part of the United States. Japanese were commonly rejected with the line, "I don't mind hiring you myself, but my employees would object."

So the Nisei took jobs within the ethnic community. Japanese college graduates manned the fruit stands in the Los Angeles produce markets, and Japanese employers demanded a college education from their $60 a month salesmen.

Ironically, the wartime evacuation played a major part in changing both the kinds of jobs the Nisei expected to get and the kinds of jobs they in fact got. In the evacuation centers, a whole range of occupations was open to them that had never been available before. For the first time, with their race no longer a factor in competition, Nisei were able to fill every job a community requires (except the administrative, reserved for Caucasians). Japanese competed against other Japanese, so that education, training, and ability determined success. Although the jobs in camp were low paying—$16 to $19 per month—the Nisei worked on all levels. For example, Japanese Americans with teaching credentials, who had never been able to get jobs in California, were needed in camp. For many, the experience and training in camp jobs served to help them relocate later in Eastern communities.

Perhaps the most important thing gained from camp job experiences was confidence. Nisei found they could do good work in varied and important roles. The satisfaction of being allowed to do what they were capable of doing and trained to do ultimately made them dissatisfied with anything less. The "cognitive discrepancy" and the occupational discrepancy could best be resolved by upward mobility for this generation once they were released from camp. Fortunately, the other part of the discrepancy—the availability of job opportunities in the employee's market following World War II—also worked in favor of the Nisei. After the war they found occupations more congruent with their qualifications both in the East and in the West. In some fields, such as architecture, Nisei gained prominence. For many, the civil service, previously difficult to enter, was the answer.

GO EAST, YOUNG MAN

The Japanese who have settled in the East have done much better in certain respects. When one hears of a Japanese in an administrative, executive, or prominent position it is highly probable that he is working east of the Mississippi.

There is also evidence that Japanese living east of the Mississippi are doing better financially than those who have stayed in California.

Income figures for 1960 from the U.S. Census Bureau show that Japanese between the ages of thirty-five and forty-four living in the Northeast—New York and Washington, D.C., principally—had a median income of $4887. Those in the North Central area (Chicago) made $5178, and those who stayed in California made only $4555. The 1970 census compared median Japanese male income in major cities as follows: Chicago, $8295; New York, $7826; San Francisco, $7337; Los Angeles, $7209.[7] Interestingly, the highest median income was in San Jose, California ($9390). Other data drawn from the 1970 census, such as the urban-rural proportions; the overall geographic distribution; the sex ratio; male and female marriages within their own ethnic group by age; occupational distribution by sex and nativity and poverty characteristics are in the Appendix. There are, in California, still some unofficial forms of job restriction. We interviewed a Nisei newspaperman who holds a prominent position in a major Rocky Mountain newspaper. When asked to compare job opportunities away from California with those within the state, he commented:

> I think it works several ways. I'm almost certain that a major Los Angeles or San Francisco newspaper would not appoint me to this position. I'm even more sure that if I were a newspaperman in those cities I'd never apply or expect to fill this position.[8]

His feeling is indicative of the suble underexpectancy among many Japanese along the West Coast. It is still rare to find Nisei in executive and administrative positions; partly perhaps because of the lack of opportunity, but also because of their low expectations of filling such positions. The income figures for the Japanese in California show the discrepancy between their education (the highest) and their income (lower than the less-educated white population). Although "reaching for the stars" may be dysfunctional in that it sets up conditions for possible frustration and despair, underexpectancy, or reaching for the lower rungs of the ladder, may also prove to be a hindrance to any group over the long term.

There are also other noticeable tendencies among many Japanese employees on the West Coast. Many feel that they have to be better than white employees—"better" often defined as more conscientious, more productive, and more efficient. Therefore, in certain lines they have become especially sought after; for example, it is difficult to hire an office

---

[7]*Japanese, Chinese, and Filipinos in the United States*, p. 55.
[8]Harry H. L. Kitano, private interviews with members of the Japanese community, 1964.

girl or secretary of Japanese ancestry because the demand for them is so high.

Nevertheless, the type of discrimination faced by the West Coast Japanese, although subtle and often difficult to validate, is there, as perceived from Japanese eyes. For example, a summary of an article written by Daniels, appearing in the *Los Angeles Times* of March 21, 1967, emphasized that Orientals were generally slighted, undervalued, and treated unequally, both in terms of history and at the present time. Within one week of the newspaper article, Daniels reported that he received over twenty letters from Japanese, thanking him for reporting a fact that needed more publicity.[9] The number of letters from a traditionally non–letter-writing population attests to the sensitivity of some Japanese to the unequality of their treatment.

The letter-writers included several with high-paying, high-status positions and a Ph.D. physical scientist. They all cited personal experiences, and their general complaint was that Japanese were ignored, or promoted much more slowly than whites of equal or even lower training and ability.

A doctoral dissertation by Wong[10] in 1974 illustrates the subtle effects of discrimination. Wong found that Japanese (and Chinese and blacks) earn less at each level of education than do whites. Minority male workers generally have lower earnings because they receive lower returns on their education; they are excluded from high-earning occupations; they are prevented from advancing within particular occupations; and they experience greater unemployment. Further, the situation has not improved appreciably, since the relative economic standing of the minorities is in fact not much better than it was for previous generations.

There are several ways of analyzing the "progress" of the Japanese. One common method is to use the past as the base line; from this perspective there has been continuous upward mobility and "success." Incomes have risen, the standard of living has changed, and the current Japanese American appears bigger, stronger, better educated, better fed, and better dressed (taking into account the changes in dress styles) when compared to previous generations.

However, if progress is measured in relation to other groups, especially the white majority, a different picture emerges. It can be argued that for every step forward that the Japanese American takes, the whites may be taking two, and it is from this perspective that the economic mobility and "success" of the group may be questioned.

[9] Roger Daniels, personal conversation.
[10] Harold H. Wong, "The Relative Economic Status of Chinese, Japanese, Black and White Men in California." (Ph.D. diss., University of California, Berkeley, 1974).

THE "KAI-SHA" AND
THE INFLUENCE OF JAPAN

We have previously mentioned the *Kai-sha* Japanese. They are a special group, usually made up of Japanese representing large Japanese corporations. Many of these companies have both Japanese-American and Caucasian employees, although in general the top management positions are filled by citizens of Japan.[11] These companies have been in the United States ever since trade became important between the two countries, and, typically, the major headquarters have been in New York.

Our main reason for considering the Kai-sha is that they had an influence on American attitudes and perceptions toward the Japanese. Although businessmen as a prestigious social class are a relatively new development in Japan, the rapid rise of industrialization, urbanization, and modernization placed enormous power into the hands of business in that country. The Japanese businessman was therefore able to communicate and interact with American business on a relatively equal basis, especially in New York markets. These business transactions often led to social interaction. Miyakawa notes that many of the exclusive social clubs in the New York area have had Japanese members for many years.[12] The popular West Coast image of the Japanese as laborers and peasants has not been an integral part of the Eastern image.

Other Japanese nationals, such as those representing the diplomatic corps, the temporary college students, and visiting members of the royalty and upper classes, have also presented a different image of the Japanese, especially to the Eastern United States. Therefore, another perception of the Japanese image—a subtle but perhaps significant factor in social acceptance—came from Japanese who were only temporarily in the United States. The irony is that few of these Japanese have had much to do with Japanese Americans and vice versa.

In this sense, the area of settlement is an important variable in the assimilation process. In general, we see the East as being more color blind but also more class conscious, so that a visiting member of the Japanese nobility would probably find a more ready social acceptance in the East than, say, a newly rich immigrant from southern or Eastern Europe. For example, Miyakawa describes a recent talk with a second-generation Italian from Boston who felt that the Japanese was much "luckier" than the socially "inferior" Italian from a lower-class background.

[11]Matsukichi Amano, "A Study of Employment Patterns and a Measurement of Employee Attitudes in Japanese Firms in Los Angeles" (Ph.D. diss., University of California, Los Angeles, 1966).

[12]T. Scott Miyakawa, personal conversation. Professor Miyakawa was the first director of the Japanese-American Research Project operating from UCLA, 1962–1965.

Conversely, the West Coast is less classbound but much more race conscious, so that there a visiting member of Japanese nobility may still be "just another Jap." This is true even though West Coast values may stress a more equalitarian and liberal attitude in other areas.

In any case, since the end of World War II in California and elsewhere, the Nisei have not suffered the overt discrimination their fathers faced, and have therefore been able to alter drastically the statistical occupation-income patterns for the Japanese group as a whole. Predictably, the Nisei complaints of discrimination have moved toward the subtler areas of promotions and advancement to administrative and supervisory responsibility.

Very few Sansei have faced overt discrimination, so that their job opportunities are determined primarily by their education and training and the overall employment picture. Therefore the sudden surplus of teachers and engineers in the early 1970s may alter the historical pattern of college training, since the most popular majors were teacher training for the Sansei females and engineering for the males.

JAPANESE-AMERICAN
FIELDS OF ENDEAVOR

Small Business

Erickson, through an interview with the manager of the Los Angeles Japanese Chamber of Commerce, describes Japanese business progress.[13] In 1958 the Japanese Americans in Los Angeles owned 6800 businesses (80 percent by Nisei) representing seventy-eight fields of endeavor. The largest number of these were in private contract gardening (5070), followed in order by 250 apartments and hotels, 129 grocery stores, 65 laundry shops, 60 service stations, 60 insurance offices, 54 restaurants, 46 dental dispensaries, 44 real estate brokerages, 34 florist shops and flower growing, and 7 travel agencies. The broad professional field listed 11 opticians, 15 lawyers, 5 practicing physicians (excluding those primarily in institutional settings), 24 accounting firms, 7 firms in the building engineering field, and 2 banks. There were also 13 companies in newspaper and other publishing, 12 in theater and amusements, and 1 Japanese-owned hospital. The estimated Japanese population in Los Angeles for 1958 was 45,000. In other words, more than 1 out of every 7 Japanese owned his own business. This is clearly an expansion of the prewar trend toward self-employment in urban centers.

After the war many Japanese managed to reestablish small businesses. But opportunities had changed. The pressures of the supermarket

---

13Al Erickson, "L.A.'s Nisei Today," *California Sun Magazine* (Summer 1958): 3.

on the small family grocery, the disproportion between work and reward, labor costs, and more attractive alternatives—these factors have drastically altered the small-business picture. Japanese shops are now often unionized, and the former Japanese employees have not come back to work in them. They have found wider opportunities elsewhere, and many note special disadvantages in going to work again for a prewar employer. We talked with a man who had returned to the same cleaning establishment, and who found his own attitudes vastly changed. He told us:

> Now we're all unionized. When I went back to work the quitting time was 5:00. All of the non-Japanese would begin putting things away so that by 5:00 they would be out. Unfortunately, all of the previous old timers [Japanese only], even if they were in the union, were expected to clean up or continue working until the day's work was done. This meant that even though I was in the union, I found myself still working past closing time with no extra pay. It was expected of me. It got to be too much so I finally quit.[14]

Exposure to other types of business models during the evacuation and differing expectations and increased opportunities were significant factors in producing the change in this individual's reaction. The 1970 census shows that the first-ranked employment category of urban Japanese males was in the "professional, technical and kindred workers" category, followed by "craftsmen, foremen and kindred workers" and "managers and administrators."[15]

Gardening, however, has assumed a new prominence since the war. Japanese returning to the West Coast found they had not been replaced here as they had in other areas and were indeed faced with a growing demand. Furthermore, the prewar stereotype had not changed at all: people continued to think that all Japanese were good gardeners. A large number of Issei and Nisei who had never been interested in gardening before now entered the field. In 1946 Bloom and Riemer, surveying a small geographical area around Sawtelle Avenue in Los Angeles, found that of the 388 employed males living there, 294, or over 75 percent, were doing contract gardening. Before the war only 48 percent of the men in this neighborhood were in this field.[16]

The 1970 census illustrates the urban-rural distribution of the Japanese. The great majority, or 88 percent, of families lived in cities, followed by 9 percent in rural nonfarm areas, while only 3 percent were on

[14]Kitano, private interviews.

[15]*Japanese, Chinese, and Filipinos in the United States*, p. 38.

[16]Leonard Bloom and Ruth Riemer, *Removal and Return* (Berkeley: University of California Press, 1949), p. 64.

rural farms.[17] The majority of those who have remained on the farms are likely to be classified as farmers and managers, rather than as farm laborers.[18]

EDUCATION AND
THE TEACHING PROFESSION

A number of Nisei have gone into teaching, an occupational choice that is also related to the traditional Japanese attitude toward education. It would appear logical that a group with a high respect for learning and for academic excellence would itself turn to teaching in fairly large numbers. Before World War II, however, lack of opportunity was the major deterrent. Nisei were excellent students and would have made excellent teachers, but timid school districts would not hire them. As late as 1950, Nisei were told by the education department of the University of California, "It's better if you don't go into teacher training. We just won't be able to place you."[19] And, unlike the situation in such professions as banking, where Japanese could find employment in Japanese firms, Nisei could not teach in Japanese-language schools because they did not really know the language.

Today the Japanese have made rapid progress in the teaching field. A successful Nisei teacher told us:

> When I came to UCLA [1936] I had to pick a college major so I chose elementary education. I always wanted to be a teacher, so even when they told me there would never be a job for me, I went ahead to work for my teacher's certificate. Actually, some of the other girls were in sociology, or economics and they'd never be able to get a job either. So I guess you can say we were all even.
>
> After I got my degree in 1940, I didn't even look for a job in teaching since there were no openings for Japanese. Soon after, I was evacuated. While in camp, they needed teachers very badly and somehow or other, they knew I had teacher training and the state sent over a teaching certificate. So I taught for several years in camp—when I relocated to Idaho, that state kept after me to teach.
>
> I came back to California in 1946 and tried to find a teaching job. It was still discouraging but I stuck to it and finally landed a position. I still remember that first day . . . as I was walking into the teachers' lunchroom, one of the teachers said in a voice loud enough so that I could hear, "Look who we're hiring now, we really must be hard up."
>
> It wasn't a pleasant situation but I knew I could teach and my experiences in camp helped out. Now that I look back on it, I always wanted to teach, I finally got the opportunity, and I'm glad I stiuck it out.[20]

17*Japanese, Chinese, and Filipinos in the United States*, p. 38.
18Ibid., p. 38.
19Kitano, private interviews.
20Ibid.

The story provides a striking contrast to the 1940s. Of the approximately thirty girls (95 percent Japanese) at an all-Oriental sorority in UCLA, over half are majoring in teacher training, and there is no difficulty in job placement. There are Nisei principals, vice-principals, and administrators in the Los Angeles school system—a remarkable achievement for a group that was systematically turned away from teaching as late as 1950, and one that says a great deal about the rapid evaporation of majority prejudice. The history of Japanese-American educators in Hawaii, as discussed in Chapter 10, was dramatically different so that in that state, they have achieved a dominant status.

In similar fashion, other Japanese college graduates—those going into engineering and accounting and numerous other fields—do not appear any longer to have difficulty finding jobs. We would expect, however, to find certain changes in the educational expectations of the Sansei generation.

Evidence is meager and often contradictory, but, as the Japanese grow in affluence, we would expect their children to choose college majors that are less concretely job-oriented and more often involved with the liberal arts, social sciences, and literature. We would expect more to leave the West Coast to attend schools and colleges in the Midwest and the East without the impetus of another wartime evacuation. For by the 1970s, the effects of the forced dispersal of several decades before had vanished, and even the Japanese who relocated away from the Pacific Coast have followed the general tendency to move toward California. The educational choices and advantages provided by the State of California in the past—the tuition-free junior college, the state colleges, and the University of California system have been instrumental in their success in education. The current generation no longer has the tuition-free advantage, but they still remain a high college bound group. In a *Los Angeles Times* article by Trombley based on a Ford Foundation report, the Asians (presumably Chinese and Japanese) were overrepresented in the college population.[21] Although they constituted .8 percent of the United States population, they were 1 percent of the undergraduate student body and 2 percent of the graduate school enrollment. In contrast, the blacks constituted 11.1 percent of the population and 6.9 percent of the college group.

OCCUPATIONAL STRATEGY

The Japanese have never directly striven for occupational mobility and expanded job opportunities. They have instead used an adaptive process—education, training, and patience, low expectations, hard work,

---

[21]William Trombley, article, *Los Angeles Times*, August 26, 1974, p. 1.

and more patience—until opportunities were available. Then a legion of already trained and qualified people poured in to meet the opportunities. Such a "strategy" depends, of course, on having a well-trained and patient labor force that has alternative opportunities during the waiting period. The Japanese emphasis on higher education, the use of jobs in the ethnic system, and patience have served them well in this way. As in the case of many "strategies," however, the process of waiting and adapting was less "planned" than "forced" by the realities of the Japanese position.

Finally, the characteristic Issei expectation of owning a small business or running one's own small farm has for the Nisei changed to a preference for a "clean job" and a "white collar." For the Sansei, this in turn has changed to occupations providing both status and security—professions such as medicine, engineering, dentistry, architecture, and teaching. And, with changing occupational expectations by generation, we begin to see subtle changes in the social-class structure.

It is difficult to speculate about the future of the Japanese in gardening. Today many gardeners hold other part-time jobs, and many think of it as a temporary occupation. However, the attempts of gardeners' associations to standardize fees and upgrade the profession have been highly successful. Income is high, especially for those willing to work long hours and who are geared toward contracts. A national magazine in 1966 mentioned that incomes of $15,000 were not uncommon for Japanese gardeners.

Nevertheless, it appears that the Sansei will not voluntarily follow in the footsteps of their parents and grandparents in this profession. Social status in this case appears more important than income alone. However, there are willing replacements. Many of the newer Japanese immigrants (the new Issei who have emigrated to the United States since 1954) have become gardeners, and an occupation that offers a combination of relative independence, adequate income, and a dimension of creativity will not remain empty for long.

One other occupation deserves special mention because of Japanese dominance in this field. It is the interesting ability to discriminate between female and male baby chicks. "Chicken sexing" has been a popular occupation for a small but specialized segment in the Japanese community. The demand for chick sexers was especially high during World War II and the postwar era.

Agriculture: The Major Occupational Contribution

Notwithstanding the rapid progress of the Japanese into many other occupations, their major quantitative contribution to America thus far has been in agriculture. Iwata, writing in 1962, summarizes the contributions thus:

Today, in their 70's and 80's [referring to age], the remaining Issei can only reminisce of their own life of struggle to gain a position, usually humble, in agriculture. Very few, however, even among the Japanese themselves, realize the important role the Japanese immigrants collectively played in California agricultural history. . . . They filled the farm labor vacuum and thus prevented a ruinous slump in those lines of agriculture for which California is noted, namely in the growing and harvesting of intensive crops. As indepenent farm operators, the Japanese with their skill and energy helped to reclaim and improve thousands of acres of worthless lands throughout the State, lands which the white man abhorred, and made them fertile and immensely productive. They pioneered the rice industry and planted the first citrus orchards in the hog wallow lands in the San Joaquin Valley. They played a vital part in establishing the present system of marketing fruits and vegetables, especially in Los Angeles County, and dominated in the field of commercial truck crops. From the perspective of history, it is evident that the contributions of the Issei to California's economy far outweigh the evils that have been attributed to their agricultural activities. They were undeniably a significant factor in making California one of the greatest farming States in the union.[22]

Those who have continued in agriculture have done well, too, but the pattern is somewhat different from that which existed prior to World War II.

Whereas before the war Japanese dominated the produce markets, especially in the Los Angeles area, they have now dispersed their activities. In some sections where Issei pioneered, such as the Imperial Valley, they have not returned at all; the loss of valuable leases and equipment proved too great an obstacle. But now, most Japanese in agriculture own the land they work. This has caused them to become better integrated with the white majority community than Japanese in many other occupations. They have joined interethnic rather than ethnic cooperatives, and are taking prominent roles in the affairs of agricultural communities. Predictably, too, they reflect the common concern of the agricultural entrepreneur to find the "ideal farm laborer," so many now find themselves looking for the docile, yet efficient, worker. In all probability, they would now view their own Issei parents in the same light as the California farmer viewed them in the 1920s—as ideal laborers except for their desire to own land and to rise above the laboring class.

To the current third generation of Japanese (Sansei), agriculture does not seem so desirable. A farmer is often thought of as a bumpkin, and the *inaka* (country) is spoken of derisively. It is said that the same phenomenon is occuring in Japan, too, so that the old question "How're you going to keep them down on the farm?" is a realistic one. The irony

---

[22]Masakazu Iwata, "The Japanese Immigrants in California Agriculture," *Agricultural History* 36, no. 1 (1962), p. 13.

of this is that, although agriculture currently has less status, the Japanese who are farming today are usually prosperous. The author remembers, during his student days at Berkeley, being somewhat envious of the big cars and liberal allowances of Nisei students who came from the agricultural communities.

A recent study of socioeconomic mobility by Levine and Montero offers insight into the importance of generational ties.[23] One of the most important predictors of upward mobility for subsequent Japanese generations was the level of education of the Issei—the higher their education, the higher the probability of their Nisei children achieving higher positions.

The continued emphasis on education among the Sansei would appear to insure continued socioeconomic success, although the other half of the equation, appropriate opportunities, should not be ignored. For it was not that long ago that college-educated Nisei were unable to find positions congruent with their education and training so that recessions, depressions, and discrimination remain as factors beyond the control of any minority group.

Downward mobility, a rarity in the earlier days, is another present day reality among some Japanese. The high educational and professional achievement of Nisei has meant that for some Sansei, the expectation of equalling or surpassing their parents is neither realistic nor desirable. The picture of a proud, less educated parent showing off his child's college diploma can be joined by the picture of professional parents attempting to understand why their child has resorted to drugs or dropped out of school.

DEVELOPMENT OF
SOCIAL-CLASS DIFFERENCES

In respect to social class, what is happening to the Japanese is typical of what has happened to other immigrant groups. From a base of relatively homogeneous occupation, income, education, and social-class backgrounds has developed a clearer set of differentiating factors that encourage social-class divisions. Although these boundaries are fluid, there is an increased awareness among the Japanese of the various styles of life and values associated with social class. It is perhaps an irony that many Issei emigrated to the United States to escape the relatively rigid class structure of Meiji Japan only to find that their children and grandchildren are developing a similar, although more fluid, structure here in this country.

23Gene Levine and Darrel Montero, "Socio-economic Mobility among Three Generations of Japanese Americans," *Journal of Social Issues* 29, no. 2 (1973): 33–48.

One exception regarding the homogeneity of the immigrant population was a group known as the *eta*. DeVos and Wagatsuma describe some of the "out" groups of Japanese society, such as the *buraku-min, hi-nin* (nonpeople), and eta, and it is believed that a few members of the latter group were among the early migrants to the United States.[24] The eta were similar to an "untouchable" class in Japan, but research into this facet of the Japanese-American social structure has been difficult to conduct. For example, Ito tried to gather evidence of eta adjustment in the United States and met with such resistance that his project was abandoned.[25] He suggests that the amount of resistance exhibited by the Issei to this topic was evidence for the importance of the subject of the "untouchables" in social interaction.

Interestingly enough, Ito suggests that Issei of possible eta background reacted toward their disadvantaged status in a "typical" Japanese manner. Rather than fleeing into the American culture, they instead attempted to become "better Japanese" by engaging in Japanese cultural activities at a higher proportion than their peers. He concludes that eta background was probably of only minor consequence among the Nisei and that prejudice against this group has disappeared among the Sansei.

It is our impression that eta background, or for that matter, even ken background, is unimportant to the current generations. We have noted that very few of the Sansei and Yonsei know the ken of their forbearers, although a small group is quite interested in Japan and their ancestry.

SUMMARY OF PRESENT-DAY
OCCUPATIONAL TRENDS

At the present time, several generalizations concerning occupations among the Japanese ethnic group in America appear valid. First, although there has been rapid progress, Japanese Americans are still not fully integrated into the occupational structure of the society. A full range of occupations is not accessible (nor perhaps desired) by the Japanese. For example, except in all-Japanese businesses, very few are executives or administrators or in publicly visible positions. Few have entered into those occupations typically known as "blue collar," as operatives in large factories. Although the major center of the Japanese population surrounds Hollywood, few Japanese are found in the entertainment industry, except when an occasional *Flower Drum Song* requires an Ori-

[24]George DeVos and Hiroshi Wagatsuma (eds.), *Japan's Invisible Race* (Berkeley: University of California Press, 1966).
[25]Hiroshi Ito, "Japan's Outcastes in the United States," in *ibid.*, pp. 200–21.

ental cast. The Japanese actor, like the Negro actor, is as yet restricted to Oriental type-casting, and does not find roles reflecting assimilation into everyday American life.

It would be difficult not to ignore the importance of more realistic and less stereotypic portrayals in the mass media for ethnic groups, especially one as small in size and of restricted geographical distribution as the Japanese Americans. The probabilities of most Americans ever meeting them on an intimate basis are almost nil, therefore most information about the Nikkei will come through the movies, television, and books. Unfortunately, the most widespread exposure of Japanese occurred during the propaganda period of World War II, and these movies continue to be shown to new generations of Americans. Most distributors and screenors have been cooperative when approached about the possible negative effects of continuing to show a racist stereotype, but others question the "supersensitivity" of the ethnic group and insist that they cannot bow down to censorship or threats. It is probably impossible to share with majority group members the feeling of seeing one's own ethnic group portrayed exclusively as second-class citizens, servants, spies, traitors, villains, and suicidal maniacs, or of seeing Japanese females invariably ending up in the arms of Caucasian heroes. Therefore, it was no surprise that when Japanese like Toshiro Mifune, or characters like Zatoichi and other samurai portrayed a more heroic Japanese image, they found a ready market among their ethnic peers in Hawaii and on the mainland.

We have also observed that talent is frequently a case of majority group membership. For example, while in Japan we observed the large number of untalented people appearing on television—the announcers, the hosts, and some of the performers had little talent by whatever standards. But if the performer happened to be from a minority group, for example, from Taiwan, the chances were high that one would see a first-class performance. Similarly, on returning to the United States we observed the large number of dull, shallow, toothy, majority group hosts, announcers, and performers with little talent. But membership in the majority group allows for wide latitudes in the definition of talent, whereas a minority group individual has to stand out in order to be given a chance.

Overall generalizations concerning occupations are still dependent on the geographical area of residence. Japanese Americans living in other parts of the country, being better distributed in terms of education and training, have a wider variety of choices and opportunities than those living in California. But certain broad trends appear to hold for Japanese in all geographical areas. Current major sources of employment include civil service, gardening, and agriculture. Those who aspire to professional status do so mostly by becoming pharmacists, engineers, dentists, schoolteachers, doctors, and nurses. Several have become prominent in architecture. Very few have become politicians, firemen, policemen, or professional athletes, although all of these occupational categories have been widely used by other immigrant minorities to achieve status.

It is also deceiving to glance at the types of occupations held by many Japanese, especially in the large California cities. Jobs connected with real estate, insurance, specialty shops, banks, savings and loan associations, law, and medicine sound like true middle-class positions, and they are. But they are primarily dependent on the ethnic community. In these areas we are apt to find that the job sounds 100 percent American, acculturative, and integrative to the middle class, but in fact reflects a structural pluralism and remains dependent on the support of the ethnic community.

By the 1970s one could "scratch a Japanese American" and not be able to predict what was underneath. For there might be any one of four generations, the Issei, Nisei, Sansei, or Yonsei, and to add further confusion, an Issei might now be a new, young immigrant fresh from Japan. For the history of the Japanese in the United States has encompassed four generations, so that acculturation, multiple experiences, and differentiation have had a chance to be felt over a span of more than seventy years. Similarly, Japan has experienced constant changes, and previous generalizations about its culture may have to be modified.

It is within this context that we will present a picture of the current Japanese family and community. Starting with the structure brought from Japan the most reasonable observation is that of acculturation and change. But acculturation has not followed a simple linear pattern; rather it has varied in terms of place and situation, so that variables like ethnic power, numbers, cohesion, goals, and expectations must be considered. There is also the degree of permeability of the American system, which has varied in terms of time, place, and situation so variables like prejudice and discrimination have to be included in any explanation of acculturation. It is the hypothesized interaction among all of these variables that helps to explain the current stage of the Japanese family and community.

The Current Japanese Family and Community

THE FAMILY

The Japanese family was never a monolithic structure, although during the early days it displayed a relatively high degree of homogeneity. By the 1970s, the Japanese were as diverse as any American group. The surviving Issei were generally retired and facing the problems of old age; the Nisei were ensconced in their middle years and attempting to understand the behavior of the Sansei, while the Sansei were in the process of raising their own families (Yonsei). In a few families all of the generations would remain close; in others all generational ties would be cut off; while the majority was somewhere in between. With the mix of the generations, there would also be variations by social class, by urbanization, and by area of residence.

TABLE 3

JAPANESE-AMERICAN OUTMARRIAGES IN
LOS ANGELES COUNTY, 1924–1972*

Year	Percentage Japanese Outmarriage
1924–33	2
1948	12
1952	14
1955	21
1959	23
1971	47
1972	49

*Akemi Kikumura and Harry H. L. Kitano, "Interracial Marriage: A Picture of the Japanese Americans," *The Journal of Social Issues* 29, 2 (1973): 69.

INTERRACIAL MARRIAGE

Perhaps the most formidable barrier in the interaction between races is that of marriage. Terms such as "mixing oil with water," of racial dilution, and of mongrelization are indicative of the deep feelings against this practice, and the phrase "Do you want your daughter to marry one?" has become symptomatic of the ultimate barrier. Antimiscegenation laws have legalized societal discrimination.

The negative feelings about intermarriage are often held by both sides. For example, Maryland had an antimiscegenation statute as early as 1661, and even though state bans on intermarriage are no longer constitutional, sixteen states still held such laws in 1967. Although the Japanese were "victims" of such practices, they also preferred that their children marry within their own group, so it would be reasonable to conclude that interracial marriage would be one of the most formidable barriers in the path of assimilation.

Prior to 1960, the outstanding tendency of the Japanese Americans was to marry within their own group. For example, Los Angeles County Marriage Statistics (see Table 3) indicate that in 1924, Japanese Americans outmarried at a 2 percent rate, and as recently as 1959, the rates were at a relatively low 23 percent. But there were generational and acculturative changes in the Japanese group as well as changes in the majority community that resulted in a dramatic increase in Japanese outmarriages.

By 1971, Japanese rates of outmarriage in Los Angeles were 47 percent, which then rose to 49 percent in 1972.[1] The Los Angeles experience was not an isolated phenomenon. Fresno's interracial marriage rates were

[1]Akemi Kikumura and Harry H. L. Kitano, "Interracial Marriage: A Picture of the Japanese Americans," *The Journal of Social Issues* 29, 2 (1973): 67–81.

always below 20 percent through 1963, but in 1969 they reached 58 percent.[2] Similar high rates characterized Japanese-American outmarriages in San Francisco (58 percent in 1971)[3] and Hawaii.[4] It should be emphasized, however, that these figures pertain to recent years only and that the total picture still shows a high in-group marital pattern. The 1970 census indicates that over 88 percent of Japanese marriages (over sixteen years of age)[5] were to spouses of the same race.

In the early days, the female chose non-Japanese partners, but by 1972 the Los Angeles males contributed 44 percent of the total. The majority of outmarriages were to Caucasians, followed by Chinese spouses.

A number of hypotheses explain the rise in outmarriages. The barriers erected by the larger society have lessened. Laws preventing miscegenation have been ruled unconstitutional. There appears to be a more tolerant attitude concerning intimate Japanese–Caucasian interaction. Interracial marriages are also affected by such variables as group size, geographic propinquity, the male–female ratio, acculturation, the cohesiveness of the ethnic community and family, ethnic identity, status, and power. It is interesting to note that the current rise in outmarriage is taking place at a time when there is a reemphasis on ethnic identity. It may very well be that love does not recognize racial boundaries.

THE SIZE OF THE FAMILY

Another variable that is directly linked to acculturation is the size of families. In 1970 the average size of the Japanese family was 2.67.[6]

Much of the early fear of Japanese centered around such notions as "they want white women," and "they breed like rabbits." California, it was predicted, would be overrun with yellow hordes even if immigration were prohibited. Elaborate mathematical tables were constructed to prove this, and, indeed, in the early period there was an apparent, although misleading, basis for this prediction. Young, rural immigrant populations do tend to have large families. However, as the population began to take on a more normal distribution—as it came to include the aged and children—birth rates also began to level out. The average size of the Japanese family in 1960 was 4.0, which can be compared to the mean of

2John N. Tinker, "Intermarriage and Ethnic Boundaries: The Japanese American Case," *The Journal of Social Issues* 29, 2 (1973): 49–66.

3Glen Omatsu, "Nihonmachi Beat," *Hokubei Mainichi*, San Francisco, January 12, 1972 (English section).

4Kikumura and Kitano, "Interracial Marriage."

5U.S. Department of Commerce, Bureau of the Census, *Japanese, Chinese, and Filipinos in the United States*. 1970 Census of the Population, PC (2)-1G (Washington, D.C.: Government Printing Office, 1973), p. 17.

6Ibid., p. 38.

3.5 for whites, 4.1 for Chinese, 4.3 for Filipinos, 3.8 for blacks, and 4.2 for people with Spanish surnames.

One interesting prediction in the 1920s was made by V. S. Mc-Clatchy, a major California newspaper publisher, a director of the Associated Press, and one of the most dedicated Japanophobes.

> Careful tables of increase of the Japanese population in the United States . . . place the total . . . in 1923 at 318,000; in 1933 at 542,000; in 1943 at 875,000; in 1963 at 2,000,000; in 2003 at 10,000,000; and in 2063 at 100,000,000.[7]

The overall Japanese population total of under 600,000 in 1970 falls far short of the prediction that the Japanese would soon be over-running the country.

ADOLESCENCE AND DATING[8]

The most accurate generalization of current adolescent and dating practices is that there are as many patterns for the Japanese American as there are for the population at large. Ethnicity, however, remains an important "other" factor, and how this "Japaneseness" (primarily in terms of physical identifiability) is perceived and treated remains a critical problem in terms of dating and marriage. Generally, physical identifiability becomes a salient issue during adolescence.

One pattern is described by Wakatsuki Houston[9] in her autobiographical novel. It is the Japanese child growing up in a "white" world and suddenly recognizing that she (or he) is different. Although her description focuses on events several decades ago, the theme is a timeless one. She has a close girl friend who is white. While in their pre-teens they share their lives, and the Japanese-American girl "helps" the other, in this case by teaching her baton twirling. But the relationship changes as the girls grow older; suddenly the blonde, blue-eyed girl becomes the center of attention. She is the more "desirable," while the Japanese-American child gets pushed to the background. Feelings of frustration, of envy, and of questions concerning ethnic identity are a common result.

At the other extreme is the child who grows up in an ethnic world. Close friends are Japanese Americans, which is isomorphic with the pa-

[7]Roger Daniels and Harry H. L. Kitano, *American Racism* (Englewood Cliffs, N.J.: Prentice-Hall, Inc., 1970), p. 52.

[8]Harry H. L. Kitano and Akemi Kikumura, "The Japanese Family Life Style" in *American Minority Life Styles*, ed. Robert Habenstein and Charles Mindel (New York: Holt, Rinehart and Winston, Inc., on press).

[9]Jeanne Wakatsuki Houston and James D. Houston, *Farewell to Manzanar* (Boston: Houghton Mifflin Co., 1973).

rental world. Attendance at public schools and universities does not significantly alter the pattern, even though there are probably no schools where they constitute even a sizeable minority. Extracurricular activities and social life revolve around ethnic organizations and structures. Athletic leagues, voluntary groups, and the church provide an ethnic base, especially in communities like Los Angeles and the San Francisco Bay area. Dating and marriage are likely to remain within the group in this pattern.

The "new pattern" of delaying marriage, yet living together, is also familiar to some Sansei. One extended family of our acquaintance has over fifteen children of marriageable age, yet only three are married. Several are living together without a formal marriage, and the expectation of having children and raising families is of low priority to the entire group.

A former pattern (prior to World War II) of sending children back to Japan for upbringing (the Kibei) has now disappeared. But a substitute pattern—of tourism, of longer visits, and of some schooling in Japan—is emerging. There are numerous group tours to Japan, and the number of Japanese Americans who have visited Japan is constantly rising. The University of California Tokyo Study Center, established a decade ago for University of California students, started with almost no Nisei or Sansei students. But in 1973, 75 percent of the group were of Japanese ancestry. Their experiences in Japan will undoubtedly influence their attitudes and behaviors.

The important difference in the current pattern of interethnic dating and of visiting Japan is that of voluntarism. Whereas most of the earlier choices were forced because there was almost no other way, the current patterns reflect a freer selection among alternatives.

DIFFERENCES AND PROBLEMS

The divergences in experiences, values, life styles, and perceptions among the three generations—the aged Issei, the middle-aged Nisei, and the younger Sansei—are vast. Views of the world are different and create strain. For example, although there is a nostalgia about the role of grandparents, there are also practical realities that must be faced by many Japanese families in regard to the aging. Generally, grandparents are less acculturated and more "Japanized," so there are practical problems of language, reading materials, and food preferences.[10] As the elderly become more dependent on their children, problems of their care arise. Placing them in majority-group institutions is not an attractive prospect,

[10]Richard Kalish and Sharon Moriwaki, "The World of the Elderly Asian American," *Journal of Social Issues* 29, 2 (1973): 187–209.

and the development of ethnic institutions remains at the planning stage. The "in-law" apartment is one answer for those who can afford it; another pattern is for the survivor to spend a portion of time with each of the children. Some elderly retire and take their social security checks to Japan, but the increasing cost of living in their former homeland is a limiting factor.

The 1970 census provides the following demographic picture of the Japanese. The median age was 29.5 years for the males and 33.2 for the female.[11] More than 68.8 percent were high-school graduates,[12] and the rates of separation and divorce were 4 percent for the male and 6 percent for the female.[13] The mean family income (male head) was $13,511.[14] Only 7.5 percent had incomes below the poverty level[15] (as defined by the census), with the preponderance of low incomes in the sixty-five years or older category. The median value of their homes was $27,900.[16]

In general we can summarize our view of the Japanese-American family:

1. That it has remained an intact family unit with low rates of separation and divorce, although there are changes toward the American model of relatively high rates of separation and divorce.

2. That the structure of the family was initially vertical, with father and males on top. It could be likened to a traditional family model, in contrast to the modern urban American family. Entertainment and recreation often took place in the family and extended family units. Families were larger; problems were often handled within the unit, and the use of outside professionals was a last resort.

3. That the ie unit was adapted in America to include larger units, including village, ken, and even the entire Japanese community. It served as an effective social-control device; it provided socialization opportunities through ethnic language schools and cultural recreational opportunities. The Japanese community became a reference group; the functions were similar to those of an ie.

4. Socialization and child rearing took into account minority group position, power, and the continuation of the Japanese culture. Those values, norms, and behaviors most likely to persist were those of the Japanese culture that interacted with the power position of the Japanese in the United States and their visibility in a race-conscious society. Many of these behaviors have also been reinforced by the majority group, so they

[11]*Japanese, Chinese, and Filipinos in the United States*, p. 5.
[12]Ibid., p. 9.
[13]Ibid., p. 17.
[14]Ibid., p. 42.
[15]Ibid.
[16]Ibid., p. 46.

have become stereotypes of the Japanese. These include quietness, conformity, loyalty, diligence, maximum effort, good citizenship, high school achievement, and a group orientation.

5. The situational orientation has been an important part of Japanese-American behavior. Learning how to behave to those above, below, and equal has meant learning appropriate styles.

The situational approach is intimately related to power. The less powerful have to learn many adaptations; the powerful can afford to use one style. Americans expect others to adapt to their norms, and their power can often command or buy this recognition. Therefore, Americans often assume that there are social science universals—"the personality" and "the truth"—whereas the search may be more a reflection of the power position than a social scientific reality. Minority groups must learn the time, the place, and the situation for sheer survival.

6. That acculturation has been the most powerful single influence on Japanese behavior. But it has not been a simple linear movement; the variables of power and visibility have resulted in different behaviors, so that Japanese Americans in Hawaii are different in many instances from their peers along the Pacific and Atlantic seaboards. There is a current reawakening of an ethnic identity and a militancy among the Sansei[17] that may slow the trend toward acculturation.

One of the most influential events hastening acculturation was the evacuation of the Japanese during World War II. It broke up the power of the Issei and the ethnic ghettoes; altered family life; scattered Japanese throughout the United States through resettlement; sent many males into the armed forces and overseas; and made many renounce everything Japanese.

7. Social class has always been a factor in the Japanese culture, but it is difficult to transcribe into the American scene. The ies tried to make appropriate matches, and "good" families were class conscious. Although most of the immigrants started at the bottom of the American class structure, they did not identify with the life styles of the lower classes. Rather, they brought with them many of the values associated with the middle class: high educational expectation for their children; respect for those in authority, including the police; desire to own property; emphasis on banking and savings; and a future orientation. They seldom fully adopted a lower-class style, even though their incomes and housing were clearly in the ghetto areas.

However, the Japanese-American community is becoming more heterogeneous and developing a more formal social-class system (debu-

17Minako Kurokawa Maykovich, "Political Activation of Japanese-American Youth," *Journal of Social Issues* 29, 2 (1973): 167–85.

tantes, professional organizations). It remains much more open than the white community, but with continued differences in education and income among the Japanese groups, it may soon become more crystallized.

Finally, it is important to emphasize that just as there is no one American family there is no one Japanese or Japanese-American family. Therefore, acculturation means different things to different families, and these will be reflected in their attitudes and behaviors. Perhaps the most appropriate generalization is that the Japanese families in the United States were different to begin with and that length of time in the United States has been just one of the many influences leading to further change.

THE COMMUNITY

The changes in the family are reflected by similar changes in the community. There are still visible "Japanese towns" (referred to as J-towns) in West Coast cities, but now they serve primarily as places of business, and the proprietors retreat to the suburbs after hours.

The effects of acculturation are clearly seen in community organizations. Although many remain structurally pluralistic, the issues and the styles are similar to majority group organizations.

The Japanese-American Citizen's League

With acculturation, increased affluence, and diminishing hostility from the larger community, the JACL currently finds itself forced to redefine its functions and goals. Many of the unifying issues, such as payment of wartime evacuation claims and citizenship for Issei, have been resolved, and the attention of the group has turned to problems that are not specifically Japanese. This has introduced new divisive factors. For instance, some JACL members are interested in the problem of *bracero* labor in California; that is, the importation of Mexican agricultural labor. The majority tend to favor a liberal position, which supports the interests of the Mexicans, but other members reflect the attitudes of agricultural employers, so that any JACL stand cannot be unanimously endorsed.

Another perennial and unresolvable issue deals with JACL's role regarding Japan and the United States. Is there a role for a powerless ethnic organization between two powerful countries? Of more recent origin is the debate concerning expansion from a Japanese group into a pan-Asian organization. This dissension is probably a reflection of the general acculturation and the stratification of the group into a plurality of interests.

The JACL can be compared to organizations representing other minority groups, such as the Anti-Defamation League, and appears especially similar to the National Association for the Advancement of Colored People (NAACP).[18] For example, both organizations maintain lobbies in Washington; both lodge legal protests against discriminatory practices; and both stand ready to protect and aid their respective ethnic groups.[19] Both organizations rely on a predominately accommodative strategy, so that the value of maintaining their tax-free status often takes precedence over stands on other issues. Finally, both organizations have achieved an aura of respectable middle-professional and upper-classness.

It will be interesting to observe the relation of the JACL to the third- and fourth-generation Japanese. The Nisei were able to break away from the paternalistic control of the Issei and to develop their own organizations based on their own perception of needs. The barriers of communication, generation, and culture functioned to the advantage of the Nisei in this respect, since ready-made Issei structures and organizations were not handed down to them. There is, however, a strong tendency on the part of the Nisei to provide such organizations for the newer generations (for example, a junior JACL), with subsequent problems of goals, control, policy, and membership that might not develop if the Sansei were permitted to evolve their own groups out of their own needs.

The JACL remains the only national organization for the Japanese, although it does not have any chapters in Hawaii. Other organizations represent the blend of acculturation and structural pluralism that so typically portrays the current stage of development of Japanese-American culture. The names, values, and goals of the organizations are synonymous with acculturation, but the membership remains primarily ethnic. For example, there are the Los Angeles Optimists, the Los Angeles and San Francisco Japanese Junior Chambers of Commerce, the Nikkei Lions in the San Francisco Bay area. All of these groups are typically "American" except that their membership is primarily Japanese. The broad term *Nikkei* is interesting; it refers to the Japanese as a whole, rather than the more restrictive generational terms of Issei, Nisei, and Sansei. The use of this word is an indication of the blurring of previously distinct generational divisions.

Possibly the most pressing reason of the Japanese Americans for maintaining their own social groupings revolves around the problem of dating and marriage. "Do you want your daughter to marry one?" is a question that is asked not only by the majority group but also by ethnic parents. This concern has led to the development and maintenance of many Japanese organizations.

For example, the Japanese in Los Angeles made an unsuccessful

18Louis E. Lomax, *The Negro Revolt* (New York: Signet Books, 1963).
19The term *Jap* is an especially sensitive one for the Japanese and the JACL.

attempt to organize a Japanese Country Club, and the 1960s and 1970s have witnessed many successful "coming out" parties for crops of Sansei debutantes. The all-Asian sororities (mainly Japanese) at California universities are very popular—the teen-age and young adult groups of all organizations are providing settings for the potential exposure of marriageable-age Japanese to each other. It is an inevitable response to a social need and an acculturative step, for it follows the model of social clubs, cliques, and marital and social patterns of the American society. What are more middle-class American than sororities, church socials, and the country club?

But many Japanese and non-Japanese appear worried over the development of the parallel social structure (structural pluralism). They believe that integration and increased social interaction between the Japanese and the Caucasian groups represent a higher order of functioning than presently exists. It should be noted, however, that the comprehensive parallel Japanese structure apparently is most typical of Los Angeles and Hawaii, the only two areas with large enough Japanese populations to support such groups. Other Japanese communities have modifications in community function and structure appropriate to size and area. The important point concerning acculturation, integration, pluralism, and the like may be the availability of Los Angeles and Hawaii for those Japanese more comfortable with a pluralistic system, while other areas of the country offer other opportunities for those Japanese preferring a more integrated existence.

But as long as race, visibility, and discrimination continue to be realities in the Japanese experience, the need for some type of ethnic organization will continue to exist. For example, we talked with a young Sansei whose ambivalence reflects the problem:

> The loneliest time for some of us is the Easter recess. We're pretty well accepted in the classroom and some of the social and athletic groups. But it gets kind of hard at Easter—most of the guys and gals (white) take off for Newport or some place like that. . . . There are two problems. One is I don't know whether my parents will let me go. But the main problem is what would happen if I went. One Sansei went with a group (non-Japanese) last year and he told me he felt left out on certain things. . . . He didn't have a good time so he's not going this year. . . . But, I don't want to go out with an all-Japanese group either.[20]

PRESENT RELIGIOUS PROBLEMS

An interview with the minister of a large Japanese Christian church emphasizes the current similarity of the Japanese and other popula-

---

[20]Kitano, private collection.

tions.[21] Interests and problems reflect age and generation rather than ethnicity. The concerns of the Issei are appropriate to the aged, and those of the Sansei are those of a young, but not necessarily Japanese, group. For example, the Issei, whose average age is now in the middle 70s, attend both Buddhist and Christian churches in large numbers and appear to be seeking reassurance in the face of aging and death. Prayer and study groups are well attended. Many regret the spiritual poverty of their pasts and feel that their previous concern with work and advancement left them unprepared for the philosophical considerations of later life.

Some Issei have turned to the Sokka-Gakkai, a fast growing religious movement from Japan that combines nationalism and simplistic solutions to metaphysical anxiety. The ultimate importance of this religion is difficult to predict at present, but it seems mainly to involve new immigrants and older Issei.

The Nisei, however, have different concerns. Most are in comfortable economic positions, and many appear to be more interested in social status than in the welfare of their souls. It seems likely that many tend to think of religion primarily in these terms. Some regard the ethnic church as conferring less status than that conferred by attendance at an all-white church in Brentwood, Bel-Air, or other high-status suburban areas. However, for a gardner, no matter what his income, Bel-Air is not a comfortable place. Many resolve this conflict by dropping church attendance altogether or by remaining inactive in the ethnic church. The social status of one's occupation is likely to influence church-going patterns in this way. Sharp social-class differences between Japanese churches have not yet developed.

Religious integration is showing another interesting trend. The Japanese churches reflect the financial solidarity of their memberships and are therefore likely to have new, attractive buildings and impressive social programs. Many have therefore begun to attract non-Japanese. Of the thirty-four active churches comprising the Southern California Ministerial Fellowship (a Japanese Protestant body), over one-half report Caucasians among their congregations. The different religions are also developing a more cohesive spirit. In Southern California the Buddhist and Christian ministers meet regularly with each other to discuss their mutual interests, concerns, and problems.

The Sansei generation is not especially active in any church. Many have dutifully gone to Sunday school and have been baptized, but few commit themselves to serious churchgoing. Many "shop around" and join either Christian or Buddhist churches that have good social or athletic programs. In general, they appear no more, and no less, religious

[21]Ibid.

than the youth of the larger community. But they may become active when they are older and have families.

A study by Kiefer[22] indicates that outside of the family, the ethnic church was the most influential collectivity among a group of San Francisco Japanese. The highest church attendance was by the Issei, followed by the Nisei, then by the Sansei.

In general terms, it is possible to say that while Japanese churches have played an important role in acculturation and in the development of community solidarity, they have retained their pluralistic structure, so that while members of a given faith participate in the matters affecting that denomination throughout the country, they remain surrounded by members of their own ethnic group. In this, the Japanese churches have followed a pattern similar to that of other Japanese institutions.

THE FUTURE

Japanese groups have been following and will probably continue to follow middle-of-the-road policies. Extremist organizations, either of the left or of the right, have not flourished in this ethnic community, although if there has been any direction, the tendency has been toward the conservative, especially among the Issei organizations.

Certain ethnic institutions will probably continue in modified form, while others will eventually disappear. Specialization and rising costs in fields like medicine, psychiatry, and social welfare mean that the ethnic community will have to turn to larger community resources. As these formal contacts with the outside community increase, primary level contacts with Caucasians and others will probably increase. Some of the structural barriers will inevitably break down, so that, in the long run, increased face-to-face contacts should lead to integration. But integration may still move at a slow pace because of resistance from all groups.

The wartime evacuation in 1942 destroyed the "old" Japanese communities, but there has been a current rebirth, albeit of a somewhat different nature. The newer communities may be titled "for the tourist," and in this sense may be similar to the "Chinatown" of San Francisco or Olvera Street of the Mexicans in Los Angeles—designed primarily for business purposes. The relative ease in securing desirable housing will continue to lead to dispersal, but toward small clusters of Japanese Americans. The absence of a single, large ethnic concentration might be somewhat deceptive, since communication and identification within the ethnic group will remain relatively high. Social, recreational, and economic organizations continue to flourish. Japanese both in the United

22Christie Kiefer, *Changing Cultures, Changing Lives* (San Francisco: Jossey Bass, 1974), p. 34.

States and in Japan have taken up golf with a vengeance, and notices of numerous fishing trips and derbies attest to the popularity of these activities among the group. The more sophisticated and powerful versions of the *tanomoshi*—the savings and loan associations—include several financed and controlled largely by Nisei; capital from Japan has developed banks, hotels, and businesses. The latter endeavor has not been without its complications. For example, the redevelopment of Los Angeles' Little Tokyo meant the displacement of many poor, elderly Issei from their low-rent lodgings by buildings and establishments geared for other populations. The conflict was exacerbated by the fact that the major developer was a company that was based in Japan. Some Japanese Americans feel that Japanese-based companies continue to discriminate in favor of their own countrymen.

But the major changes continue to reflect the processes of acculturation, so that by the mid-1970s very few community groups are Japanese in the Issei sense. Interestingly enough, the more "Americanized" activities like fishing, golf, and the Little Leagues, may remain structurally pluralistic, as are the fraternities and sororities, whereas those more traditionally Japanese interests like the martial arts and flower arranging may include larger proportions of non-Japanese.

DIFFERENCES BETWEEN JAPANESE IN JAPAN AND THE UNITED STATES

It is difficult to understand acculturation and changes among the Japanese generations in the United States without referring to changes in Japan. Although partial knowledge of Japan can be obtained through books,[23] through personal observations and experiences, and through interview material and emperical studies,[24] the changes experienced by the people in Japan have undoubtedly been much more dramatic than those faced by Japanese immigrants to the United States. Perhaps the safest generalization is that the Japan that the Issei left in the early 1900s bears but a minimal resemblance to modern-day Japan.

For example, the all-English Tokyo daily, *The Japan Times*, of March 23, 1967, reported the statistical results of a survey concerning the role of the husband in Japan: 78 percent brought home their paychecks intact; 84 percent told their wives if they expected to come home late; more than 50 percent spent their leisure time with their wives; and 60 percent consulted their wives first when they were in trouble. The survey

---

23Edwin O. Reischauer, *Japan Past and Present* (New York: Alfred A. Knopf, 1964); Leonard Mosley, *Hirohito* (Englewood Cliffs, N.J.: Prentice-Hall, Inc., 1966).

24The writer has made over five trips to Japan and has conducted a cross-cultural study of child-rearing attitudes and a study of mental illness. The most recent stay was as the Director of the University of California Tokyo Study Center, 1972–73.

notes that the image of the drinking, socializing, geisha-entertained Japanese husband may only survive in Kabuki plays, and it concludes with the prediction that within twenty years, 65 percent of the opinion leaders in Japan will be women, a figure that is believed to be comparable to the role of women in the United States. The stereotype of the dominant Japanese male appears to be only a myth. Nevertheless, it is our impression that the Japanese culture remains male-dominated and that no amount of statistical data will alter this fact. The society is geared to cater primarily to male egos and male needs, especially when compared to male–female relations in the United States.

Important impresssionistic differences may also exist between the Japanese in Japan and the Japanese in the United States. For example, although his purchasing power is much less than that of his American-born counterpart, the middle-class, urban Japanese male appears more "modern." His clothes are of the latest style, and he often demands the "best." Ironically, his cigarette lighter will be an expensive import, whereas the American-born Japanese may be content with an inexpensive Japanese lighter. He has at least one expensive camera (made in Japan), and often laughs at Issei and Nisei tourists who come to Japan with the American-made "Brownie." He spends money much more freely than his California-born peer and gives the impression of being more "American" in many ways that the conservative Issei, Nisei, and Sansei are not.

The differences between the Japanese in the two cultures can be attributed to many factors. One of the most important is majority-minority status—the Japanese Americans living as a small group within a white majority have constantly adapted to a weaker position through servility, conformity, conservatism, and a willingness to please. Their behavior often resembles that of the colonized as described by the Tunisian-born novelist Albert Memmi,[25] just as the behavior of some Americans toward minority cultures resembles that of the colonizer. However, the important exception to the colonized-colonizer model was the ability of the Issei to transfer their hopes of success in terms of citizenship, social status, and the like to their American-born children, and the ability of American democracy to offer opportunities for mobility.

Another plausible explanation for the differences relates to the relative isolation of the Japanese in America. Because of this isolation, their values, representing the Meiji Japanese era, have remained relatively intact and unchanged, while the people in Japan have seen rather dramatic changes. It is not an uncommon phenomenon; a Japanese scholar in Japan remarked that a good place to study nineteenth-century

25Albert Memmi, *The Colonizer and the Colonized* (New York: The Orion Press, 1965).

France was probably in certain parts of Canada, and the best place to study Meiji Japan was in California. Therefore, the socialization, the values, and the shaping of the behavior of the Japanese American are presumably closer to "old Japan" than to "new Japan," although the generalization is obviously affected by the degree of Japanese isolation, interaction, and communication with the American society.

Our observations lead to the conclusion that change in Japan has been more dramatic than change for the Japanese in the United States. Some recognition of the rapid change in the modern Japanese society can be gathered from a quote in the Yomiuri Shimbun, a large Tokyo newspaper, of September 15, 1966, concerning the newly designated national holiday for the aged: "In the case of Japan, the fall of the family system in postwar years is responsible for the lack of respect for the aged."

Although this is an oversimplification of a complex problem, the family and community life that many Issei remember as a part of old Japan has obviously changed. This may mean that, ironically, "acculturation," if measured in terms of moving away from the old, traditional Japanese culture, may be more rapid in modern Japan than it has been for the Japanese in the United States.

Culture means different things in different contexts. Some people think of art, plays, and books. The archaeologist finds evidence of it in the artifacts—pottery and statues—left behind by extinct peoples. The sociologist may mean the behavior of certain current groups, as when he speaks of the "teen-age culture." The psychologist may think in terms of culture and personality. In a sense, of course, all these aspects—behavior, products, achievements, and personality are of importance in defining a culture in its widest sense—that is, to relate to the social heritage of man. Thus the focus of the entire book relates to the Japanese-American culture—from its historical roots to the development and maintenance of its economic, political, social, and religious structures, to its institutions, to Japanese-American norms, values, personality, and behavior.

The

Culture

In this chapter, the emphasis will be on narrower aspects of ethnic culture, namely, Japanese norms, values, and personality. These intervening variables help to explain Japanese-American behavior, just as knowledge of the Japanese-American social structure aided in an understanding and explanation of their behavior. Gordon sees norms and values as the other side of the coin to structures and institutions and their interdependence to be so marked that knowledge of one without the other is only half-knowledge.[1] In a social learning-model sense, the structures and institutions act as agents, shapers, socializers, and reinforcers; norms and values help determine the content, the direction, and the how and the what that is being taught.

The way a man behaves, how he will communicate and what he values, will vary with different cultures and even differ within the same culture. Nevertheless, the relative homogeneity of Japanese adaptation to America can be attributed to the strength of their culture—to their ability to teach, shape, and reinforce certain behaviors over others. The power of their social structures has already been discussed, and a further clue to the effectiveness of its social system lies on the other side of the "coin"—in Japanese-American norms and values.

FREQUENT MISCONCEPTIONS

To many people, Japanese culture suggests mainly tea ceremonies and flower arranging.[2] As often happens, the quaint, the unusual, and

[1]Milton M. Gordon, *Assimilation in American Life* (New York: Oxford University Press, 1964), p. 32.

[2]An all-Japanese sorority asked a Nisei professor to be their faculty sponsor.

even the trivial become so firmly associated in people's minds that complex explanations of behavior are often built on pursuits that may in fact represent only the interests of a select population. In the same way, certain cultural myths develop and are perpetuated by our general ignorance. Things that seem incomprehensible to Western eyes are often attributed simply to the "curious, mysterious, and inscrutable ways" of the East. For example, Americans generally believe that during the last days of World War II, hordes of Japanese volunteered to become human bombs—the famous *kamikaze*—and were delighted to give up their lives for emperor and country. This suicidal behavior is often dismissed as an "aspect of Japanese culture," wherein to sacrifice one's life is an important part of the value system. In actual fact, surviving kamikaze tell a more understandable story, albeit a less romantic and exotic one.[3] Kamikaze pilots were selected, in general, in the good old army way— they were ordered to volunteer—and then were systematically conditioned to expect death. And, propaganda to the contrary, the kamikaze unit was never a popular one to belong to.

Of more relevance to the Japanese American is the common notion that suicide is for Japanese a culturally acceptable way of solving problems. We are acquainted with the case of an Issei who recently committed suicide by throwing himself in front of a moving automobile. This act was reported in the metropolitan press as suicide, but the local Japanese-American newspapers delicately reported the death as an accident and raised not so much as a hint of suicide. This raises some doubts about whether suicide is socially acceptable in the Japanese-American culture, at any rate. And, of course, suicide rates within this group are no higher than in the majority.

The measurement of norms, values, and personality, and their relationship to behavior, remain a major problem in social science. Any method of measurement has limitations, and no instrument, however sensitive, can hope to record precisely things so intangible, fluctuating, and variable as human thoughts and feelings. Nevertheless, the limited available empirical evidence about the Japanese American has certain characteristics that suggest that it is, as far as it goes, reliable and useful. For example, there is the fact that researchers, whether working with Japanese populations in Chicago, Los Angeles, or Hawaii, arrive at con-

When asked why they didn't ask a Caucasian, their answer was quite revealing. "Most of the ha-ku-jin [white] profs who might be interested might want us to practice Japanese "culture"—you know, the tea ceremony, putting on kimonos for special days and things like that. We think you [a Nisei] would be much more relaxed about those things and wouldn't force us into being Japanese. Of course, we'd do them if you'd want."

[3]Yasuo Kuwahara and Gordon Allred, *Kamikaze* (New York: Ballantine Books, 1957).

sistently similar empirical conclusions. These findings are themselves congruent with what we know generally about the Japanese-American groups, so that the problems of reliability and validity, although inevitably present, have consistent empirical reference points.[4]

There is also one other important point to keep in mind as we discuss the Japanese-American culture. Many of its norms are not wholly Japanese in either a literal or technical sense, but they are real in the behavioral sense—that is, these were the messages that Issei passed on to the Nisei and Sansei. Purist savants of the Japanese culture often delight in finding discrepancies between the Japanese meaning of certain norms and their translation by the Issei, with the inference that the Issei understanding was "wrong." But obviously the meaning of these prescriptions in relation to Japanese-American behavior, not the wrongness or rightness of such prescriptions, is the matter of importance.

NORMS

"Norms" are shared meanings in a culture that serve to provide the background for communication; values refer to clusters of attitudes that give a sense of direction to behavior; and personality refers to the characteristics of persons that remain relatively stable and provide the individual with an orientation to the world. The primary purpose of a social norm is to provide a guide for interpersonal behavior so that an individual has an acceptable way of interacting with others and, conversely, is able to judge the acts of others.

Studies of Japanese social norms reveal some of the following features: Japanese patterns of social interaction are highly personalized;

[4]Studies of Japanese Americans in Chicago include: William Caudill, "Japanese-American Personality and Acculturation," *Genetic Psychology Monographs* 45 (1952): 3–102; George DeVos, "A Quantitative Rorschach Assessment of Maladjustment and Rigidity in Acculturating Japanese-Americans," *Genetic Psychology Monographs* 52 (1955): 51–87.

Studies of Japanese Americans in Los Angeles include: Harry H. L. Kitano, "Passive Discrimination: The Normal Person," *The Journal of Social Psychology* 70 (1966): 23–31; Harry H. L. Kitano, "Japanese-American Crime and Delinquency," *The Journal of Social Psychology* 66 (1967): 253–63.

Studies of Japanese Americans in Hawaii include: Walter D. Fenz and Abe Arkoff, "Comparative Need Patterns of Five Ancestry Groups in Hawaii," *The Journal of Social Psychology* 58 (1962): 67–89; Gerald M. Meredith, "Amae and Acculturation among Japanese College Students in Hawaii," *The Journal of Social Psychology* 70 (1966): 171–80; Gerald Meredith and Connie Meredith, "Acculturation and Personality among Japanese-American College Students in Hawaii," *The Journal of Social Psychology* 68 (1966): 175–82; Gerald Meredith, "Observations on the Acculturation of Sansei Japanese-Americans in Hawaii," *Psychologia* 8 (June 1965) (Department of Psychology, Kyoto, Japan): 1–2; Richard Kalish, Michael Maloney, and Abe Arkoff, "Cross-Cultural Comparisons of College Students and Marital-Role Preferences, *The Journal of Social Psychology* 68 (1966): 44–47.

there is a definite hierarchy of status positions with a corresponding regard for the importance of status; the status systems are relatively permanent; and behavioral reserve and discipline are highly regarded.[5] Further, certain norms have been incorporated into the Japanese national school curriculum as ethical doctrine, so that exposure to these teachings has been widespread. These codified norms were *on* (ascribed obligation), *giri* (contractual obligation), *chu* (loyalty to one's superior), *ninjo* (humane sensibility), and *enryo* (modesty in the presence of one's superior).

These norms, if followed religiously by Japanese individuals and groups, might describe a culture with an aggressive, probably arrogant, ruling class; conforming, obedient ruled classes; and a high degree of order through hierarchical structures and external sanctions. Further, in order to enforce these norms, there might be a network of smaller structures (for example, cliques, families, villages), each with similar normative interactions so that socialization procedures could be consistent and effective. The maintenance of such a system would depend on relative stability among classes, high values placed on the system by all members, clear role prescriptions, a desired modal personality structure emphasizing conformity and obedience, and a symbolic "head" (the emperor) at the top of the hierarchy of structures. Obviously this describes the Japanese culture of the Meiji era. There is still evidence of these normative patterns in Japan today, especially among the older generations.

It would be inaccurate to say that all or even most Japanese behaved in accordance with the prescribed norms, just as it would be an overgeneralization to indicate that most Americans behave strictly according to the prescribed democratic norms of our society. Nevertheless, a knowledge of the Japanese Meiji period norms is important because it provides the background for understanding Issei behavior.

Probably the one outstanding characteristic of Japanese norms is their adaptiveness to fixed positions and to external realities. Rather than a stream making its own course, the stream follows the lines of least resistance—their norms emphasize duty and obligation; their values include conformity and obedience. Part of the "success" of Japanese adaptation to the United States was their ability to respond to the problem of lower status with those normative patterns learned in Japan.

For example, the immigrant's lower status was similar to his role position in Japan so that a transfer of high-status positions to the "white man" and subsequent patterns of deference and humility were relatively easy transitions.

[5]Ruth Benedict, *The Chrysanthemum and the Sword* (Boston: Houghton Mifflin Co., 1946); John Bennett, Herbert Passin, and Robert McKnight, *In Search of Identity* (Minneapolis: University of Minnesota Press, 1958).

A lower status in the Japanese structure is often associated with humility, a service orientation, and a high sensitivity to the needs of the superior. Some of the consequences of this structure, where rewards and punishments are distributed by the whim of superiors, are hypothesized by Iga.[6] One characteristic is insecurity, which means that Japanese tend to be indifferent to other people's troubles and tend not to become too involved with others because of their own need for security. Another characteristic is a lack of commitment to abstract and absolute ideals. Instead, there is a substitution that leads to a blind following of government or other officials, with little criticism of "superiors." The third characteristic is that of opportunism, since authorities define what is right, and the "inferior" is constantly caught in the position of having to adapt to the new variations. Iga feels that these three characteristics of Meiji Japanese culture and personality help to explain the lack of Nisei involvement in the civil rights struggles of the black, the present voting behavior of Japanese, and other facets of Japanese acculturation as well.

Conversely, a higher status in the Japanese system may be accompanied by paternalism and arrogance. However, these status differentials with consequent effects on personality and behavior are not only typical of the Japanese system but are probably present in most autocratic structures, and the old adage about power and corruption, and relationships between the "superior" and the "inferior," appear to be characteristic of many cultures.

The Enryo Syndrome

Among the many norms that shape Japanese behavior, the norm of enryo appears to be one of the most important. Even the present generation of Japanese Americans uses the term, whereas other norms such as giri and *on* have long been forgotten (except as resurrected by Caucasian researchers). The concept originally referred to the manner in which "inferiors" were supposed to behave to "superiors"—that is, through deference and obsequiousness. As with many norms, however, the meaning and the use eventually expanded to cover a variety of situations—from how to behave toward the white man, to what to do in ambiguous situations, to how to cover moments of confusion, embarrassment, and anxiety.

Enryo helps to explain much of Japanese-American behavior. As with other norms, it has both a positive and a negative effect on Japanese (social interaction.) For example, take observations of Japanese in situations as diverse as their hesitancy to speak out at meetings; their refusal

[6]Mamoru Iga, "Do Most Japanese-Americans Living in the United States Still Retain Traditional Japanese Personality?" *Kashu Mainichi* [California Daily News], Los Angeles (June 21, 1967), p. 1.

of any invitation, especially the first time; their refusal of a second help-ing; their acceptance of a less desired object when given a free choice; their lack of verbal participation, especially in an integrated group; their refusal to ask questions; and their hesitancy in asking for a raise in salary —these may all be based on enryo. The inscrutable face, the noncommit-tal answer, the behaviorable reserve can often be traced to this norm, so that the stereotype of the shy, reserved Japanese in ambiguous social situations is often an accurate one.

Ha zu ka shi is a part of the enryo syndrome. It is observed in terms of embarrassment and reticence. The motive for this feeling is centered in "others"—how other people will react to self so that there remains a feeling of shame, a feeling that one might make a fool of himself in front of others. Childhood discipline emphasizes ha zu ka shi—"others will laugh at you"—and the norm is used as a means of social control. It may lead to a lack of aggressive behavior and to high dependency because the cues for shame come from the outside, especially from parents. One result of this kind of behavioral norm is the nod of agreement with which a Japanese often implies a "no" answer. This can cause much difficulty, since Americans assume that the nod means "Yes, I understand," whereas it may mean, "I don't want to cause you embarrassment or trouble by disagreeing" or some other variation of the enryo syndrome. American teachers soon learn that even in classes made up of Sansei it is an error to say, "All right, are there any questions? If there are none, I assume you all understand," since there will be no questions and often, little under-standing.

Hi-ge, also a part of the enryo syndrome, leads to social interaction that is difficult for many Americans to understand. For example, if an American praises the Japanese wife, the husband may respond, "Oh no, it's not true." Or the Japanese husband may introduce his wife as "Here is my stupid wife." Or the Japanese may denigrate his children or him-self or others close to him because his norms preclude the praising of self or family. Such praise, especially in public, is considered to be in very poor taste, except in certain formalized circumstances.

The difficulty with the enryo syndrome relates to the possible effects on the Nisei and Sansei. In Japan the messages, the cues, the presence of others who would understand the culture and play the game accordingly (for example, others may then praise children or the family)—the entire system—would operate in this manner. However, in America, the full consequences of the enryo syndrome—including its devaluation of self and family—have never been fully understood by the population. It has helped the Japanese "look good" in Caucasian eyes because of its lack of aggression and high conformity, but for the Japanese American the cost of the goodness may have been very high. A full development of an individual's potentialities would surely be hindered under such a norm.

Another concept, that of *amae*, has been described by Meredith and Doi as critical in understanding the basic dependency of the Japanese.[7] The term refers to the need to be loved and cherished, but is difficult to translate accurately into English. It was frequently used by the Issei mother to describe the behavior of her children—sometimes with approval, sometimes with impatience.[8] From the child's side, it was a technique of interaction asking for love, for attention, for approval, and for recognition. It was one of the few acceptable ways that individuals had to cope with the enryo norm.

We conducted a discussion of the term amae with a group of Japanese college students in Tokyo in 1973, and their reactions were diverse and vehement. Some felt it was a negative type of interaction; others thought of it as a positive term, denoting a "softer" type of response between unequal power positions. All agreed that it was used constantly in Japan, and phrases like "begging," "gaining attention," "asking for approval," "coquetry," and the like were broached, but with no agreement as to the most appropriate definition.

Perhaps the critical part of amae is the way it is perceived and responded to in the Japanese culture. If the parent sees the behavior of her child as amae, she may not have to respond by spanking or yelling, since it is understood as an important factor in a relationship, whereas if she defines it in some other way, a different interaction may be involved. The term is currently equated among Nikkei with "being spoiled" and is therefore considered an undesirable action to be restricted or eliminated. But it may also deprive the child of a "soft" technique for gaining attention or asking for a favor.

There are many other ways of handling the power relationships within the Japanese system, and one of the most critical is related to independence and dependence. One goal of socialization in Japan is to establish a dependency on the family, the group, the company, and the mutual responsibility that goes along with such a perspective. Conversely, the goal of socialization in the United States appears to be the establishment of independence and autonomy as early as possible. The conflict between these two goals is often reflected in Japanese-American families.

[7]Meredith, "Amae and Acculturation among Japanese College Students in Hawaii"; L. T. Doi, "Amae: A Key Concept for Understanding Personality Structure," *Psychologia* 5 (1962) (Department of Psychology, Kyoto, Japan): 1–7.

[8]For example, a mother might indicate that all her children have to amae so that she would pamper and "baby" her children. In other situations she might indicate that her children are asking and behaving with too much amae and refuse their requests or ignore their behavior.

CONFRONTATION AND INDIRECTION

Functional norms help a group to adapt and to survive. The less-than-equal power relationships faced by the Japanese meant that they had to develop ways of dealing wtih this problem.

A technique that is associated with less power is the avoidance of direct confrontation. People, cultures, and countries with less direct power have avoided the "eyeball to eyeball" type of conflict, whereas those with more power—technology, resources, numbers, and firepower—generally welcome the direct confrontation.

The Japanese have had to adapt to less powerful positions constantly. The size of their country, the lack of natural resources, and their smaller stature has usually meant that there is a preference for indirect tactics, rather than meeting force head on. One of their martial arts, aikido, stresses relaxation, deflection, and the interaction of mind and body as sources of inner strength in defending against an outside aggressor. It is an appropriate technique for neutralizing the force of much larger and aggressive individuals. To meet strength with strength means that both sides will be hurt and that the stronger will eventually win, whereas aikido attempts by deflection to use the strength of the aggressor against himself.

Socialization into the Japanese culture takes into account the art of deflection and the avoidance of direct confrontation. We have observed one consistent technique in their child rearing that encourages deflection and cooperation.[9] Rather than the direct confrontation by the more powerful parent against the child ("You do what I say, or else"), the Japanese parent is more apt to use indirect techniques. They may introduce a diversionary stimulus or attempt to bring about cooperation by saying, "Let's do it this way," or "A good child will do it this way."

For example, the differential modes can be illustrated by how a Japanese and an American family might handle the case of an eight-year-old son who is watching television beyond his allotted time when he should be doing his homework. In the American family, there might be the direct statement, "Why don't you turn off that TV and study?" If there is not the desired response, it may escalate into a conflict between the power of the parent and the power of the child. Eventually it may be resolved by "showing the child who's boss around here," and power threats like "Turn off that TV or else . . ." are common interactions. In

[9]Gail Shimamoto, participant observation and interviews with Japanese families (Class paper, International Christian University, Tokyo, Japan, 1973); Ezra Vogel, *Japan's New Middle Class: The Salary Man and His Family in a Tokyo Suburb.* (Berkeley and Los Angeles: University of California Press, 1965).

the Japanese family, a different type of interaction (and often just as ineffective) is used. The parent may indicate to the child that "Isn't that a boring program?"; or "I think Jun-chan [a close friend] must be doing his homework now"; or mother might say, "I think father wants to watch his favorite program." There may be an attempt to bring in another member of the family, so that father might ask his daughter to tell her brother to study. She may be praised as a good girl because she is studying and not watching television, and this praise and recognition is probably more effective in socializing her rather than bringing about the desired response in her brother. But direct confrontations between parent and child remain rare. One parent may turn to the other and remark how bad children are getting to be, loud enough for the child to hear but not directed at him.

It is difficult to evaluate the effectiveness of these techniques in isolation, for they are within the context of each of the cultures. One of the ultimate weapons used by Japanese parents to get children to behave is the threat of banishment from the family circle. Children are threatened by putting them outside, or in a closet, or in a basement. This appears to be an effective device, whereas such threats may have little noticeable effects on an American child. In fact, the American technique is often the opposite; rather than the threat of banishment, the threat to "keep in" is often used so that a child is told "You can't go out and play" if he has been misbehaving.

Concepts such as losing or saving face, the difficulty of getting clearcut yes or no answers, and the vagueness of the language itself, are other manifestations of the use of indirection in the culture. Although these themes exist in all cultures, they appear to be central to the Japanese system. The indirectness can have both healthy and unhealthy consequences. Among Japanese Americans, the lack of direct statements often leads to confusion, misinterpretation, and misunderstanding, but it also avoids those direct attacks that often lead to irreconcilable differences. The current therapeutic techniques of confrontation, of expressing "honesty" and true feelings will be difficult for many Japanese Americans to handle.

Direct Confrontations

We have mixed evidence concerning direct confrontations between husband–wife and parent–child. We never witnessed a direct screaming and yelling interaction between husband and wife in Japan. Instead, the anger came out in much subtler forms, such as the wife half-jokingly remarking about the ineptness of her husband's driving and he in turn making a general remark about how women with a good education could not read a simple road map. In America, we could expect remarks directed squarely at each other. However, Shimamoto[10] indicates that although such direct confrontations are rare in Japan, they are not completely absent.

Similarly we have mixed evidence concerning the direct spanking and beating of children by Japanese parents. Most of the literature on child rearing in Japan emphasizes tolerance during the early years, and any rider of Japanese trains will vouch for the relatively high degree of tolerance and permissiveness given to Japanese children by their parents. Part of the reason may be the general conforming behavior of most Japanese children, so that few major disciplinary incidents arise in public. But a major proportion arises from a different style of discipline.

The role of the father is central in the disciplinary schema. The mother is forced to handle most of the everyday happenings and in the process loses a degree of social control and effectiveness because of the tireless repetition. The father, however, often appears self-indulgent with a high degree of tolerance for almost any behavior, especially that of his sons. But there is also a limit to his tolerance, and once the boundary is crossed, discipline may be immediate, severe, and demanding. We have been surprised by the sudden change in tone and behavior of a previously tolerant father when his children finally strain the limits, and one of the childhood skills is to sense when the mood changes will occur.

Perhaps the major difference between the Japanese and the American way (controlling for in-group differences based on social class, generation, and the like) is that there may be constant verbal reminders to the American child including spanking at a relatively early stage, whereas there is a higher initial tolerance in the Japanese family. However, once the limits are surpassed, Japanese discipline may be quite severe.

VISIBILITY

How to deal with visibility problem and physical identification was another problem for the group. Because of the nature of American racism[11] and the problems faced by the Japanese, one important adaptation of the group was through invisibility. The dictum was "Don't bring attention to us," and if public attention were warranted, the phrase was then expanded to "Only for good deeds and not one that would embarrass the community." The same prescription held for families.

The problem of visibility and invisibility is an interesting one relating to figure–ground perceptions. Most movie viewers see the lone

10Shimamoto, Interviews.
11Roger Daniels and Harry H. L. Kitano, *American Racism: Exploration of the Nature of Prejudice* (Englewood Cliffs, N.J., Prentice-Hall, Inc., 1970).

Japanese samurai as the main figure—stoic, noble, loyal, with the ability to repress his passions—while in the background are the thousands of others who connive, fornicate, lust, cry, break down, and openly behave with the full repertoire of human emotions. Yet it is important to note that generalizations concerning the Japanese are usually drawn from the more visible, single samurai, rather than the numerous others.

The Issei choice of being less visible was shaped by their culture (one knew his place in the Japanese social structure and conducted himself accordingly) and reinforced through their interaction with the American social structure. Competing on equal terms with the white man usually meant additional discriminatory treatment, so that one strategy for survival was the "low posture" and staying in the background in order not to bring undue negative attention on themselves. Therefore, life styles were conservative, and those visible behaviors that would reflect on the community were discouraged (for example, crime, delinquency, mental illness, flashly clothes, ostentatious spending), whereas behaviors like good grades in school and membership in scholarship, honor, and good citizenship groups were strongly reinforced.

As a result, it was unusual to see Issei and Nisei riding in Cadillacs, purchasing large, expensive homes in exclusive districts (even if such were available), and using money in a way to draw public attention. Clothes were often dated and conservative in style, and for many, the less expensive was chosen with the inference that the "best" was reserved for the Caucasian. The unstated inference "Who does he think he is, a ha-ku-jin [Caucasian]" was often strong enough to discourage those who violated the norms. However, for many of the new generation, a reaction formation to some of the Issei prescriptions has developed. Many demand the "best" (translated into the most expensive) from the most prestigious stores, so labels have become extremely important.

The desire for invisibility is related to a number of other socialization goals. Japanese are expected to be quiet, conforming, obedient, and to avoid loud, attention-getting behavior, especially in public places. And Japanese students in class—whether in Tokyo or Honolulu or Los Angeles—retain much of their invisibility by their lack of overt participation.

OTHER FACTORS

There was also a strong emphasis on filial piety. It was originally a reciprocal obligation, but many Issei have felt that in the United States it has been somewhat unilateral: the story of Issei parents denying their own needs for their children is common, whereas the converse is less likely to occur. Nevertheless, it is our impression that many families have absorbed grandparents (the in-law apartment is a popular feature in want ads aimed at the Japanese American.)

There were other facets of both the Japanese and Japanese-American systems that may be more closely related to income (and subsequent living conditions) rather than to some other explanation. One concerns sleeping arrangements: Maeda (personal communication, 1972) indicates that in Japan, children sleeping with their mothers (usually the youngest child) and their fathers (the older child) is common, even to relatively older ages. A group of Nissei were asked about their present sleeping arrangements; the emphasis is on separate rooms for each child (even babies), but in their own upbringing, most remembered, some with embarrassment, that they slept with their parents and then with other siblings up to the beginning of school and even later. These closer living arrangements are related to economic conditions, however the possibility of psychological benefits arising from this intimacy may also be hypothesized.

ATTITUDES TOWARD WORK

One of the most salient features of the Japanese culture, which cuts across the parallel structures, has been attitudes toward work. It was and still remains such an important part of the Japanese culture that one anonymous professor is quoted in the *Japanese Times*: "Japanese work as if they were addicted to it. Japanese forced to retire because of age often face a lonely life because they have lost the most meaningful part of their existence."[12]

When compared to the Protestant ethic and the value it places on work, the roots of the Japanese work orientation apparently go back much further. The work ethic may stem from the teachings of Confucius and Buddha; other forces that shaped the practice included the very survival of an island culture with limited natural resources where the greatest asset was the people themselves. Some Japanese we have talked to include other explanations, including that of "blood," meaning that they feel it is a hereditary characteristic that can be transmitted.

There is little question that the social structure was designed to take advantage of Japan's human resource. The value of work was part of the Meiji school curriculum, and one of the main reasons behind the dramatic rise of present-day Japan as an economic power has been the productivity of its labor force.

The Issei immigrants brought over this attitude to the United States, and for many, the problem of sheer survival reinforced this per-

12*Japanese Times*, Tokyo, Japan (1973:3).

spective. Hard work was looked on as a desirable goal in itself, and there was often a feeling that occupations that somehow appeared unrelated to sheer sweat and toil (music, show business) were less desirable. We know some surviving Issei who still refuse to purchase a completely automatic washing machine because they feel that something is vaguely lacking (work and effort) in the procedure. Work has played a prominent part in the socialization of most Japanese Americans, and it was reinforced in their contacts with the American culture.

It is our belief that the combination of a Japanese culture emphasizing norms, or the "how to behave" aspects of life, coupled with the content of the norms such as in the enryo syndrome, help to achieve understanding of Japanese behavior in the United States. The cooperative docile behavior of the Japanese during the wartime evacuation is an example of the consequences of socialization within this pattern. Although we have emphasized some of the possible negative effects of enryo, it also has many positive features, and many Japanese must privately wish that Americans would learn more about the practice of enryo.

The Importance of the Ethnic System

It would be relatively easy to forecast the personality, the self-concept, and the behavior of the Japanese if they had continued to interact with others on a perpetual "inferior" basis. They might eventually exhibit the common characteristics of a culturally deprived group—low self-esteem, high alienation, and a desire to escape from a negative self-identity.

But, in the final analysis, it did not quite work out this way. An Issei working in a white man's home would hear his name mispronounced, or be called "Hey you," or "Hey, boy." On his way home from work he might hear the phrase "damn Jap," and while riding in the streetcar others might carefully avoid sitting next to him until all seats were filled. A constant awareness of "inferiority," of being a "nonperson," might permanently affect the personality. However, on coming home, the Issei was now *papa-san*, the head of the household with all of the rights, duties, responsibilities, and obligations of this position. In the ethnic community he might be the president of his local *ken-jin-kai*, an active member of his Buddhist church, and very likely to be called on for advice and counsel. His credit rating at the ethnic store was beyond question—his identity, his status, and his position within the ethnic system provided a different set of cues and reinforcements. Therefore, his self-concept, his position, his status, and his personality were not permanently affected by his dealings with the larger world. The saving grace for the Issei, during the early troubled years, was his ethnic community.

Conversely, for the Nisei, somewhat the opposite procedure may be described. In his family he was the child, the inferior, and in his dealings with the ethnic community he was the "son of an Issei," rather than an individual in his own right. He was taught to behave "Japanese," which meant in a relatively narrow, conforming orientation to the world. But the Nisei's world was not wholly within the ethnic community—he went to American schools and dealt with people and institutions outside of the ghetto. He saw and participated in different situations, and even though some experiences were negative, he identified with American values.

Therefore, neither of the Japanese generations was permanently restricted nor psychologically damaged—both perceived and used alternatives that provided reasonable opportunities for growth and self-esteem. There are elements of a "schizophrenic adaptation" on the part of the Japanese to life in the United States. But most physically identifiable groups are also faced with the same problem—the how-to-behave problem when interacting with the majority and the behaviors when with one's own group. Therefore, within one individual there is often the many personalities—the "Uncle Tom" to the white man, deferential and humble; the "good son" to his parents, dutiful and obedient; and the "swinger" to his peers, wise-cracking, loud, and irreverent. And all of the behaviors are real, so none can be said to give a truer picture except in terms of time, place, and situation.

The issues facing the Sansei and Yonsei are much more subtle. They are not Japanese in the Issei or in the Nisei sense. Very few have faced overt discrimination; the concentration camp experiences are second or third hand at best; and their knowledge of the Japanese language and culture is minimal. Yet they are a part of an "ethnic revival" that includes a reassessment of an ethnic idenity, a participation in ethnic studies, and a reevaluation of the "melting pot" goals of American society.

Some respond by becoming interested in Japan and taking a trip to their ancestral homeland. They generally find that they are not fully accepted there and may even face more rejection, since they have "Asian faces" but do not speak or behave in a manner expected by the Japanese. Others obtain a sense of identity with the Third World and a participation in solving community problems. But the bulk have been acculturated into the mainstream of American society and are seeking their identities in typically American ways, so that employment, security, and status are primary concerns.

VALUES

In describing the general values of the Japanese group, we refer particularly to two studies, that of Iga, in which he compares values of

Nisei, Sansei, Japanese in Japan, and a California Caucasian group;[13] and a study by the author, which describes value changes in Japanese Americans by generation.[14]

Iga hypothesizes a number of values thought to be held in common by most Japanese, and then subjects these to empirical test. Each of these values is related to certain personality characteristics.

One value derives from the difference between a collective and an individual orientation. Self-needs for the Japanese are deemed to have a lesser priority than group needs—in athletic terms, one can be a team player or play primarily for individual glory. The Japanese tends to be a "team player."

The terms of particularism and universalism are related to group loyalties and identification. The question is, are Japanese values more related to specific institutions or are they related to more universal value systems? The answer for the Japanese is apparently toward particularism. For example, there seems to be no universal concern with religion among the Japanese, and loyalties are instead to the house, the family, and related specific groups. The extension of paternalistic loyalty is seen in the attitudes of self-sacrifice by employees, and in the attitudes of benevolence and obligation on the part of Japanese employers.

Another value is conformism, regard for conventional behavior, and obedience to rules and regulations. Related to this is the frequent development of dependent personalities. Compromise and yielding to others is highly approved, and disruptive behavior is censured. Further, discipline and obedience are mandatory, so that self-control, resignation, and gratitude are highly desirable. Many Japanese also feel that suffering and hard work are necessary ingredients of character-building.

There is also a heavy Japanese emphasis on status distinction and "knowing one's place," so that age, sex (masculine superiority), class, caste, family lineage, and other variables of social status are important in the Japanese culture. Finally, much value is attached to aspiration and competitiveness, but also to obligation and dependency, especially within the family circle.

As with most value system schemata, there are conflicts and incongruencies that are difficult to resolve on the conceptual level. Nevertheless, on the basis of these hypothesized values, Iga feels that the Japanese individual will have certain personality traits: fear of power, insecurity, obedience, cliquishness, and an inability to make forceful decisions.

[13]Mamoru Iga, "Changes in Value Orientation of Japanese Americans," paper read at the Western Psychological Association Meeting, Long Beach, California, April 28, 1966.

[14]Harry H. L. Kitano, "Japanese-American Mental Illness," in Stanley Plog and Robert Edgerton, eds., *Changing Perspectives on Mental Illness* (New York: Holt, Rinehart and Winston, 1969), pp. 256–84.

Iga's findings provided general validation for his major hypothesis. For example, the Japanese in Japan were found to hold the most "Japanese values," followed by the Japanese American, then by the Caucasian. Significant differences between the Japanese American and the Caucasian were found among the following: conformity, compromise, success, aspiration, obligation, and dependency. The Japanese American was closer to hypothesized Japanese values on each of these measures.

GENERATIONAL CHANGES

The writer administered an instrument to groups of Issei, Nisei, and Sansei for the purpose of describing value changes by generation. A group of American college students were also given the same instrument for comparative purposes. The attitudes tested were toward ethnic identity, mean-ends, masculinity and responsibility, individual-group orientation, passivity, and realistic expectations. The results are presented in Table B of the Appendix.

Ethnic identity refers to the degree of Japaneseness, and the preference, by generation, for things ethnic over things American.

Means-ends refers to forms of ethical behavior wherein the way of doing things is considered as important as the result of doing them. In other words, "how" is as important, or more important, than the "why."

Masculinity-femininity refers to the definition and acceptance of clear distinctions between male and female roles. The American culture probably provides a less clear-cut male role, which results in more role confusion. *Individual-group conformity* refers to individual and collective behavior.

Passivity is related to a fatalistic orientation. An individual resigns himself to external conditions as diverse as a wartime evacuation or reverses in business with the Japanese phrase *ski-ka-ta-ga-nai* (it can't be helped) and a shrug of the shoulders.

Realistic expectations refers to the discrepancy between expectations and reality. Expectations are especially difficult to quantify because abilities and opportunities differ widely from individual to individual. However, from this perspective, we have the impression that the Japanese are an "underexpectant" group—that is, that goals are set low so that it is easy to attain them. For example, it is common for a young man, qualified to be a doctor, to choose to become a pharmacist. The consequence of this is that Japanese are frequently overtrained and overqualified for the jobs in which they find themselves. In the long run, both overexpectancy and underexpectancy are dysfunctional—reaching for the unattainable stars is as immature as not reaching at all.

The data from Table B strongly support a point of view indicating a change of values with each succeeding Japanese generation. In each case, the direction is toward acculturation. A further refinement of the inventory resulted in the isolation of nine factors, which we labeled duty and obligation to family, ethnocentrism, trust in parental authority, independence of family, internal locus of control, responsibility and self-reliance, guilt and family authority, alienation from community authority, and social acceptance versus achievement.

In general, the empirical evidence on values supports what we know and observe about the Japanese. There is a high degree of conformity, obedience, a manifestation of ethical behavior, and respect for authority, and a corresponding low degree of acting out, overt rebellion, and independence.

There are other values that also help to explain Japanese behavior. One is the concept of *ga-man*, which refers to internalization of, and suppression of, anger and emotion. The author's father often tells of early episodes of discrimination and mistreatment to which he was subjected. A simple walk down the street, in 1919 in San Francisco, often resulted in being shoved into the gutter and called a "damn Jap." But father would *ga-man*, that is, take no retaliatory action, and the incidents never escalated into serious conflict.

Another characteristic value of Japanese Americans has been competitiveness. This would at first seem to be in conflict with values of conformity and group loyalty, but, as in the case of most values, there are combinations that are difficult to resolve conceptually. The encouragement of personal excellence—"do the best you can, no matter what you are doing"—can be interpreted to mean both "be a credit to the Japanese group," or, simply, "be best." Interestingly enough, the competitive behavior of most Japanese is seen primarily in relation to other Japanese. Many Sansei prefer to enroll in college classes that have no other Sansei because they will feel more relaxed there. Japanese families have to keep up with the Watanabes, but don't worry so much about keeping up with the Joneses.

Certain rules also seem to govern competition within the Japanese group. An economically successful Issei would more likely drive an Oldsmobile than a Cadillac. The more expensive car would be considered "flaunting his success." It is important to be a winner, but equally important that the winner be humble, modest, and self-deprecating.

But acculturation has modified the older ways, and there is now a wider dispersion of life styles in the Japanese community. Some have the wealth and flaunt it, but others in the same income level prefer more modest life styles. The equating of the "best" with "name brands," "name stores," and the most expensive is strongly felt in the community, and although such styles may be functional for those with the income, they become additional burdens for those less affluent.

PARENTAL CHILD-REARING ATTITUDES

Two studies by the author, using the Parental Attitude Research Inventory (PARI), illustrate changes in parental child-rearing attitudes by Japanese generation. The first study compares child-rearing attitudes of an Issei and a Nisei sample.[15] There was a significant difference between the two groups on the overall scale—the Nisei mean score was 12.89 compared to the Issei mean score of 16.88, with the higher score representing a more restrictive way of raising children. The Issei view of child rearing is more "old-fashioned"—children are viewed as dependent, quiet, unequal, and to be raised with strictness. In contrast, the Nisei view is more "modern" and more American—children are viewed as comrades with a subsequent sharing of experiences; they are encouraged to ask questions; and they are permitted a higher degree of sexual exploration.

The second study, using the same PARI scale, compares a younger and old Nisei generation with similar age populations in Japan.[16] The findings were somewhat surprising—the significant differences were between age rather than national groups. Older Japanese, whether in Japan or America, held similar attitudes, and so did the younger population in both countries. It may well be, at least in the area of child-raising attitudes, that we are measuring age-generation changes as well as acculturative ones. The findings also suggest that age-sex groups, across national and other structural boundaries, may have more attitudes and interests in common than do age-generation groups within a structure.

PERSONALITY MEASURES

One of the many serendipitous results of the wartime evacuation was the migration to Chicago of a number of Issei and Nisei. Here, many were given personality tests by Caudill and DeVos. Their findings opened up an area of study for those interested in personality and acculturation.

Caudill's study showed a logical continuity between the values and the adaptive mechanisms of the Issei and Nisei.[17] Both values and adaptive mechanisms clearly pointed toward "middle-class American" life. One important finding related to the compatibility of Japanese to American values, rather than their degree of sameness.

DeVos found personality differences among the Issei, the Kibei, the

[15]Harry H. L. Kitano, "Differential Child-Rearing Attitudes between First and Second Generation Japanese in the United States," *The Journal of Social Psychology* 53 (1961): 13–16.

[16]Harry H. L. Kitano, "Inter- and Intragenerational Differences in Maternal Attitudes towards Child Rearing," *The Journal of Social Psychology* 63 (1964): 215–20.

[17]Caudill, "Japanese-American Personality and Acculturation."

Nisei, and American norms.[18] His Issei group stressed the submergence of individual needs in the face of family and group expectations and the use of rigid social role definitions. The Issei could function relatively well in terms of well-defined expectations and situations but were relatively inflexible in the face of new experiences. Intrapsychic difficulties were more apt to show up in their personal and family lives, since the overt economic and social lives were much more amenable to ritualized behavior. The other generations showed acculturative changes toward American norms.

Some personality research has centered in Hawaii. Arkoff[19] and Fenz and Arkoff[20] noted that Sansei males expressed high need for deference, abasement, nurturance, affiliation, order, and exuberance, and a correspondingly reduced need for dominance, aggression, autonomy, exhibition, and heterosexuality when compared to Caucasian males. Sansei males also held a more traditional "Japanese" view of male dominance in marriage, and in this respect were at odds with views held by Sansei females and American college students.[21] Sansei females expressed a need for deference, nurturance, and order, and less need for aggression, abasement, autonomy, exhibition, and heterosexuality than Caucasian females.

Meredith and Meredith investigated the Sansei in terms of multivariate personality theory and found Japanese-American males more reserved, more humble, more conscientious, and more regulated by external realities than Caucasian-American males.[22] Conversely, Caucasian-American males are more out-going, more assertive, more expedient, more venturesome, and more imaginative than Japanese-American males. Japanese-American females are more affected by feeling, more obedient, more suspicious, and more apprehensive than Caucasian-American females. Conversely, Caucasian-American females are more emotionally stable, more independent, more trusting, and more self-assured than Japanese-American females. The majority of these findings appear congruent with general observations about Japanese behavior.

The author compared the personalities of Sansei delinquents (those on probation from the Los Angeles County Probation Department, 1964)

18DeVos, "A Quantitative Rorschach Assessment of Maladjustment and Rigidity in Acculturating Japanese-Americans."

19Abe Arkoff, "Need Patterns in Two Generations of Japanese Americans in Hawaii," *The Journal of Social Psychology* 50 (1959): 75–79.

20Fenz and Arkoff, "Comparative Need Patterns of Five Ancestry Groups in Hawaii."

21Kalish, Maloney, and Arkoff, "Cross-Cultural Comparisons of College Students and Marital-Role Preferences."

22Meredith and Meredith, "Acculturation and Personality among Japanese-American College Students in Hawaii."

and a matched sample of nondelinquent Sansei. The California Psychological Inventory (CPI) was used. Significant differences between the groups were found on responsibility, socialization, tolerance, achievement via conformance, achievement via independence, intellectual efficiency, flexibility, and femininity (see Table C of the Appendix).

The overall Sansei delinquent profile is similar to the norms of California adolescent delinquents, while the Sansei nondelinquent personality scores are similar to those of the normative California high-school population.

Several generalizations concerning values, attitudes, and personality appear important. First, there is a continuity in the change of "Japanese culture" toward American norms, so that most empirical evidence on all of the above-mentioned variables reflects this trend. Second, most results indicate the similarity of Sansei to American norms, so that from the point of view of selected psychological variables, the Sansei have acculturated. Finally there remains a number of questions concerning the use and interpretation of personality tests based on Caucasian norms. It should be remembered that the Japanese American is operating from a less powerful, or "dominated," position, whereas many test interpretations are based on the assumption of a "free" individual with few "racial" restrictions.[23] The tests also tend to ignore behavioral variations in time, place, and situation; otherwise how could a group so constantly analyzed as quiet, submissive, and self-effacing be so different when seen away from the testing and more formal situations?

COMPATIBILITY OF JAPANESE AND AMERICAN MIDDLE-CLASS VAUES

Caudill stresses the compatibility of Japanese and American middle-class values. For example, politeness, the respect for authority and parental wishes, duty to the community, diligence, cleanliness and neatness, emphasis on personal achievement and on long-range goals, a sense of shame concerning nonsanctioned behavior, the importance of keeping up one's appearance, and a degree of "outer-directedness" are values shared by the two cultures.

However, from our evidence it appears that the acculturation of the Japanese has not been because their culture and the American middle class are the same, but rather because of the functional compatibility and interaction between the two. The Issei have not acculturated and have retained most of the ways of the old culture. Even the Sansei retain a certain degree of Japaneseness. However, the differences often facilitate rather than hinder their adjustment to American society.

[23]Daniels and Kitano, *American Racism*, pp. 5, 9–28.

For example, Iga notes that success-aspiration and obligation, both of which the Japanese American values more highly than does the Caucasian, are ideal norms of an older Protestantism, and both values help the group to become successful in America.[24] Some other characteristics in which Japanese Americans are higher than Americans are conformity and compromise. Therefore, a complex of patterns of Japanese-American culture, wherein success-aspiration and regard for rapid socioeconomic success are coupled with deference, conformity, and compromise, may explain why the group at the present time is doing well in America, but has not raised the hostility of the larger society.

An "Ethical" Culture

The American and Japanese cultures have different ways of viewing norms and goals. The American appears more goal-oriented—efficiency, output, and productivity are highly valued, and the primary object is to win or to achieve success. The Japanese system appears much more norm-oriented—the how, the style, and the means of interaction are important—so that playing the game according to the rules is as important as winning it.

The norm-oriented culture may prove to be quite adaptable to external changes (for example, the Issei immigrant, or the behavior of the Japanese during the wartime occupation of Japan), provided that some social structure remains, because interrelationships have meaning in themselves. How to interact with others—superiors, inferiors, and equals —can be relatively easily transferred from one structure to another, so that such a system may be less stressful to its members than one that is more success-oriented in terms of goals. For when goals are blocked or are unreachable, or when the lack of success in terms of "output" is glaringly apparent, the individual in such a position may be placed under very high stress.

Our previous illustration of the employer–employee relationship provides an example of the possible difference between the two cultures. A Japanese firm will tend to keep an inefficient employee, since Japanese norms encourage the notion of obligation; the *oyabun* (parent) and the *ko-bun* (child) relationship obtains between employer and employee and is a goal in itself. Conversely, an American firm will not hesitate to fire an unproductive employee—the goals of the system are productivity, and can be summarized in the familiar phrase, "I'm running a business, not a welfare agency."

In a similar vein, American baseball players who have played in Japan feel that the Japanese will never be major leaguers until they de-

---

[24]Iga, "Changes in Value Orientation of Japanese Americans."

velop a greater will to win. By this the American means that Japanese pitchers should throw at batters more often; Japanese players should slide with spikes high, challenge umpires, and play a more aggressive game. There is little question that if the worth of a culture is measured in terms of efficiency and productivity, the American model is vastly superior, but one may also question the possible emotional cost of such a system to those who cannot "make it" there. However, there are indications that the modern Japanese business and economic world is rapidly moving toward the American model.

Assimilation of the American Culture

The present trend away from the Japanese culture in terms of norms, values, and personality means that in the near future there will be almost complete acculturation. For example, although Japanese and Americans have differed in the past in their collective and individualist orientations, the collectivity orientation has diminished among Sansei and at present is similar to that of Caucasian samples. Egoistic behavior and the importance of self over others has developed to such an extent that, in a study discussed earlier, on a question dealing with the family and the nation, the Sansei held a more individualistic position than did the non-Japanese American! Similarly, standards of discipline, paternalism, status distinction, and other parameters of the "American" value system show that the Sansei are for all practical purposes completely acculturated. Iga states:

> Their [the Sansei] desire to be assimilated appears to be so complete and their knowledge of Japanese culture so marginal that we cannot anticipate their return to traditional Japanese cultural interests. The only factor which prevents them from complete assimilation seems to be the combination of their physical visibility, and racial prejudice on the part of dominant group members.[25]

But parts of the Japanese culture undoubtedly remain. The tea ceremony, flower arranging, ondos and other dances, sukiyaki and other Japanese dishes, have become firmly a part of the Japanese-American culture. Certain traditions are already lost. Nisei and Sansei remember fondly the public singing performances of their otherwise restrained Issei parents at festivals and picnics, but the self-conscious Nisei have not stepped in to fill the role. Some values—responsibility, concern for others, quiet dignity—will hopefully survive, but other less attractive aspects—authoritative discipline, blind obedience to ritual, extensive use of guilt and shame to shape behavior, and the submissiveness of females—will not be much regretted in their passing.

[25]Ibid.

Finally, although most empirical tests indicate the similarity of the Sansei to his American peers, the groups are by no means identical. Hopefully, in a culturally pluralistic society, the Sansei will find an effective combination of Japanese and American values, a personal value system for maintaining a mature and responsible attitude toward themselves and the world.

During the Issei period, the Japanese were not popular in America. Early complaints against them alleged, in particular, dirtiness, disease, and poor living conditions, irreligion (after the manner of the "heathen Chinese"), and, most serious of all, reluctance to keep to a modest lower-class place in the white society. The Japanese, it was thought, were too pushy, and ought not to have wanted the things that white men want—to own land, to be a citizen, to be treated as equals. For all these reasons they were regarded as undesirable immigrants.

Since that time, however, the behavior of the Japanese has generally been described as "good." Goodness means different things in different contexts, of course. To the schoolteacher it means that Japanese students are quiet, obedient, and diligent. An employer considers his Japanese employee good because he is well trained, well educated, and highly motivated to work. Public health officials now find the Japanese clean, disease-free, and living in sanitary housing. In terms of the general society, the Japanese are good because they do not get into trouble and keep in their place.

Social Deviance

But conceptions of goodness and badness often lead to peculiar generalizations. For example, the Japanese behavior during the evacuation could be considered good because it was so docile, just as, from the Nazi point of view, the Jews were very good about Auschwitz and Buchenwald. Conversely, the black revolt is not characterized by "good" behavior because it is nonconformist and uncooperative. And, of course, to be labeled "good" by the dominant culture is often fraught with danger—in previous eras, the good Indian was the dead Indian; the good "Chinaman" was the one who packed up his belongings and went back to China.

Obviously, whether Japanese, Jewish, and black behavior has been good or bad depends on the perspective from which it is judged. And because this is often true in making moral judgments of goodness and badness, it is necessary to look for some sounder criteria pertaining to social deviance; that is, rates of violation of generally respected social mores. Social deviance in this chapter refers to aberrant behavior as measured by rates of crime, delinquency, and mental illness, and also to nonconforming behavior, such as the creative and the unusual.

ABERRANT BEHAVIOR

Several general difficulties are inherent in all studies of crime, delinquency, and mental illness. They must necessarily rely on official statistics, and these statistics often reflect consistent biases. Who is caught and who is hospitalized may not reflect the actual incidence of problem behavior. Intermediaries—policemen or psychiatrists—play a major role in the determination and processing of a potential "statistic."

Also, the validity of official statistics often changes with the level at which they were gathered. Cressey describes this as the "funneling effect," which simply means that data are screened by various processes until those emerging at the bottom or final point are less apt to reflect the actual incidence of deviant behavior than those data which are fed in at the top.[1] For instance, an analysis of the inmates of a prison or mental institution corresponds to the bottom of the funnel, and its results may bear little resemblance to analysis of rates of arrest or outpatient care. Yet funneled statistics are often the most readily available, and therefore are most commonly used.

Adult Crime

With these limitations in mind, it is possible to make a simple overall generalization about the Japanese. They are low in criminal behavior. They are infrequently arrested, seldom imprisoned, and seldom on parole. This may not have always been true. The *San Francisco Chronicle* on August 2, 1900, reported:

> Japanese Interpreter Wanted
>
> District Attorney and Police Judges have joined in petition to the Mayor and the Board of Supervisors to take immediate steps to create the position of interpreter of the Japanese language for the Police Courts and criminal department of the Superior Court, alleging as a reason the great increase in crime among the Japanese owing to the large immigration.

It should be remembered that the early immigrants were young, male, and unmarried—a group highly vulnerable to asocial behavior. But they also brought with them a series of stories that, although possibly idealized, may have been true. Issei stories of unlocked doors in old Japan—the safety of dropped wallets and forgotten purses, the infrequency of robberies and violence, at least suggest high group expectations of noncriminal behavior. The early "increase in crime" among Japanese immigrants did not reflect much serious felony.

And, on the level of official statistics, the Japanese then and since have been a noncriminal group. Their lack of crime is striking, especially when compared to other groups. For example, if we use FBI statistics for 1940, 1950, 1960, and 1970, comparing arrests per 100,000, the Japanese

---

[1]Donald R. Cressey, "Crime," in R. Merton and R. Nisbet, eds., *Contemporary Social Problems* (New York: Harcourt, Brace and World, 1961), p. 28.

are lower than any other group studied[2] (see Table 4). The rates for Japanese for these years were 347, 202, 187, and 656. Other groups show the following patterns: whites—372, 429, 1461, 2460; blacks—1078, 1366, 5642, 7477; Chinese—1332, 719, 871, 593; Indians—1092, 2136, 13687, 16523. Comparable statistics from other official sources provide similar data. For example, arrest records of various police departments and data on California prison populations rank the adult Japanese among the lowest group rate. Another source of data is the Los Angeles County Probation Department, where we can compare Japanese adult crime rate with non-Japanese adult crime for ten-year periods. Rates, adjusted per 100,000, show the Japanese with *15* in 1920, *53* in 1930, *149* in 1940, *111* in 1950, and *67* in 1960. Non-Japanese rates were *190* in 1930, *518* in 1940, *589* in 1950, and *793* in 1960. Comparative rates for Honolulu, the other center of a large Japanese population, are similar.

Two generalizations can be made from these statistics. First, the overall Japanese rate of crime is very low, and second, the trend for the Japanese adult is toward even lower rates. While non-Japanese rates con-

TABLE 4

ARREST RATES OF SELECTED ETHNIC GROUPS IN THE UNITED STATES (Census Year 1940–1970)*

Year

(Rates per 100,000)

Ethnic Group	1940	1950	1960	1970
Total, U.S.	462	524	1,951	3,079
Japanese	347	202	187†	656
White	372	429	1,461	2,460
Black	1,078	1,366	5,642	7,477
Chinese	1,332	719	871	593
Indian	1,092	2,136	13,687	16,523

*Computed on the basis of: Federal Bureau of Investigation, *Crime in the United States*, Uniform Crime Reports, 1940, 1950, 1960, 1970, and U.S. Census Bureau, U.S. Population Census, 1940, 1950, 1960, 1970. It should be noted that not all cities are reported in the Uniform Crime Reports. However, population figures used to compute rates are for the total U.S.
†Since 1959, the Uniform Crime Reports have included Hawaii and yield a rate of 1,200. Because the Islands contain a large Japanese population, the inclusion of their figures drastically alters the total rate for the Japanese. In order to get an approximation of the Japanese rate for the United States, less Hawaii for 1960, the number of Japanese arrests for Honolulu County (not all of Hawaii) was subtracted from the FBI figures and the rate was computed using the Japanese mainland population as a base. This calculation yielded a rate of 187.

2U.S. Department of Justice, Federal Bureau of Investigation, *Uniform Crime Reports for the United States, 1940–1970* (Washington, D.C.). The Chinese rate for 1970 was lower than the Japanese.

tinue to rise, the Japanese adult rates peaked in 1940 and have shown a
steady drop since this time. These trends are consistent on various levels
of the funnel. However, the sharp rise in crime in 1970 may portend
another trend.

The kinds of crime committed by the Japanese adult are consistent.
Federal Bureau of Investigation data show almost no change in the nature of Japanese crimes from 1940 through 1970; drunkenness and gambling were the two most common offenses. Other groups, such as the
white and the black, also show drunkenness as a common crime, but
members of these groups are not so likely to be arrested for gambling.
A common local offense for the Japanese is traffic violation.

It should be noted that drunkenness and gambling appear to be
culturally based. Both of these behaviors are tolerated in Japan; for example, Belli reports that a drunk driver arrested for having an accident
in Japan may defend himself on the ground that he was too drunk to vio-
late the law intentionally.[3] However, when I was in Japan in 1974, the
police were extremely strict about drunken driving. Gambling was the
number one offense in Japan from 1907 to 1931, and even today, a form
of gambling, the *pachinko* (pinball machine) parlor remains extremely
popular.[4] The gambler's "specials" leaving from San Francisco and Los
Angeles for Nevada continue to draw a good proportion of Japanese
Americans, and once there, they may be joined by their ethnic peers from
across the sea.

Juvenile Crime

The same generalizations concerning the rates of official Japanese adult
crime appear relevant in regard to data on Japanese juvenile crime. Los
Angeles County Probation records for Japanese juveniles, adjusted to
reflect rates per 100,000, show *300* in 1930; *119* in 1940; *180* in 1950; and
450 in 1960. In comparison, non-Japanese were *1709* in 1930; *1069* in
1940; *1291* in 1950; and *1481* in 1960. The trend for the Japanese and
non-Japanese rates are similar—relatively high in 1930, a drop in 1940,
with steady increases up through 1960. However, the Japanese rate is
consistently lower than the non-Japanese figures. Earlier studies by
Misaki[5] and Beach[6] also show the Japanese rates of juvenile delinquency

[3]Melvin Belli and D. R. Jones, *Belli Looks at Life and Law in Japan* (New
York: Bobbs-Merrill Co., 1960).

[4]M. Miyaki, *Outline of Japanese Judiciary* (Tokyo: The Japan Times Mail,
1935).

[5]H. K. Misaki, *Delinquency of Japanese in California*, Stanford University Series
in Education-Psychology, vol. 1 (Stanford, Calif.: Stanford University Press, 1933).

[6]W. C. Beach, *Oriental Crime in California* (Stanford, Calif.: Stanford University Press, 1932).

in California to be substantially lower than for other groups.

Arrest rates for Japanese juveniles under eighteen years of age remain virtually nonexistent. From 1964 to 1971 they were .1 percent of all arrests and in 1972 and 1973 they had dropped even lower.[7] Federal Bureau of Investigation rates per 100,000 show the following arrest comparisons; whites—613; blacks—1641; Indians—1719; Chinese—164; Japanese—264.

There appear to be recent changes in the type of delinquent acts committed by the Sansei juvenile in Los Angeles. Assault and battery, narcotics violations, and disorderly conduct by gangs have increased over previous periods.[8]

Crime by Generation

A final generalization applies to Japanese statistics on crime and delinquency. There are fluctuations in rates even within the Japanese groups, and these changes appear to be related to generations. If we analyze each generation separately, we find that the high rates, in the relative sense, are concentrated during the juvenile years. The Issei, few of whom were juveniles, were low in law violations throughout; the Nisei were high in 1930, when their estimated age was five through fifteen, and in 1940 when it was fifteen through twenty-five. The same appears to be true for the Sansei, whose rates were high in 1960, when the estimated age span for this group was ten to twenty years of age.

These figures appear consistent with one of the "facts" in criminology—the variations by age as presented by Cressey.[9] It does show that for the Japanese, as well as for the general American population, high criminality occurs during the adolescent period.

Another fact is that juvenile delinquency is usually higher among the American-born children of immigrants than the immigrant group itself. This appears to be true for the Japanese, too; however, the largest rise appears to be a generation later than for other immigrant groups, since it is the Sansei, rather than the Nisei, who show the largest increase. It may very well be that for some non-European groups, the acculturation process, which leads to possible conflicts and to a rise in crime and delinquency, is delayed.

The types of crime also appear to be related to generation. For example, Issei crimes were mostly "immigrant crimes," that is, related either to ignorance of the law and/or to behaviors less severely punished

[7] *Uniform Crime Reports for the United States, 1964–1973.*

[8] Harry H. L. Kitano, "Japanese-American Crime and Delinquency," *The Journal of Social Psychology* 66 (1967): 253–63.

[9] Cressey, "Crime," p. 31.

in the old country and in the immigrant community, particularly drunkenness and gambling. Since their adult crimes also remain predominantly in the areas of drunkenness and gambling, the Nisei appear to follow the same pattern. Overall, as the Japanese become more acculturated, their deviant as well as conventional behaviors should conform more closely to that of the majority culture. For example, although statistics remain unreliable, there is high concern about drug problems in the Japanese community. Several ethnic agencies were established in Los Angeles to address the problem, so that the previous "immunity" of the group to the aberrant behavior of the larger community appears to have been erased.

DIFFERENCES BETWEEN "NORMAL"
AND "DELINQUENT" JAPANESE

A further question for analysis deals with the "delinquent" Japanese-American population. Who are they? How different is this group from nondelinquents? Why did they turn to delinquency?

In an effort to answer some of these questions, the writer compared thirty-five Japanese-American delinquents in Los Angeles with a matched group of nondelinquents of the same ethnicity (Japanese); age (late adolescent); sex (male); and social-class backgrounds. By delinquent, we refer to those Japanese Americans who were on file with the Los Angeles County Probation Department.[10]

The research analyzed both the children and parents, and the following generations are drawn from the study.

More of the delinquent sample came from broken or separated homes (32 percent) than the nondelinquents (0 percent). The delinquents constantly perceived their homes in unfavorable terms—poor relationships, unhelpful parents, poor and ineffective discipline. Further, they also saw their schools and neighbors in negative terms when compared to the nondelinquents.

There were similar differences between the parents of the delinquents and nondelinquent samples. The parents of the delinquents perceived self, family, school, and community in negative terms.

Personality scores (California Psychological Inventory) also showed consistent differences between the two groups. The delinquent sample performed similarly to the "delinquent norms" of the test, while the nondelinquent scores were similar to "normal" scores. There were no significant differences between the samples on self-concept except for one

---

[10]Further information is available in Kitano, "Japanese-American Crime and Delinquency."

response where the delinquents perceived themselves as less "lucky" than the nondelinquents.

Although the terms *delinquent* and *nondelinquent* are open to question, the findings of the study were congruent with what is known about the group.[11] For example, all of the parents (primarily Nisei) discussed the hard times of their youth—strict Issei parents, poverty, and discrimination, and most of the adolescents had the usual complaints (lack of communication and understanding) about their own parents.

The overall description of the delinquent Japanese sample was related to the concept of marginality. By marginality, reference was made to both the sociological (individuals who do not belong to either the Japanese or the American middle class) and the psychological (personality deviations).

As we commented:

> The delinquents in the present study were the marginal population. They did not identify with their ethnic community; nor were they a part of their families, or their neighborhood, or the schools and other institutions. Their personality and self-perceptions also reflected this marginality. The broken home, high family conflict, minimal intercommunity interaction, and disturbed personality syndrome significantly differentiated the probationer from his non-probationer peer.
>
> Clinical impressions provided further validation for this point of view. Our interviewers often mentioned the apparent "non-Japaneseness" of the delinquent sample—especially in terms of talking (e.g., high use of lower-class argot); of dress (e.g., sloppy, extreme forms of apparel); and of physical appearance (e.g., hair style and general physical impact). Their social participation patterns were typically with non-Japanese lower-class populations. There is, of course, the question of whether the status of being a probationer has led to this marginality or whether this pattern was apparent before the probation role.
>
> Basically, the marginal person does not identify with the major institutions of his culture and is, therefore, relatively immune to the social control influences of these forces. The problem is of identification, of socialization, of opportunities, and of reinforcement.[12]

Such an explanation relies heavily on a social-control theory of crime and delinquency.

Several other observations can be made in relation to Japanese crime and delinquency. One is that there is little evidence of large-scale organized crime, or of a delinquent subcommunity; second, the role of

---

[11]We included an item in the interview that asked for admission to certain behaviors that could be labeled delinquent. One hundred percent of the delinquent sample admitted to "delinquent behaviors," while only 42 percent of the nondelinquents admitted to similar behavior.

[12]Kitano, "Japanese-American Crime and Delinquency."

the gang is still minimal in contributing to illegal behavior. The importance of these overall reinforcements for the development and maintenance of delinquent roles cannot be overemphasized. Finally, as we will further explore in the section on mental illness, preferred behavior for the Japanese is not "acting out." By this term we refer to behavior like hitting and stealing. This controls to a great extent the form of the rebellious, overt acts that play such an important part in determining rates of delinquency.[13]

MENTAL ILLNESS

The funneling effect also operates statistics relating to mental illness. Generally, Japanese rates of mental illness seem to be consistent. Whether data is drawn from hospitalization records, or from the records of "preventive" agencies, such as child guidance clinics and family service agencies, or from impressionistic evidence by professionals in the ethnic community, the conclusion is the same: the Japanese are among the lowest of all identifiable groups in reported incidence of mental illness.[14]

Data on hospitalization provide the least complete reflection of the problem, but it is the most readily available and has limited usefulness. For example, since hospitalizations can be precisely quantified, it is possible to compare rates among Japanese in California, Hawaii, and Japan, although because of differences in definition, diagnosis, and the availability of medical care and the objectives of treatment, such cross-cultural comparisons may be quite deceptive. Statistics on hospital admission, using rates per 100,000 population, indicate the low incidence among Japanese. In 1960, the California Japanese rate was 40, compared to 150 for Caucasians, 40 for Mexicans, 150 for Indians, 70 for Chinese, and 190 for blacks. In 1965, the rate was Japanese, 40; Caucasian, 180; Mexican, 40; Indian, 180; Chinese, 90; blacks, 280. Admissions to the Hawaii State Mental Hospital in 1960 showed a rate of 88 for Japanese, 63 for Chinese, and 99 for the Caucasian.

Californian hospitalization statistics (see Table D of the Appendix) show that in 1964 the Japanese rate was 198; the Caucasian, 213; the Mexican, 74; the Indian, 174; the Chinese, 361; and the blacks, 296.

---

[13]One other comparison of the Japanese delinquent was made. We compared IQ, school grades, marital status of parents, parental occupation, and housing among matched probationers representing the Japanese, Mexican, black, and the Caucasian. The Japanese and Caucasian were similar in most respects in that they were more "normal," while the Mexican and black probationers scored much lower in all categories.

[14]Harry H. L. Kitano, "Japanese-American Mental Illness," in Stanley Plog and Robert Edgerton, eds., *Changing Perspectives on Mental Illness* (New York: Holt, Rinehart and Winston, 1969), pp. 256–84.

Hospitalization rates for mental illness among the Japanese in Japan for a comparable period are 130.

The State of Hawaii's Mental Health Division statistics show that in 1974, Japanese Americans comprised 16 percent of the active in-patient population and 8 percent of the out-patient population. The most common diagnosis was schizophrenia. For patients suffering with alcoholism problems, the Japanese were represented by 4 percent.[15] It should be remembered that the Japanese comprised more than 28 percent of Hawaii's population, so that they are consistently underrepresented in these "mental illness" statistics.

In general, the data support a generalization that the Japanese contribute a very small proportion to the hospitalized, mentally ill population. However, it also appears that once they are hospitalized, they remain there longer. A hypothesis for future exploration suggests possible differences in the severity of the Japanese illness. It is possible that since their rates are so low, only the most severely disturbed end up at the hospital, and once there, they tend to remain. There is also the possibility that the Japanese family may be slow in reaccepting a hospitalized member.

We have made some attempt to gather evidence from the other end of the funnel—that is, from within the Japanese community. This evidence is mostly impressionistic. A poll of sixteen Nisei professional people yielded a general impression of low rates of mental illness in the Japanese population with whom they worked.[16] We probed incidents of *ki-chi-gai* (crazy) behavior among the family, extended family, and Japanese friends, encouraging the professionals to recall observations of their own developmental years and to analyze incidents in the intimate day-by-day interaction in wartime relocation camps. All agreed that if mental illness were defined as hospitalization or the use of therapeutic resources outside the Japanese community, the Japanese were a mentally healthy group. However, there was disagreement among professionals as to whether the fact that Japanese did not go to agencies, psychiatrists, and mental hospitals perhaps might reflect factors other than mental health. Several felt that the traditional husband–wife and parent–child roles, especially among the Nisei and Sansei, were potential sources of much conflict for Japanese Americans. And although statistics from community agencies support the contention that Japanese do not show up in child guidance and mental health clinics, and because of their "good" behav-

15I would like to thank Lily Shigezawa, research statistician for the Department of Health, State of Hawaii, for providing the print-out data for these statistics. The mental health print-out is dated August 12, 1974; the alcohol data, August 21, 1974.

16Four psychiatrists, two psychologists, and ten social workers, all working in Los Angeles, 1966.

ior, are seldom referred there by schools and doctors, the records of Japanese community agencies provide an interesting contrast.

The social worker employed by the Japanese Chamber of Commerce in Los Angeles handled more than six hundred cases in the early 1960s, and classified well over one hundred of them as mental illness. Most of these cases involved older, male Issei, with low income, from lower-status occupations, such as janitor or laborer, and with relative isolation from a peer group. Even in the area of mental illness we find a typical Japanese pluralistic pattern—that is, to develop their own structures to take care of their own problems.

Classification of Mental Illness

The classification of mental illness is probably even more unreliable than attempts to determine its incidence. The absence of reliable criteria and differences in the training, tools, and insight of the professional produce a wide variation in descriptive labels for specific illnesses. Generally speaking, however, the most frequent form of Japanese mental illness, whether in California, Hawaii, or Japan, is schizophrenic. Many of the cases conform to a typical pattern, of which the following history is representative:

> Mr. H., owner of a small hotel in the "Little Tokyo" area of Los Angeles, begins to notice the gradual deterioration of Mr. Watanabe (fictitious name). Mr. Watanabe had moved into the hotel with two other bachelor Issei. Although information was difficult to obtain, it appeared that all three had come from the same ken in Japan, and had worked as fruit pickers most of their lives. Now that they were too old to continue, they had come to Los Angeles for retirement. The low rates at the hotel (an average rent of $45 a month) and a communal kitchen helped to stretch the dollar. The nearby Japanese community, the recreation rooms at the Chamber of Commerce Building (*go, shogi, hana*—all Japanese games) filled some of their time. Their lack of money precluded gambling, a once-favored pastime. Savings were meager.
>
> When his two friends died last year, Mr. Watanabe withdrew further and further from the outside world. He soon failed to get up from bed and developed problems going to the bathroom, getting up to eat, and finally, of cleanliness.
>
> Eventually Mr. H. contacted the Japanese social worker, who in turn brought Mr. Watanabe to the County Hospital. Diagnosis was schizophrenia and Mr. Watanabe was sent to a state hospital. There were no known relatives in the United States.[17]

Common symptoms of Mr. Watanabe and similar cases would in-

[17]Kitano, "Japanese-American Mental Illness," pp. 6, 7 of original manuscript.

clude hearing the voices of dead friends in Japanese, emotional crying, heightened irritability, loss of toilet control, and withdrawal.

There is some research evidence that the Japanese mental patient when hospitalized is much more inhibited and restrained than non-Japanese patients, and more frequently has ideational rather than action responses. For example, in a study comparing schizophrenic Filipino and Japanese mental patients in Hawaii, Enright and Jaeckle found that the Filipino behaved more outwardly, or alloplastically, so that his attempts to resolve conflicts were through environmental manipulation.[18] He expected to change the world. Conversely, the Japanese behaves inwardly, or autoplastically, attempting to resolve conflicts through modifying his own feelings and behavior.

In a study comparing the hospitalized mentally ill Japanese in Japan, Okinawa, Hawaii, and Los Angeles, Kitano found some consistent patterns.[19] The best predictors toward hospitalization were job loss, disruption of family life, and violent behavior in all four of the settings. The most common diagnosis was that of schizophrenia.

The following picture emerges in relation to Japanese-American mental illness. There is initially a relatively high tolerance for "crazy behavior" within the family. Much of the tolerance is related to "shame" and the blemish on the family name, so that attempts at suppression may be rather high. However, once a level of tolerance is reached, the individual may be sent to a mental institution with the feeling that "it's now someone else's problem." Therefore, once a Japanese is sent to an institution, he is likely to remain there for a long time.

Another facet of mental illness relates to the use of larger community institutions. Most Japanese prefer to use ethnic community resources before depending on the resources of the larger community. Other generalizations concerning the Japanese and mental illness are:

1. Official statistics indicate that mental illness is not a major problem for the Japanese.
2. Those afflicted are likely to be old, lower-class males.
3. The rates of hospitalization, although subject to systematic biases, appear to be remarkably similar among Japanese in the United States and Japan.
4. Schizophrenia, with symptoms of withdrawal, is the most frequent illness.

18J. Enright and W. R. Jaeckle, "Ethnic Differences in Psychopathology," paper presented at the Pacific Science Congress, Honolulu, Hawaii, August 23, 1961.

19Harry H. L. Kitano, "Mental Illness in Four Cultures," *The Journal of Social Psychology* 80 (1970): 121–34.

RELATIONSHIPS AMONG CRIME,
DELINQUENCY, MENTAL ILLNESS,
AND SUICIDE

There is an oversimplified description of behavior that predicts a balance between "withholding" or "acting out." By this is meant that cultures may either value repression or suppression so that very few emotions or impulses are acted on, or encourage the release of impulses, so that feelings are "acted out." From this perspective, delinquency (e.g., "acting out") and mental illness (e.g., withdrawal) are looked on as a single dimension, so that a negative correlation is thought to exist between the two variables. Therefore groups who are high on one end of the continuum are assumed to be low on the other and vice versa. Obviously, the Japanese American does not fit into this model, at least according to official statistics.

Another oversimplified view sees deviance as an escape valve, analogous to the valves on a steam engine, necessary to prevent explosions in the social system. If this were true, one would expect a monstrous explosion within the Japanese group, for there is little deviance. But there is no indication that such an explosion will occur. Even suicide, thought to be a typically Japanese form of release behavior, although frequent in Japan, is no more frequent in the Japanese-American population than in the American population as a whole. In general, the Japanese population simply minimizes "acting-out" behavior.

We do, however, describe other forms of acceptable "release" behavior among Japanese Americans. Most common is somatization—that is, the development of psychosomatic symptoms and undue concern with bodily functions. Although the evidence is only impressionistic, all that one knows of the Japanese group tends to support this observation. The widespread use of patent medicines, obsession with high blood pressure, hot baths, masseurs, the practice of acupuncture, and concern for the stomach and other internal organs is typical of Japanese whether in the United States or Japan.

Further, the rather formal, stylized social interaction among Japanese, with a minimum of personal affect, presents diagnostic difficulties. For example, one Japanese-American psychiatrist related:

> Because of the relatively rigid, set ways for social interaction, it's often difficult to diagnose where the role-set ends and possible psychiatric symptomatology begins. The person who reacts to extreme stress with a pattern of unemotional and ritualistic behavior may be relatively easy to diagnose

psychiatrically in another culture, but for the Japanese (especially the Issei), it's really hard to figure one way or the other.[20]

The choice of occupations is also protective for many Japanese. The stereotyped Japanese gardener has an occupation where the amount of social interaction can be held to a minimum and where ki-chi-gai, or crazy behavior, can be widely tolerated.

But possibly, the most relevant hypothesis concerning the Japanese and their overall lack of deviant behavior relates to their family and community structure; their "culture" and their ability to control marginality. Gordon writes that the marginal man, from the sociological perspective, is the person who stands on the borders or margins of two cultural worlds but is fully a member of neither.[21] Marginal positions may develop from mixed or interfaith marriages or from those who seek contact in worlds other than their ethnic culture.

Psychological indications of marginality, hypothesized but not empirically validated, are possibly related to marginal sociological positions and would include symptoms like anxiety, frustration, alienation, and anomie, as well as the commission of deviant acts.

The ability of the Japanese family and community to provide ample growth opportunities, to present legitimate alternatives, to provide conditions of relative tolerance and treatment, to provide effective socialization and control, as well as the relative congruence between Japanese culture and the middle-class American culture, has aided the group in adapting to acculturative changes with a minimal marginal population. Relatively few Japanese seek social friendships in the social cliques and organizations outside of their own ethnic group. And those who do seek outside contacts appear to have many of the necessary requisites for such activity—high education, good training, and adequate income.

We do not wish to infer that the marginal position is necessarily a negative one. For example, in a study of interethnic contacts (e.g., such as dating or marriage), those Japanese who were marginal in terms of ethnic identification and psychological orientation were found to be much more "liberal" in crossing ethnic boundary lines than their more "normal" cohorts.[22]

Of our cases of deviance—the mentally ill, the suicide, and the delinquent—a great many fall into the marginal classification. For example,

[20]Kitano, "Japanese-American Mental Illness," p. 24 of original manuscript.

[21]Milton M. Gordon, *Assimilation in American Life* (New York: Oxford University Press, 1964), pp. 56–57.

[22]Harry H. L. Kitano, "Passive Discrimination: The Normal Person," *The Journal of Social Psychology* 70 (1966): 23–31.

Japanese delinquents can be differentiated from a matched group of non-delinquents on certain variables. The delinquent tends to be characterized by broken or conflict-ridden homes, a lack of ethnic identity, and incongruent life-styles. Cases of suicide and mental illness also show a surprising degree of similarity. A recent suicide case involved a thirty-five-year-old man from Japan who had little income or job security, was not a member either of the ethnic community or the majority community, had no close relatives or friends, and finally killed himself over an unhappy love affair with a Caucasian divorcee. A recent case of mental illness that came to our attention involved a forty-year-old female, married to a non-Japanese, who after the death of her husband, finding herself rejected by both families and unequal to the task of raising several young children by herself, had a psychotic break. A twenty-two-year-old Sansei male, unable to get along with his parents, left home, married a black woman, and was recently arrested for robbery. These are fairly typical patterns, and, it will be noticed, are similar to one another in most respects except the ultimate form of the expressive behavior.

The essential similarity of case histories of deviant Japanese appears to be more than coincidental. For this reason we feel that certain predictions can be made. It would seem to be relatively easy to differentiate between the "normal" and those with prospects for "deviant" behavior, so that most clinicians, in analyzing case histories, would be able to decide very accurately who is normal and who is potentially deviant. In other words, it will be relatively easy to predict that many future deviants will come from the group that has been selected out on such variables as broken homes, lack of ethnic identity, and marginality. But it is more difficult to predict what direction the eventual deviance will take—whether an individual will become delinquent, criminal, or mentally ill—because these behavior patterns seem to derive from essentially similar histories. But, finally, there are very few deviant individuals among the Japanese, because the ethnic community has been effective in providing a large enough umbrella to cover and control the development of a significant marginal group.

There are explanations of low deviant behavior among the Japanese American other than the social control and the community-family hypotheses. One deals with the definition and treatment of trouble. A culture that tries to avoid "trouble," and has therefore geared a social system toward minimizing troublesome behavior, may be effective in repressing or hiding these problems to outside sources and even to themselves. As long as "trouble," be it poverty, mental illness, delinquency, or family conflict, remains private, it will remain unrecognized.

Another explanation for low "official" rates of deviant behavior concentrates on the low use of community services by a group. Miranda and Kitano[23] write that although the Mexican American and the Japanese American represent two different "cultures," both are similar in their low use of community mental health services. It is the hypothesized interaction among the lack of information about mental health, ethnic styles, the fragmentation and discontinuity of services, their unaccessibility, and their unaccountability that explains Chicano and Japanese American nonuse of community mental health resources.

REASONS FOR THE SMALL
MARGINAL POPULATION

Why have the Japanese been able to acculturate with such a small marginal population? Why have so many Japanese retained their ethnic identity? Why have so many remained with their ethnic community? Why have child socialization techniques been so effective? We have attempted to answer these questions in the broadest terms—the physical visibility of the Japanese; the difficulty they have had in entering the opportunity structures within the larger society; their relatively small numbers; the Japanese culture itself, with its cohesive family and community systems; and the effective enforcement of certain norms and values.

Some additional features of the Japanese culture also bear on the problems of social control and social deviance. For example, the opportunities within that culture were open to virtually everybody with the correct ancestry, so that there was a place for everybody, no matter what his degree of talent, success, rank, or personality. If he was Japanese, he belonged. For instance, the typical Nisei basketball team of the 1930s included excellent, good, mediocre, and poor players who "belonged" equally—they bought the same club jackets, they shared in its activities, and they felt the same degree of club loyalty and acceptance. The current emphasis on winning is a recent phenomenon and brings with it selective criteria—high athletic ability, selectivity, and small squads.

These changes reflect an important phase of acculturation. An American goal-orientation that values efficiency, success, winning, is taking over from a system more oriented toward ethical interaction, a system that valued means more than ends. And as the group changes from an inclusive system, in which most everybody belongs and that conduces to social control, to exclusive, where some are left out, it will face one common American dilemma—the maintenance of excellence and yet attempting to get everyone involved. It is difficult to retain social control

23Manuel Miranda and Harry H. L. Kitano, "Barriers to Mental Health Services: A Japanese and Mexican-American Dilemma" (in process).

over groups and individuals who feel no stake in the practices of that culture.

NONCONFORMING BEHAVIOR

For many of the same reasons that the Japanese show little negative deviant behavior (aberrant), such as crime, delinquency, mental illness, and suicide, it would be reasonable to suppose that they also show little positive behavior (nonconforming), such as creative forms of rebellion, disagreement, and individualism. This seems to have been generally true. Their docile behavior during the wartime evacuation and the absence of widely recognized persons of creative genius tend to support the observation. In a highly educated, highly trained, skilled population, one would normally expect to find more individuals involved in the so-called rebellious and "creative" areas of artistic, scientific, and academic contribution. This has not been the case. During the student protests at the University of California at Berkeley in 1965, Sansei were notably absent. Only very recently do we begin to find an occasional "unusual" Japanese, such as Minoru Yamasaki, a ranking architect.

Significantly, the majority of "unusual" Japanese have developed outside of the centers of Japanese population. Area of residence and size of ethnic community is highly related to acculturation and marginality. Of the 100,000 persons interned during the war, only a handful lodged protests. None of the cases that eventually were tested in the Supreme Court involved individuals from Los Angeles or San Francisco, although the majority of Japanese resided there. And it is a rather common observation among Japanese in Los Angeles that "outsiders" (Japanese Americans reared elsewhere) have "taken over" (that is, taken leadership positions). The financial leader of the Los Angeles ethnic community grew up in Oregon; the former publisher of the all-English Japanese newspaper grew up in Riverside, some miles away from Los Angeles' Little Tokyo; and various others who have become "leaders" are also products of outside environments. In the final analysis, the value of conformity and goodness must be weighed against the loss of the potentially valuable, creative, and expressive aspects of nonconforming individuals as well as against the absence of its disruptive aspects.

ACCULTURATION AND BEHAVIOR

Another interesting fact concerning aberrant behavior and acculturation is the initial starting point for the Japanese. For many other populations, acculturation means a move toward "good" behavior. That is, their initial rates of aberrant behavior may be high, and there is the hope that continuous exposure to and identification with American institutions and values will eventually lead to a modification of the problem behavior in question. For the Japanese, an interesting reversal is taking place—their initial rates of behavior like crime and delinquency have been low, so that acculturation is associated with rising rates of problem behavior. Not only is this true in the area of crime and delinquency but it is also true of a wide range of other behaviors. For example, acculturation may mean a rise in the number of accidents for Japanese-American children,[24] it may mean a lowering of school achievement,[25] and it may mean a rise in stomach cancer and heart disease.[26] There is also a finding that at the present time in California, the Japanese child at birth can expect to live about six to seven years longer than the white and ten to eleven years longer than the black.[27] As a group he has the lowest infant mortality as well as the lowest mortality rates throughout his life span. This last finding is difficult to explain in terms of acculturation alone.

MARGINAL GROUPS

The Kibei

Within the Japanese system, however, are groups who by definition are marginal. They include the Kibei and some recent new immigrants.

The Kibei are technically Nisei—born in the United States—but differ in having spent their early years in Japan, usually with grandparents. Because members of this group differ in regard to sex, particular experiences in Japan, and length of expatriation, it is difficult to arrive at meaningful generalizations about them. Their number was estimated by Leighton to be over 9 percent in one of the evacuation camps, which is probably a typical distribution. Therefore, they are a group of significant size.[28]

The practice of sending at least one child back to Japan to be educated was most popular between 1920 and 1940. This was the period

24Minako Kurokawa, "Proposed research in the field of childhood accidents" (unpublished proposal, Department of Sociology, University of California, Berkeley, May, 1964).

25Harry H. L. Kitano, "Changing Achievement Patterns of the Japanese in the United States," *The Journal of Social Psychology* 58 (1962).

26"High Rate of Stomach Cancer among Japanese—State Report," in the *Nichi-Bei Times*, April 23, 1959, English section, p. 1.

27H. H. Hechter and N. O. Borhani, "Longevity in Racial Groups Differs," *California's Health* 22, 15 (February 1, 1965).

28Alexander Leighton, *The Governing of Men* (Princeton, N.J., Princeton University Press, 1945).

of rampant nationalism and patriotism in Japan. Therefore, many Kibei returned to the United States with strong pro-Japanese feelings. Here, since their perceptions of Japan were greatly different, they came into inevitable conflict with the Nisei, and even with many Issei. Some of the overt conflicts that arose in the wartime relocation centers were the result of Kibei-Nisei clashes.

Naturally, after the beginning of World War II, no more Japanese Americans were sent back to Japan, and the practice was never resumed. The Kibei population has therefore remained static and is currently indistinguishable from the middle-aged Nisei population. Certain impressions suggest that a higher proportion of them remain in Japanese "cultural activities," such as the judo, kendo, and aikido clubs, and they may not, in general, be as well acculturated as their Nisei peers. The Kibei did face many of the problems associated with marginal populations, especially during and directly after World War II (for example, Tule Lake, the stormiest evacuation camp, was made up of a high proportion of Kibeis), but the passage of time and the changing conditions have done much to resolve the major issues.

The "new" interaction has been the increasing volume of visits to Japan by the Nikkei. Chartered tours, education abroad programs, business trips, and visits to relatives have become common, so that many Japanese Americans have a first-hand, albeit fleeting, experience of the mother country.

Some Sansei have attempted to understand their heritage by spending a longer time in Japan. We sat down with a group of them in Tokyo in 1972 and heard their experiences. We also met with a group of Nisei who had settled down in Japan after World War II, and the question of their identities was a constant issue. The problem was especially acute for their children: should these Sansei be raised as Japanese, Japanese Americans, or Americans, including language, reading material, values, and dating, since the Nisei parents were expecting to return with their families to the United States sometime in the future? We also met individual Kibei who had never returned to the United States, and as an example of fixed roles they probably represented the way that the Nisei in California were socialized in the 1930s. So, if one of the ways of studying Meiji Japanese values is to look at Japanese immigrants in the Central Valley of California, then a way of studying Nisei socialization in California prior to World War II may be to study those Kibei who went to Japan during this period and never returned.

Recent Immigrants

The New Issei. Since the immigration legislation of 1954, many new Issei have come to the United States. Some have been quota immigrants, others were relatives of citizens, others emigrated under the refugee relief act of 1956, and more recently with the elimination of quotas, there are those with training and skills deemed to be important for America.

Unlike the first immigrants, who were homogeneous in terms of age, sex, social class, and residential background, the new Issei are a more heterogeneous group. Therefore it is difficult to generalize about them.

They have come, however, at a time when Japanese Americans have few occupational and residential problems, and have naturally benefited from this circumstance. Nevertheless, the adults will probably never fully acculturate. There is also a relative coolness between the new immigrant and those Japanese who have been here for a long time. The new Issei often bring with them a sense of the new and modern Japanese nation that is much closer to the American world than was the Japan of the first Issei. They already probably have more in common with American Nisei than with American Issei. Their children, of course, will be largely indistinguishable from American Nisei and Sansei.

War Brides. An estimated 25,000 Japanese war brides were in the United States by 1960. This is a heterogeneous group in terms of background, for the motivation for marrying out of the Japanese culture varied widely, but a relatively homogeneous one in terms of sex and age.

The experiences of these war brides vary.[29] Those who marry Nisei probably have merged imperceptibly into the ethnic community. However, there is some evidence of greater mother-in-law problems in this group.[30] Others have scattered throughout the country with non-Japanese husbands, and probably account for the wide geographical distribution of Japanese at present.

It is interesting to note that although this group represents marital and structural assimilation in a manner not commonly found among the Issei, Nisei, and Sansei groups, they were initially less well acculturated. Their sociological position is marginal: the ethnic community has generally not accepted them, and their primary ties are to the husband's social group. In general, these groups probably regard them as exotic, too. Certain behaviors commonly associated with marginal populations (e.g., less stable occupations) are sometimes seen in this group. One common pattern of employment involves serving as waitresses in Japanese restaurants.

Temporary Japanese: Kai-sha, Students, and Visitors. The temporary Japanese population is a heterogeneous one in terms of age, sex, and geographical location. Some represent a wealthy and privileged Japanese class and therefore play a subtle role in shaping the American conception

---

29Chizuko Tsutsumi, "World of Mrs. Kiyoko Smith," Japanese-American Marriage Study Report. Mimeographed. (San Francisco: The International Institute, 1962).

30Richard Kalish, Michael Maloney, and Abe Arkoff, "Cross-Cultural Comparisons of Marital Role Expectations," *The Journal of Social Psychology* 68 (1966): 41–47.

of Japanese people. This was especially true in the earlier days, when social interaction with upper-class Americans, especially along the East Coast, was available to powerful Japanese businessmen and members of royalty. Such contacts, of course, have never been available to the typical Issei immigrant.

Present-day Japanese visitors reflect the many changes in Japanese culture in Japan. The student today is different from his counterpart of 1920; he is often accused of being lazier, more carefree (non-ki), and less studious. Nonetheless, many modern students are even more successful at their studies than those of an earlier day. Finally, as we will discuss in Chapter 10, another new "immigrant" is Japanese capital, with (its) ability to purchase hotels and other facilities.

In general, all of the newcomers—visitors, students, and the new Issei—have little intimate contact with the local ethnic communities. American Sansei often refer derisively to the new Issei, even those of their own age, as FOB's (fresh off the boat), even though these FOB's dress in "mod" and other current fashions and have many more "American" attitudes than their critics. Many appear at least superficially to be more acculturated than the Sansei, especially in terms of personality. Where many Sansei still demonstrate reticence and reserve, the new Issei, reflecting changes in modern Japan, often seem more open and receptive to new ideas.

The problem for these younger Issei is their marginal position in relation to both the Japanese-American culture and to the white middle-class one. Several recent cases of shootings, and the establishment of no-mi-yas (bars) with barmaids similar to those in Japan, have raised the eyebrows of the ethnic community. However, we know of several cases where the newcomer (in each case female) has bypassed the ethnic community to participate directly in the larger society. In this sense, they have achieved both structural and marital assimilation more rapidly than have the longer established Nisei and Sansei. And as we have previously noted, the Japanese with "marginal personalities" and with little interaction with the Japanese institutions are less discriminatory toward outgroup members than their more "normal" counterparts.

In this chapter, we have presented data concerning some of the behavioral "outputs" of the Japanese-American culture. By "outputs" we refer to behavior like crime and delinquency and titled aberrant, as well as creative or unusual behavior titled nonconforming. The very low rates of Japanese behavior on either the aberrant or the nonconforming ends were interpreted in terms of the effectiveness of the social-control mechanisms of the Japanese system and their ability to control the growth of a large marginal population. We also attempted to emphasize both the positive and negative of aspects of marginal individuals and groups.

It is assumed that with continued acculturation and the gradual breakdown of ethnic structures and institutions that the social-control powers of the Japanese system will diminish. Such a change should be associated with a rise in social deviance—both in terms of the aberrant and the creative.

It is difficult to understand the omission of Hawaii when there is a discussion of the Japanese American, but such a practice is common. Perhaps there is a feeling that Hawaii is an exception to many of the generalizations concerning the Japanese American, or that it is so small that it is not worth counting. But a glance at population figures shows how erroneous such impressions are; in 1970, 217,307, or 37 percent, of the 591,290 Japanese in the United States were residents of Hawaii.

But the numbers alone do not begin to reflect the importance of the islands. The most prominent politicians of Japanese ancestry come from Hawaii, and the sight of Japanese faces sitting in both the United States Senate and House of Representatives must be a surprise to those who view America solely as a white nation. And the experiences in Hawaii have been different, so that they provide another frame for looking at the Japanese.

The Japanese in Hawaii

For example, the Japanese in Hawaii were never a small, scattered minority in a vast land but were a large, sometimes majority group on a few concentrated islands; they entered into a more racially tolerant society than their peers in California; and they were one of a large number of imported nationality groups. Further, they were geographically close enough to Japan so that homeland influences were much stronger than on the mainland. Therefore, the Japanese in Hawaii offer an opportunity to evaluate the effect of variables like power, a more tolerant social structure, a relative degree of social isolation, and closer ties to the homeland on a Japanese population.

KOTONKS

But the question of different experiences would remain academic if the Japanese in Hawaii turned out to be identical to their mainland counterparts. Most close observers indicate that differences do exist and that a person acquainted with the Japanese can distinguish between those from the mainland and those from Hawaii. There is even a classification system with special terms—the Kotonk for the Japanese American from the mainland, and the Buddhahead for his cohort from the islands.

One popular version of the origin of the term *Kotonk* is that the

head of the mainlander is hard and hollow so that when it hits the floor
it makes this sound. This interesting discovery occurred during World
War II when the Hawaiians of the 442nd Combat Team met mainland
Nisei on a large scale for the first time. There were the inevitable arguments and fist fights and the sound of mainland Nisei heads bouncing
off the floors must have left an audible impression.

Although the audio origin remains the most colorful, the definition
also included the feelings the islander had toward his look-alike peers
from the West Coast. The mainlander was considered standoffish and
uptight, overly concerned about surface appearances, materialistic, too
careful about impressing the majority group, too acculturated, and, in
one word, too *haolefied* (white).

For example, Ogawa presents one stereotype of the Kotonk as contrasted to the islander. In a restaurant, the islander fights to pick up the
check, or at a bar, he takes out cash and puts it on the table. In contrast,
the Kotonk carefully ascertains whether he paid the last time, or accurately figures out how much he owes and then adds the required tip. Or
if the Hawaiian Japanese had a good time he would say, "Terrific, yeah,"
whereas the Kotonk might say, "Yes, it was marvelous."[1]

The term *Kotonk* remains in use today, especially in Hawaii. The
mainlander still finds some difficulty in gaining full acceptance into the
Japanese-American social system, and his island peers will seldom let
him forget his Kotonk background. Conversely, mainland Japanese also
hold certain stereotypes about the islanders as "pineapples," but the
current ease of travel and the constant interchange have changed the
stereotypes, except among the most prejudiced.

There are some obvious differences between the islanders and the
mainlanders, whether Japanese or not: variations in language (including
pidgin), a healthier tan, and the more casual Hawaiian style of dressing
and living. But these differences are regional, and the vastness of the
United States incorporates a smorgasbord of life styles. Other differences
may reflect rural-urban contrasts, although present day Honolulu is a
big city by any standard, including freeways, overcrowding, and pollution.

But subtly, the Japanese in Hawaii make up a powerful group with
a number of alternatives not readily available to most of their peers on
the mainland. They are more comfortable in their ethnicity; they are freer
to retain their life styles by voluntary choice. Yet, they were also freer
to acculturate because the barriers toward Americanization were not as
rigid as on the mainland. Even more important, their acculturation was
to a more racially tolerant island culture, so that many profess surprise

[1]Dennis Ogawa, *Jan Ken Po* (Honolulu: Japanese Chamber of Commerce, 1973),
p. 17.

when a discussion of racial discrimination, mainland style, is raised. It is the amalgamation of these experiences that has developed the Japanese in Hawaii into something different from their mainland counterparts.

HISTORY

Hawaii was initially settled by Polynesians, believed to be from Tahiti, around A.D. 750 to 1000. Their ability to navigate the vast Pacific was an incredible feat of early seamanship. The Western world first heard about Hawaii through Captain Cook, who in 1778 named it the Sandwich Islands after his patron the Earl of Sandwich.

At the time of Cook, each island was ruled as an independent kingdom by hereditary chiefs. King Kamehameha I gradually brought the islands under his control, so that by the time of his death in 1819 he had established the Kingdom of Hawaii. A "bloodless revolution" in 1893 overthrew the monarchy, and a provisional government under the leadership of Sanford Dole, an American, requested, but was refused, annexation to the United States. The provisional government then converted Hawaii into a republic; it was annexed as a United States Territory in 1898 and became the fiftieth State on August 21, 1959.

Several factors have influenced Hawaii ever since its "discovery" by Captain Cook. First was the early influence of explorers and traders of many nations who visited this independent kingdom for rest, recreation, and trade. Lind remarks that the Westerner, if he wished to remain on friendly terms with the islanders, had to honor the customs and practices of the Hawaiians; conversely, if the natives were to enjoy those goods and services of the foreigner, he too had to use tact, compromise, and discretion. Therefore, the stage up to about 1850 was characterized by mutual degrees of tolerance by both sides.[2]

The second stream was the influence of various Western religious groups, starting with the New England Congregationalists who arrived in 1820 for missionary purposes. Although there were disagreements between the traders and the religious people, the two groups of foreigners had much in common, and they eventually supported each other against the native islanders. The Roman Catholic influence began in 1828, and Mormon Missionaries began to arrive on the islands in the middle of the nineteenth century.

A third, and the most important stream, was the importation of "labor" to work on the large agricultural plantations. By this time, the islands were essentially conquered, and business and economic considerations were of the highest priority. Peoples of various racial and national

---

[2]Andrew Lind, *Hawaii's People* (Honolulu: Univ. of Hawaii Press, 1967).

origins, "Portuguese, Chinese, Puerto Ricans, Japanese, Micronesians, Melanesians, Polynesians, Germans, Koreans, Russians, and Filipinos, among others, were imported in varying numbers to supply laborers for the expanding plantations of Hawaii, but with little thought for the complex processes of ethnic interaction which were thereby initiated."[3]

It is interesting to note the initial attitudes that some native Hawaiians held toward the Japanese. In an interview between Mr. Kapena, a representative of the Hawaiian government sent to Japan to search for

TABLE 5
THE PEOPLE OF HAWAII[a]
GROUPS "IMPORTED" (RECRUITED AS PLANTATION WORKERS)

Order of Arrival	Time of Major Immigration	Size of Group, 1960		Size of group, 1970, by percent[f]
Chinese	1878–1884	38,119	6.0%	6.8
Portuguese	1878–1887	(27,588 in 1930)[b]		N/a
Japanese	1886–1924	203,876	32.2%	28.3
Puerto Ricans	1901	(9,551 in 1950)[c]		N/a
Koreans	1904–1905	(7,030 in 1950)[c]		N/a
Spaniards	1907–1913	(*were* 8,000)[d]		N/a
Filipinos	1907–1931	68,641	10.8%	12.2
Non-Plantation-Labor Groups				
Hawaiian	approx. 950 A.D.	10,502	1.7%	N/a
Haole (Caucasian)	1878–1884, 1920–40, 1950–	202,230	32.2%	38.8
Part-Hawaiian	. . .	91,597	14.5%	N/a
Black	1940–	4,943	0.8%	1
All Other[e]	. . .	12,864	2.0%	N/a
Totals		632,772	100.0%	

[a]Information for this chart was compiled principally from Lind, *Hawaii's People*, especially p. 28; the date for arrival of the Hawaiians is from Gerrit P. Judd, IV, *Hawaii: An Informal History* (New York Collier-Macmillan Ltd., 1961), p. 21.

[b]The U.S. Census last delineated Portuguese in 1930. Since then they have been included in the Caucasian category. In 1930 the Portuguese were more than 1/3 of the Caucasian group.

[c]Included in "All Others" in the 1960 Census.

[d]Migration to California plus assimilation into Caucasian group resulted in practical elimination of Spaniards as a durable group in Hawaii.

[e]Includes Samoans, Micronesians, Indians, Koreans, and Puerto Ricans.

[f]U.S. Dept. of Commerce, Bureau of the Census, *Characteristics of the Population of Hawaii*, 1, 13 (1970), Table 18, pp. 13–29.

Source: Frederick Samuels, *The Japanese and the Haoles of Honolulu* (New Haven, Conn.: Yale University Press, 1970), p. 23.

[3]Ibid, p. 7.

immigrants, and the Japanese Minister of Foreign Affairs Inouye in Japan in 1882, Kapena sounded the following note of racial affinity:

> We believe the Japanese and Hawaiians spring from a cognate race and that Japanese children growing up and amalgamating with our population will produce a new and vigorous race, which will repeople our Islands. . . . We wish to repeople our country with an orderly, laborious [sic], civilized, law abiding and cognate race.[4]

But the feelings of Kapena were not to be shared by groups already on the islands. Some saw the possibility of Japanese domination and feared that Hawaii might become a Japanese satellite. The Portuguese considered them a menace to their position. Mechanics and tradesmen would soon note with apprehension the Japanese drifting away from the plantations to become possible competitors for lower- and middle-level positions. But as Kuykendall notes, during these early years from 1886 to 1894, the anti-Japanese sentiment was relatively minor, and the Chinese were the main targets. The Japanese were to become victims later.[5]

Hawaiian history is the story of a tolerant native population quickly losing their lands and their power to the more sophisticated, restless, ambitious, and ruthless *haole* (whites), who then began to encourage the Hawaiian government to import various nationality groups to labor on the plantations. There is a parallel between the Hawaiian experience and the treatment of the native Indian populations on the mainland. Both native groups were overwhelmed; their lands were taken away from them; both were ill-suited for laboring for their conquerors; and both were, therefore, bypassed as newer groups were imported.

RACIAL HARMONY

The ideal of racial harmony has long been a part of the Hawaiian ethos, and in comparative terms, conflicts stemming from race are perhaps less severe on the islands than in most other parts of the world. But it would also be an error to minimize its history of diverse racial and nationality groups; the plantation economy ruled by a small group of white oligarchs and the continual struggle of various immigrant groups to gain some degree of control over their lives.

Generally the theme of harmony has come from a power group perspective, and life must have been pleasant and reasonably tranquil for the ruling elites as long as the lower status groups could be kept

[4]R. S. Kuykendall, *The Hawaiian Kingdom, Vol. 3, 1874–1893* (Honolulu: Univ. of Hawaii Press, 1967), p. 160.
[5]Ibid, p. 172.

under control. One of the strategies was to cut off the immigration of one group before it got too powerful and switch to another group, and then to another, and another. Once in Hawaii, nationalities were often kept in separated plantation camps with a Caucasian overseer, or *luna*. It would be difficult to ignore the racism in such arrangements.

The native Hawaiians were also manipulated toward an anti-Oriental stance. For example, Fuchs writes that many Hawaiians responded to their own frustrations and bitterness by using the Asians as scapegoats. Rather than confronting the haole, who had taken away their land and freedom, the Hawaiians helped the haoles write discriminatory land restriction laws against the Chinese and Japanese in the late 1800s.[6]

It is our hypothesis that as more ethnic histories are discovered and publicized (especially those written in the native language), the picture of harmonious race relations will be discredited. But it is also our observation that the relative harmony among the various groups in Hawaii is so vastly superior to other areas that it still deserves the appellation of a "racial paradise," albeit with flaws.

THE PLANTATIONS

The Japanese entered into the Hawaiian plantations as contract laborers and inherited the bottom position in that system. They were assigned to the poorest houses and were the lowest paid. They were expected to work efficiently and to be highly productive. They served under impersonal Caucasian managers. It should be recalled that the Japanese were recruited as early as 1868, but the heavy influx of Japanese laborers to Hawaii occurred several decades later.[7]

Life on the plantations was monotonous and severe; the laborers soon hoped to find better jobs in the city. The plantation owners were aware of the situation, and as early as March 1903, the Executive Committee of the Republican Territorial Central Committee passed a resolution discouraging the employment of Asiatics in Honolulu because their labor was deemed necessary to the plantations.

Hunter described some of the early plantation conditions. The men lived in termite-ridden, unfit quarters, and from six to forty men were often huddled together in barrack-type rooms. Their lives were controlled by an indifferent and inaccessible plantation management in which the laborers served as specialized functionaies with little personal or individual identities. "They lived in plantation owned houses, bought their food

---

[6]Lawrence Fuchs, *Hawaii Pono: A Social History* (New York: Harcourt Brace Jovanovich, Inc., 1961), p. 82.

[7]Ibid., p. 115.

and clothing from plantation owned stores and were treated by plantation paid physicians."[8]

The appalling conditions drove some laborers to gambling and other vices. "Between April 1894 and December 1895, alone, 14,492 Japanese were arrested; 10,109 were convicted. A few . . . put an end to their misery by committing seppuku (self-disembowelment). More of them just quietly despaired. "Shikata ga Nai, it is no use."[9]

As one Buddhist bishop saw it, "the immigrant's life was a monstrous conglomeration of greed, passion and folly."[10]

Most owners felt that the Japanese made good workers, except that they were not content to remain on the plantations. There were continuous efforts to harass the Japanese to render them obedient and to prevent them from leaving the plantations.

Strategies included "maintaining a surplus, playing race against race, keeping aliens out of the city, restricting government jobs, prohibiting laborers movement to the mainland, working through foreign consuls and police officials and intimidation."[11] For example, there was the practice of establishing competing labor camps, so that "now Puerto Ricans, Spanish, Russians and Filipinos would be used to keep the Japanese in their place."[12]

The stereotype of the docile, conforming, accepting Japanese laborer was not wholly accurate. He could be obstreperous, even to the Japanese consul;[13] he could and did express his grievances in no uncertain fashion. There were numerous strikes on the plantations including two major ones known as the Oahu strikes of 1909 and 1920.

Some of the reasons given for the strikes were indicative of Japanese dissatisfaction with plantation life. The workers demanded the discharge of excessively cruel lunas; they pressed for compensation for injuries; they wanted higher pay and better working conditions; they called for the reinstatement of discharged employees; and they preferred the use of Japanese, rather than white lunas.[14]

---

[8]Louise Hunter, *Buddhism in Hawaii* (Honolulu: Univ. of Hawaii Press, 1971), p. 80.

[9]Ibid., p. 81.

[10]Ibid., p. 79.

[11]Fuchs, *Hawaii Pono*, pp. 211–12.

[12]Ibid., p. 210.

[13]The role of the official representatives of Japan (consuls, embassy officials, and the like) was often antagonistic to the immigrants. They came from a different class, so that class and national interests often placed them in conflicting positions with the Issei immigrant interests.

[14]Ernest Wakakuwa, *A History of the Japanese People in Hawaii* (Honolulu: The Toyo Shoin, 1938), p. 127.

The Oahu strikes of 1909 and 1920 were important because they were concerted efforts among Japanese working on various plantations to organize and to coordinate their resources. There was planning; the strikes were island wide; and the numbers and duration were unprecedented for those times. Part of the impetus for the 1909 strike came from an article by University of California student Motoyuki Negoro, which showed the disproportionately high profits for the plantation owner when compared to the extremely low paid but very productive Japanese laborer.[15]

The strikes often split the Japanese community, since values of loyalty and obligation to the employer, hard work, and gratefulness could not be easily integrated into a militant, adversary position.

The response of management was much simpler and appealed to racism and the American way. The owners felt that the Japanese could not be trusted because they might be allied with a foreign power, although they themselves were allied with the United States. For example, an editorial in the *Honolulu Star Bulletin* dated February 13, 1920, asked:

> Is control of the industrialism of Hawaii to remain in the hands of Anglo-Saxons or is it to pass into those of alien Japanese agitators? . . . Never lose sight of the real issue: Is Hawaii to remain American or become Japanese?

WHICH DIRECTION?

The choice of Japan or the United States was an option for the Japanese residents, but not in the manner in which the question was raised. The possibility of Hawaii becoming part of Japan was a remote one, especially when considering that that nation was just emerging from its enforced isolation of centuries, but for the immigrants there was the realistic possibility of remaining "Japanese" or becoming "American." The Japanese language and culture could survive, since there was a large community with ethnic institutions and organizations and one could identify with his Japanese background and heritage as one realistic alternative.

Conversely, there was also the possibility of becoming "American" in a way that could not be duplicated on the mainland and to move toward acculturation and assimilation since the barriers of racism were not so overpowering. These options are clearly indicated in the following biographies of two Japanese in Hawaii.

[15]Ibid., p. 169.

ETHNIC RETENTION: FRED MAKINO[16]

Makino came to Hawaii in 1899. He felt that the plantation owners were exploiting the Japanese, and rather than fatalistically accepting their position, he felt that the best strategy was for the Japanese to organize and to strike back. He helped the Japanese to found their own unions; he started lawsuits against discriminatory practices; and he was willing to go to jail for his convictions. One of Makino's priorities was to heighten ethnic awareness through promoting ethnic identity and developing ethnic cohesion. He supported Japanese-language schools where the Issei and their Nisei children could learn their native language and understand their native heritage. He held that the Japanese values of the Meiji era were superior to those of the Americans and that the Japanese should resist the attempts of the Americans to "rob" them of their culture. He advocated political organization, voting blocs, and the strategy of ethnic power as the most effective means of dealing with the white man. He believed that the maintenance of a strong and cohesive ethnic community based on the Japanese culture was the wisest adaptive strategy. Popularity with and acceptance by the white man were not important in Makino's perception of the world.

ACCULTURATION AND ACCEPTANCE: TAKIE OKUMURA

Okumura,[17] living in Hawaii about the same time as Makino, perceived the problems of the Japanese quite differently. He advocated an acculturative position whereby the Japanese could find acceptance by identifying with and acquiring the American culture.

For example, Okumura felt that one of the major barriers toward group acceptance was the maintenance of the Japanese culture. He felt that Japanese living conditions, manners, habits, and customs should be discarded. Therefore, smelly Japanese foods, noisy Japanese festivals, loud conversations in Japanese, and prominent Japanese architectural forms were to be discouraged, since they were hindrances to acceptance. From this perspective, any behavior that might be offensive to the Americans was to be controlled.

The most important guideline for Okumura was the concept of the

---

[16]The contrasts between Makino and Okumura are analyzed in Jacobs and Landau (1971) and Kitano (1972). Both were Japanese living in Hawaii, and we have taken some liberties in developing them as "models." The purpose is to show the different styles and not to advocate one position or to defame their respective positions.

[17]Takie Okumura, *Seventy Years of Divine Blessings* (n.p., 1939).

Japanese as "guests." As such, the Japanese should conduct themselves with as little visibility as possible. Attending American schools, learning the English language, and adopting the ways of the American were the highest priorities. Unpopular actions, such as labor strikes and running away from the plantations, were to be discouraged, whereas to continue to work loyally, no matter what the provocation, was a part of the Okumura philosophy.

Both positions and their numerous variations were viable alternatives for the Japanese in Hawaii. Because of the number of realistic options, it is our impression that in Hawaii there is a wider and more diversified range of attitudes and behaviors than is true for Japanese on the mainland.

THE BREAKTHROUGH

Because of their potential numerical superiority, it appeared to be just a matter of time before the Japanese broke away from their initial low position in the Hawaiian social structure. However, numbers by themselves are no guarantee for bringing about change, as witness the disorganized masses in most parts of the world. Groups with few resources, those who lack skills and those who have little cohesion and organization, seldom bring about change. Further, as in most instances where the power relationships are unequal, what the minority does is less important than what the majority does. It was the dominant group that erected the walls of discrimination, and it was they who made it impossible for the Issei to achieve citizenship. It was majority group laws that "granted this right" to the Nisei generation, enabling them to acquire a degree of power that was dramatically different from their parents. The Nisei could vote, own land, run for public office, and even try for the presidency, although such expectations lay primarily in the realm of fantasy, especially during the early days.

Education

An area that soon drew high Nisei participation was education. In many ways it provided one of the "ideal" means for upward mobility, for it combined the values of the ethnic community (the *sensei*, or respected teacher); the group had skills (school achievement was never a major problem for the Nisei); it was *open* (in contrast to the situation in California); and the initial low salaries drew away many of their potential competitors (especially the haole). In addition, many haole educators actively encouraged the Nisei to become public-school teachers, and there was the fear of discrimination in other occupations. As one Nisei related,

"Many of us felt that the big (white-owned) firms were not likely to hire us."[18]

One recently retired Japanese-American educator reflected on his own career in the public schools. He was born in 1909 and went into teacher training (then two years of higher education) with active encouragement from his immigrant parents. A shortage of funds prevented him from attending the four-year University of Hawaii. He found little difficulty in obtaining his first job as a teacher in the late 1920s, and from that beginning he served in various capacities, including those of educational consultant, Japanese-language instructor with the military during World War II, and school principal. He encountered little overt racial discrimination during his entire professional career.[19]

There were barriers, but many of the people who grew up during this era did not perceive them as such. There was the emphasis on "standard English," which meant that students with higher academic and professional goals were expected to discard their local "dialects" and learn English, mainland style. Many Nisei told us, with some hesitancy and embarrassment, of their difficulty with standard English. They recalled finishing all of their academic requirements for a degree from the university, then waiting for their diplomas until they could pass the speech requirement. Some mentioned the names of currently prominent Nisei leaders who were in the same situation. Recent statistics provide a dramatic picture of the degree of Japanese-American participation in the state's educational establishment (see Table 6).

If proportionate representation in terms of numbers in the population is a desirable distribution, the 68 percent of Japanese Americans as Department of Education (DOE) teachers and the 63 percent in the Boards of Education are well over twice these norms. Conversely, the 28.3 percent in administrative positions reflects their proportion in the population.

Ethnic representation at the university provides an interesting contrast. Samuels,[20] in a study of ethnicity at the college professor level, reported that only 11.9 percent of the University of Hawaii faculty had Japanese surnames. He presented several hypotheses to explain the low representation. One was the probability that the Japanese, as a minority

---

[18]Tom Kaser, "Japanese Americans Largest Group in the DOE," *Honolulu Advertiser, Honolulu,* July 19, 1974, Section C, p. 2.

[19]Katsumi Onishi, Lecture in class of American Studies 620, University of Hawaii, July 17, 1974.

[20]Frederick Samuels, *The Japanese and the Haoles of Honolulu* (New Haven, Conn.: Yale University Press, 1970), p. 26.

TABLE 6
ETHNIC REPRESENTATION IN THE HAWAII STATE
DEPARTMENT OF EDUCATION, 1974*

Population	Officers (administrators and consultants)	Educators (teachers)	Boards of Education
	By percent		
Caucasian	39.2	13.8	27
Japanese	28.3	68.9	63
Filipino	12.4	1.6	0
Hawaiian and part-Hawaiian	9.3	2.9	0
Chinese	6.8	11.5	0.1
Korean	1.3	1.1	0
Negro	1.0	0	0
Other	1.8	0	0

*Tom Kaser, "Japanese Americans Largest Group in the DOE," *Honolulu Advertiser*, Honolulu, Hawaii, July 19, 1974, Section C, p. 2.

group, would choose more practical fields, in which jobs could be gained immediately. Dentistry is one such field, and its attractiveness is further enhanced since it does not require a high degree of verbal proficiency. Some evidence for this hypothesis was provided by Samuels; he found that 60.9 percent of the dentists and 60 percent of the optometrists listed in the telephone directory of Honolulu were of Japanese background.[21]

Discrimination at the more prestigious university professor level was another hypothesis. Entrance to the higher status positions would be more apt to evoke Caucasian reactions in the form of rigid and higher barriers. Linked to the external barriers were lowered expectations by the group itself, so that as one public-school teacher said, "I never dreamed of being a university professor."[22] The interaction between discrmination and lowered expectations is a logical one but is difficult to validate empirically.

Japanese Americans are well represented on the university regents. Of the nine appointed Regents of the University of Hawaii as of July 1974, six were Japanese Americans, and in 1974 a Japanese American, Fujio Matsuda, was appointed president of the University. It was the first permanent appointment of a local "ethnic" to this position.

But their success in the educational field has created problems. There have been cries of a Japanese takeover and of discrimination against non-Japanese. Affirmative action programs using population pro-

21Ibid., p. 26.
22K. Onishi, lecture.

portions are sure to target in on the overrepresentation of Japanese in the field. However, sole concentration on ethnic proportions without understanding some of the historical and cultural circumstances leading to the distribution may be as myopic and unjust as the discrimination the programs are trying to change.

Economic Activity

Data in the economic area are more difficult to gather, especially in cross-ethnic comparisons. The economic growth of the Japanese American is closely tied to the growth of Hawaii, so that generalizations about the economic progress of the islands are also generalizations about the Japanese from that state.

An early tabulation of occupations, compiled by the Honolulu Merchants Association (the forerunner of the current Honolulu Japanese Chamber of Commerce) in 1912, shows the economic picture of the Japanese in Honolulu (see Table 7) and on the island of Oahu (see Table 8).

In the city of Honolulu, the most common occupations were domestics and servants, followed by laborers and store clerks. The picture is of an immigrant group just beginning its entrance into the lower rungs of the urban occupational structure.

Statistics from the island of Oahu for 1912 describe the rural occupational distribution of the Japanese. The model categories were contract cane growers and plantation laborers. The picture is again that of an immigrant group at the bottom rungs of the occupational ladder.

The 1970 census (see Table 9) provides data on the current employment picture of the Japanese American in Hawaii. Although the categories are different from the 1912 table and are limited to census definitions, the changes are apparent. The modal category for males is that of craftsmen, foremen, and kindred workers (30 percent), followed by the professionals and technicians (14 percent), and managers and administrators (12 percent). The rank of farm laborer is among the lowest (2 percent).

The proportion of Japanese Americans in some of the professions closely approximates their number in the population. Samuels[23] reported that 26.4 percent of the architects, 25 percent of the physicians, and 24.3 percent of the lawyers in Honolulu were of Japanese ancestry.

For the female, the highest category was that of clerical and kindred workers (35 percent), followed by service workers (20 percent), and professionals (16 percent). The high number in the service occupations is related to discrimination against women.

[23]Samuels, "The Japanese and the Haoles of Honolulu," p. 26.

TABLE 7 HONOLULU CITY: OCCUPATIONS OF JAPANESE, 1912*

Occupation	No. of Households	Men	Women	Occupation	No. of Households	Men	Women
Bank Employees	30	35	35	Sundry-Sales	135	265	245
Sake Shops	12	45	40	Shoyu-Sales	18	28	18
Inns	12	57	47	Restaurants	30	57	59
Physicians	11	13	10	Hatters	47	49	48
Pharmacies	17	39	24	Carpenters	295	348	209
Watchmakers	18	32	27	Ironsmiths	40	54	40
Confectioners	90	142	140	Masons	62	79	62
2nd Hand Goods Shops	36	56	43	Painters	52	72	49
Barbers	125	173	125	Fishing	177	300	132
Contractors	22	52	47	Honey Bee Raising	9	9	11
Tailors/Seamstresses	105	129	109	Noodle Mfg.	32	35	29
Dyers	50	82	57	Cooks	20	30	21
Tofu-Sales	13	24	31	Ships' Crew	80	95	82
Charcoal/Firewood Sales	28	50	55	Employment Brokers	10	15	11
Billiard Halls	30	38	40	Pineapple Growers	30	5	6
Horse Carriage Trade	122	195	174	Horticulture	25	35	32
Bicycle Shops	12	35	32	Fish-Dealers	35	54	35
Photographers	17	22	17	Rental-Carriage	12	2	8
Hardware Shops	19	24	26	Meat-Sales	10	10	12
Rental-Houses	42	46	42	Geisha	25	2	38
Milk-Sales	10	24	25	Laborers-General	722	1,988	572
Vegetable-Sales	98	144	138	Servants-Domestic	1,632	2,195	995
Bath House	23	42	35	Post Office Employees	5	8	10
Newspaper	111	140	64	Shinto Priests	5	9	9
Firms/Store Clerks	407	742	479	Automobile Industry	20	25	20
Teachers	26	35	45	Missionaries	8	18	20
Buddhist Priests	7	10	9	Interpreters	30	39	35
Hog & Poultry Farms	144	272	238	Others	389	773	474

TOTALS: No. of Households: 5,592; Men: 9,297; Women: 5,486; Men & Women: 14,733
*The Rainbow: A History of the Honolulu Japanese Chamber of Commerce (Honolulu Japanese Chamber of Commerce, 1970), p. 110.

TABLE 8 ISLAND OF OAHU: OCCUPATIONS OF JAPANESE, 1912

Occupation	No. of Households	Men	Women	Occupation	No. of Households	Men	Women
Sundry Shops	99	235	121	Priests	10	10	12
Inns	2	5	9	Interpreters	9	12	11
Restaurants	12	9	14	Hog & Poultry Farms	44	49	43
Physicians	5	9	12	Carpenters	120	157	79
Pharmacists	18	18	19	Ironsmiths	29	31	32
Watchmakers	22	30	27	Masons	22	24	23
Confectioners	47	57	39	Painters	28	30	32
2nd Hand Goods Shops	1	2	4	Fishing	41	52	32
Barbers	62	60	62	Honey Bee Raising	8	9	11
Contractors-Bldg	23	27	22	Cooks	10	10	12
Tailors/Seamstresses	45	39	58	Horticulture	22	35	21
Dyers	7	7	12	Rice Growers	88	162	99
Tofu-Sales	32	39	45	Pineapple Growers	283	489	305
Charcoal/Firewood Sales	20	25	20	Fish Dealers	12	12	15
Billiard Halls	14	9	12	Carriage Mfg.	5	8	3
Horse Carriage Trade	40	50	52	Meat-Sales	6	9	12
Bicycle Shops	2	9	5	Sugar Mill Workers	130	122	80
Photographers	12	12	10	Railroad Engineers	111	121	120
Hardware	5	6	4	Luna	25	50	47
Rental-Houses	12	12	13	Cane Contract Growers	2,435	3,498	1,475
Milk-Sales	19	22	29	Plantation Laborers	2,420	4,994	2,279
Vegetable-Sales	109	111	109	Domestic Servants	62	89	79
Bath Houses	29	32	32	Day Laborers	20	85	42
Clerks-Firms/Stores	121	172	108	Post Office Employees	8	11	11
Teachers	23	20	25	Shinto Priests	3	3	5
Newspaper	4	5	8	Automobile Industry	15	20	15
Missionaries	6	6	10	Others	79	368	350

TOTALS: No. of Households: 6,836; Men: 11,488; Women: 6,126; Men & Women: 17,614 Schools: 17, Temples 16

*The Rainbow: A History of the Honolulu Japanese Chamber of Commerce (Honolulu Japanese Chamber of Commerce, 1970), p. 111.

TABLE 9

EMPLOYMENT CHARACTERISTICS OF THE JAPANESE POPULATION, SIXTEEN
YEARS AND OLDER BY SEX AND BY MAJOR OCCUPATION IN HAWAII, 1970*

Occupation	Male	Percent	Female	Percent
Professional, technical, and kindred workers	8,156	14	7,425	16
Managers and administrators, except farm	7,258	12	2,036	4
Sales workers	3,527	6	4,251	9
Clerical and kindred workers	5,648	10	16,200	35
Craftsmen, foremen, and kindred workers	17,654	30	835	2
Operatives, including transport	6,672	11	4,645	10
Laborers, except farm	3,751	6	312	1
Farmers and farm managers	715	1	314	1
Farm laborers and foremen	1,075	2	548	1
Service workers, except private household	3,912	7	9,191	20
Private household workers	20	0	1,081	2
Total employed	58,388	99	46,838	101

*U.S. Department of Commerce, Bureau of the Census, *Japanese, Chinese, and Filipinos in the United States.* 1970 Census of the Population, PC (2)-1G (Washington, D.C.: Government Printing Office, 1973), p. 35.

But in spite of the advances of the group on all levels, the most visible breakthrough has been in the political arena. The Issei, because of discriminatory laws, were not a factor politically, but their American-born children were. It was not easy; the idea of Japanese Americans running for elective offices did not sit well with the early political Republican establishment, and the attack on Pearl Harbor put a temporary halt to Nisei political expectations. Interestingly enough, Pearl Harbor also set into motion a number of subsequent events that drastically changed the position of the Japanese in Hawaii.

WORLD WAR II

The Japanese attack on Pearl Harbor was even more dramatic on the islands than on the mainland because it was the actual site of the battle. Residents could hear gunfire, feel the bombs burst, and see the airplanes. There was an immediate roundup of suspected enemy aliens, and the web included Japanese priests, language teachers, and community leaders. A camp on Sand Island served as a temporary detention facility, and from there some Japanese were transferred to the mainland.[24]

The attack elicited a wide range of reactions among the island residents of Japanese ancestry. Some strongly identified with Japan and considered the attack a retaliation against the injustices of the United

24Lind, *Hawaii's People.*

States and their European allies, while others took the opposing position, condemning the attack and identifying totally with the United States. There were rumors of a mass evacuation of all Japanese to Molokai (the former leper colony), but realistically any drastic action against them would have been sheer folly. For in 1940, there were 157,905 Japanese, or 37.3 percent of the total population, on the islands, and their removal would have both strained the logistical capacities of the United States Navy and brought about a collapse of the island economy, thereby affecting the war-making potential of the islands.

Although there was no mass evacuation such as on the mainland, the islands were placed under martial law, so that many restrictions were placed on all of its residents. Japanese churches, language schools, and other ethnic facilities were closed. The influx of a large number of servicemen and defense workers with varied backgrounds raised social tensions and terms like *Japs, slant-eyes, yellow bellies,* and *gooks* began to be indiscriminately used without regard to ethnic sensitivities. Conversely, many natives added terms like *white trash, damn haoles,* and *dumb haoles* to their vocabularies.[25]

Rumors about the Japanese demonstrated the ethnic sensitivities of Hawaii during World War II.[26] There were the stories of Japanese seen flashing signals, and of a Japanese fleet waiting to enter Pearl Harbor. There were rumors of Japanese burning secret papers and workers cutting arrows in the fields pointing to Pearl Harbor. Many aggressive words were directed against those of Japanese ancestry, and attempts were made to boycott stores run by Japanese Americans.

One Japanese American (years later a legislator) was a teen-ager at the time of the attack. He remembers his parents' temple being sacked by American GI's and his father being hauled away. "I was a kid, but still I was the oldest so I took care of the other kids. Through the whole war we ate only rice balls and miso soup or nothing. That's why I'm in politics—I said, 'Never again.' "[27]

However, even though the combination of rumors, the restrictions of martial law, and the temporary immigration of masses of servicemen introduced stress-inducing elements into Hawaiian life, the Japanese there never suffered the indignity of a mass evacuation into concentration camps that was the fate of their countrymen on the Pacific Coast.

[25]Ibid., p. 10.

[26]Hester Kong, "Through the Deepsight of a Grocery Store," *Community Forces in Hawaii*, ed. Bernard Hormann (Honolulu: Univ. of Hawaii Press, 1968), pp. 209–13.

[27]Tom Coffman, *To Catch a Wave* (Honolulu: University of Hawaii Press, 1972), p. 16.

The Niihau Incident

An interesting incident related by Lind[28] and by Allen[29] occurred on the small island of Niihau as a direct result of the Japanese attack on Pearl Harbor. Niihau was an isolated island located off the coast of Kauai with a population of less than two hundred, which included three persons of Japanese ancestry. It was cut off from all outside communications, so that the population had no immediate knowledge of Pearl Harbor.

Several hours after the attack, a Japanese plane crash-landed on Niihau. The pilot could only communicate with Ishimatsu Shintani, born in Japan, and Yoshio Harada, a Hawaiian-born Nisei. Whether by threats or promises he eventually induced Harada to cooperate in gaining control of the island, while Shintani, fearful for his life, went into hiding.

For several days the pilot and Harada directed a reign of terror on the island. It would be correct to say that Niihau was almost occupied and conquered by the Japanese, albeit by an army of one helped by one Japanese American. Several Hawaiians eventually managed to escape by boat to Kauai, but before they could get back with American troops, another native had killed the Japanese pilot. The Nisei then committed suicide.

The Niihau incident was unusual in several ways. The idea of a Japanese pilot taking over an entire island so close to Hawaii strains one's credulity. The cooperation of the Japanese American was another surprise, since in spite of widespread rumors, there was no evidence of Japanese Hawaiians helping the Japanese in their attack on Pearl Harbor. Although the incident was a little known affair, it again portrayed the age-old dilemma of the Japanese group: were they to identify with Japan or America?

One strong Nisei response to Pearl Harbor was to "prove" their loyalty to the United States by volunteering and fighting against fascism. The 100th Battalion and the 442nd Combat Team, made up of Nisei from Hawaii (and later from the mainland), became the vehicles for active participation in the war.

The Hawaiians were initially placed in all-Japanese units under white officers, a long familiar racist army pattern. They received their basic training in places like Wisconsin, Minnesota, and Mississippi, and for many this was their first experience off the islands. They met Nisei

---

[28]Lind, *Hawaii's Japanese*, 1946.
[29]Gwen Allen, *Hawaii's War Years* (Honolulu: University of Hawaii Press, 1950).

mainlanders, and they also met thousands of poor whites. The encounters with the Kotonks, although interesting and informative, were not particularly new, since they had met and related to Japanese of all types. But the observation that there were millions of poor, uneducated, and powerless whites was new, since the majority of whites that they had encountered at home were representatives of power and privilege.

The experiences gained on the mainland, in Europe, and in the Pacific meant a changed generation of Nisei who came back from the war. Although young in age, they had their horizons broadened, and many took advantage of the G.I. Bill for further education and training. The *status quo* was about to be challenged.

POLITICS

The area of politics provided the most dramatic example of change. By 1954 the Nisei war veterans started to challenge the huge Republican majority in the legislature. The close bond established between the Nisei and some of their Caucasian friends who had supported them during harder times developed into a powerful Democratic group that eventually wrested political control from the Republicans. Senator Daniel Inouye[30] mentions some of these individuals—John Burns, eventually to be governor; Dan Aoki, a 442nd first sergeant; Spark Matsunaga of the 100th Battalion, currently senior member of the Hawaiian delegation to the House of Representatives; Masato Doi of the 442nd, chairman of the Honolulu city council and eventually appointed a circuit judge by Burns. Then, of course, there was Daniel Inouye himself, a war hero who is now a United States senator.

In his autobiography, Inouye recalls the 1954 campaign, in which the young, politically naive group of war veterans began their challenge to the long entrenched Republican political machine. The incumbents raised questions about the loyalty and patriotism of the Nisei, a dubious tactic, since most of these men had recently returned from Europe with the 100th and the 442nd. The cry of communism was another technique used by the Republicans, and in one encounter, Inouye, thoroughly disgusted with the big lie and the big scare, shook his empty right sleeve (he had lost his arm to fight fascists) and said, "If my country wants the other one to fight communists, it can have it."[31]

The Nisei, with the help of their allies, conducted a successful campaign and were able to wrest political control from the incumbents. Since that time, the Japanese Americans have remained a politically significant force.

[30]Daniel Inouye, *Journey to Washington* (Englewood Cliffs, N.J.: Prentice-Hall, Inc., 1967).
[31]Ibid., p. 249.

For example, in the 1971–72 edition of *Who's Who in Government in Hawaii*, eleven Japanese Americans were mentioned among the twenty-three members of the State Senate, and they comprised over 50 percent of the membership of the House of Representatives. Japanese Americans headed the majority of the important state departmental posts, including those of the attorney general and the secretaries of education, budget and finance, labor and industrial relations, land and natural resources, taxation, and transportation. And, as mentioned previously, their representation and participation in the educational establishment has been especially strong, so that one common stereotype of the Department of Education (DOE) teacher is that of a person of Japanese ancestry.

Another opportunity to gain a degree of economic and political power was through the International Longshoremen and Warehousemen's Union (ILWU). In contrast to the labor movement along the Pacific Coast, which sought to limit or to exclude the participation of the Japanese and other Asian groups, the ILWU welcomed the ethnics. By 1947 the union claimed a multiethnic membership of more than 30,000 members in a territorial population of 500,000.[32]

OTHER EVENTS

Many Japanese-American traditions have become an integral part of the Hawaiian scene. The Cherry Blossom Festival has a Japanese-American Queen; the *bon odori* and a wide range of Japanese foods have intermingled with other cuisine for a truly international flavor. The Japanese-language schools have diminished in importance, ironically at a time when Japan and Japanese have taken on additional importance.[33] However, courses developed by Professor Ogawa of the American Studies Department at the University of Hawaii on the "Japanese American" have held exceptional student interest. A similar, but more modest, surge of interest in ethnic identity has taken place on mainland campuses.

But it is in the area of leisure-time activities where the consistent visible difference between the mainland and the Hawaiian Japanese can be seen. If there are one hundred Japanese Americans at Golden Gate Park in San Francisco barbecuing teriyaki chicken over fifty hibachi stoves, there are over one thousand enjoying a similar outing at Ala Moana Park in Honolulu. If there are one hundred youngsters running races at Elysian Park in Los Angeles, there are well over five hundred competing at Kapiolani Park. A Japanese American sunbathing on the beach at Santa Monica searches far and wide before spotting a "brother

---

[32]Francine du Plessix Gray, *Hawaii: The Sugar Cooled Fortress* (New York: Random House, 1973), p. 80.

[33]Patsy Matsuura, "Language Schools on Shaky Grounds," *Honolulu Star Bulletin and Advertiser* (Sept. 12, 1971, Section c, p. 1.

or sister" among the carpet of white bodies, whereas at Hanauma Bay the white skin is the exception among a sea of deep tans. And even then, the light skin may belong to a Japanese tourist from Japan.

THE CURRENT PICTURE

The growth of Hawaii since its admission as the fiftieth state in 1959 has been paralleled by a corresponding increase in problems. Overcrowding, pollution, and high prices have become everyday realities, and the influx of new residents and the constant flow of tourists has contributed to the ever changing island scene. There are attempts to differentiate among the old timers (kamainas), the new residents, and those whose stay will be temporary, so that the picture of a dynamic, changing Hawaii is more accurate than that of a slow-paced South Seas island paradise. Even some of the more isolated islands in the chain are sharing in this "progress."

The new immigration has come from several sources. Immigrants from Melanesia, Micronesia, the Philippines, and Korea have added to Hawaii's ethnic and racial diversity. There has been a steady flow of whites from the mainland, so that by 1972, they were the most populous "ethnic group" with 38.8 percent, and the Japanese proportion had dipped to 28.3 percent.

But much information about the mobility and movement of the Japanese in Hawaii remains to be gathered. Many leave Hawaii, some temporarily to attend mainland schools, and others emigrate as permanent residents. There is a reverse flow of more modest proportions consisting of Japanese Americans coming to live on the islands. Then there is the interisland flow, generally from one of the outer islands to Oahu, and currently the most visible and controversial movement is the visit of tourists from Japan. The latter appear the easiest to stereotype, since they often arrive on conducted tours, all apparently headed by a tour leader with whistle in mouth and flag in hand. It is said that the Japanese tourists "saved" the island economy in the early 1970s because they filled the vacuum created by a drop in American visitors. In 1972 approximately 230,000 Japanese visited Hawaii, an increase of over 50,000 from the previous year.[34]

The influx of Japanese tourists and Japanese capital has not been without its problems. In a newspaper article, datelined Tokyo, Ishizuka writes, "Deep concern and resentment are growing among the Hawaiians over the fast increasing Japanese investments and swelling crowds of Jap-

[34]Yoshikazu Ishizuka, "Resentment Continues to Grow in Hawaii over Japanese Takeover," Nichi-bei Times, April 2, 1974, p. 3.

anese tourists in Hawaii." The article points out that the proportionate
amount of Japanese investments is small, but it is often highly visible.
The purchase of prominent Waikiki hotels by Japanese is one example.
Other complaints lodged against the Japanese included their insensitivity
to local sentiments, their indifference to local community styles, and the
closed Japanese system of operation: they owned the hotels; used their
own guides; flew in their own planes; hired their own workers; and
brought in their own managers.

Kuroda[35] conducted a telephone survey of a random sample of
Honolulu residents concerning their attitudes toward Japanese investments and tourists. She reported that the vast majority were aware of the
issue, and that even those who favored continued Japanese investment,
desired limits and controls. She also reported: "It appears as if race is
not the overriding factor in determining one's attitude toward the question raised here. Age, for example, appears to be an equally important
factor."[36] The younger respondents, especially the women, were against
foreign investment, whereas the older respondents were generally more
favorable.

The new influx of Japanese from Japan and some of the resultant
"new problems" has been a recurring theme in Japanese-American life,
whether in Hawaii or on the mainland. For even the most acculturated
third or fourth generation Japanese American still has identifiable Japanese features and is generally viewed as such by the majority group. So
what Japan does as a nation affects the Japanese American—whether it
be Pearl Harbor, or as a staunch Pacific ally, or as purchasers of hotels in
Waikiki.

But hopefully there will come a time when the ethnic group will be
able to behave autonomously, as individuals with their own needs, expectations, and goals, rather then being compared or mistaken as Japanese from Japan, or measured against the Japanese American from the
mainland.

A Hawaiian culture has developed that is a blend of the Pacific
Islands, the Asian, the native, and the haole. The proportions of the
blend are open to conjecture and probably depend on group identification and position. But even though the influences of the blend may differ, permanent residents of the islands refer to this culture as "local." Although there are ethnocentric connotations to the term, it is also a recog-

[35]Alice Kuroda, Y. Kuroda, and G. Martin, "Hawaii's Reaction to Japanese Investment and Tourism," paper prepared for delivery at seminar on Japanese investments in Hawaii sponsored by Honolulu Japanese Chamber of Commerce, Honolulu,
Hawaii, Nov. 10, 1973.
[36]Ibid., p. 31.

nition that the local—whether of Asian, islander, European, or American ancestry—has developed a way of looking at the world that is different from his countrymen across the oceans. As with most cultures, this local blend is difficult to describe, but it is probable that the modern Hawaiian has learned to live in an interracial atmosphere; that he is not too concerned about status, material success, and prestige; and that he has developed a tolerant and a relaxed style of living suited to the ambience of the islands. But the strength of this local culture is under continual testing, just as the tolerance of the native Hawaiians of centuries ago was tested, for Hawaii continues to draw new immigrants, many as aggressive and as sure that their ways are superior as were the missionaries, traders, and businessmen of a past era.

CHAPTER ELEVEN

At the beginning of the book we remarked that it must have seemed that the early Japanese came to the wrong state at the wrong time with the wrong color, religion, and nationality. And, judging from some of their early experiences, the statement held true for a long time. Now it is possible, in retrospect, to see, however, that the Japanese had some advantages too. They came in the right numbers, with a strong "culture," with strong institutions in the community and the family, and, finally, they came to the "right" country.

Even in their daydreams, it would have been difficult for the Issei to dream of such success for their group. In 1975 three Japanese Americans sat in Congress.[1] They are more than adequately represented in the professions, are successful in business, and are comfortably acculturated. Japanese family and community structure, Japanese values and culture, and Japanese expectations have proved singularly compatible with the American style of life.

Conclusions and Summary

Their record is amazing, and the most remarkable thing about it is the relative speed with which they have progressed. In a faculty lecture at UCLA a few years ago, I told the audience of a personal experience, by way of illustration:

> . . . I remember making another address approximately 19 years ago, similar in that I was doing the talking and similar because there was an audience. But there were many differences. I was much younger and it was a high school valedictory address, filled with words and ideas that only a high school youngster could comfortably espouse. And even more different was the audience and the setting; the audience was made up only a high school youngster could comfortably espouse. And even more relocation camp, a euphemism for a concentration camp. Although I have difficulty in remembering the exact words of the address (for which I am thankful) I do recall declaring with all of the dramatic power that a naïve high school youngster can: "I don't know why we're here, I don't know where we're going, but I'm sure that things will work out." . . . The question of where we were going was the crucial question. How could anybody have really guessed? For if I had thought that within the next two decades I was to be giving a lecture such as this as a member of the staff of UCLA to such an audience, it would have been just a matter of time that people in white jackets would have whisked me out of the war relocation center,

[1]Senator Dan Inouye and Representatives Spark Matsunaga and Patsy Mink, all representing Hawaii.

and into another kind of institution for handling problems of people who had somehow lost touch with reality.[2]

Many other Japanese can recall similar stories.

The story of Japanese achievement is especially impressive if we recall the thinking of many Americans of an earlier era. For example, V. McClatchy, publisher of the *Sacramento Bee*, wrote of the Japanese in 1921:

> The Japanese cannot, may not, and will not provide desirable material for our citizenship. 1. The Japanese cannot assimilate and make good citizens because of their racial characteristics, heredity and religion. 2. The Japanese may not assimilate and make good citizens because their government claims all Japanese, no matter where born, as its citizens. 3. The Japanese will not assimilate and make good citizens. In the mass, when opportunity offered, and even when born here, they have shown no disposition to do so. . . . There can be no effective assimilation of the Japanese without intermarriage. It is perhaps not desirable for the good of either race that there should be intermarriage between whites and Japanese. . . . They cannot be transmuted into good American citizens.[3]

Obviously, the record of the Japanese has challenged the early racist claims that nonwhite groups can never become good American citizens.

It should also be mentioned that the Japanese comprise a successful immigrant population, whether in the United States or in other countries. It is extremely difficult to get a Japanese to move from his beloved island of Mt. Fuji and the cherry blossoms, but once he emigrates he adapts extremely well. Brazil, which has a Japanese population approximately equal in size to that of the United States group, has been good for the Japanese, and the Japanese have been good to Brazil.[4] Similar successes have been noted in other countries. But he appears to have progressed the furthest in the United States.

ASSIMILATION BY GROUP

The term *Japanese American* of course describes many different kinds of groups and individuals, and these different groups have sometimes accultured, assimilated, or integrated in different ways. Referring back to Gordon's model, if we divide Japanese Americans along cultural,

[2]Harry H. L. Kitano, "The Japanese in America," Faculty Lecture Series: The Many Faces of Integration, UCLA, October 21, 1963.

[3]V. McClatchy, "Japanese in the Melting Pot: Can They Assimilate and Make Good Citizens?" *The Annals of the American Academy of Political and Social Science* 322 (January 1921): 29–34.

[4]*The Japanese Immigrant in Brazil* (Tokyo: Tokyo University Press, 1964).

structural, marital, and identificational lines, the following pattern emerges. The Nisei and Sansei are fully acculturated, the Kibei and war brides have partially acculturated, and the Issei have not acculturated; the Kai-sha—students and visitors—have also been placed in the "no acculturation" classification, even though there is evidence that some individuals from this group are even more "American," or at least less "Meiji Japanese," than members of the other groups.

Since the last edition, dramatic changes have occurred in the Japanese-American group. Structural assimilation has occurred on a wide scale, so that interracial dating and marriage have become realities. Perhaps the most encouraging aspect of structural assimilation is that it is apparently taking place on an equal status basis. Previously, the largest known group to have outmarried were the war brides who were generally caught in "less-than-equal" relationships.

By the 1970s there has been widespread structural assimilation (primary friendships, dating, and marital patterns outside of the ethnic community and in the larger "American community"). But interestingly enough, identificational assimilation, which refers to the hyphenated American (e.g., Japanese American), remains and may even be strengthened with the renewed emphasis on ethnic identity.

The process of achieving an identification may be hypothesized as following certain developmental guidelines. For example, Cohen, in tracing the process of identity for the Jew, describes a broad initial phase where the primary concern of certain Jewish organizations was the protection of their good name.[5] Associate concerns at this stage might include keeping a united front and not airing intragroup problems in public. A possible next stage might include the development of ethnic humor, not only for the in-group, but now performed for the larger society. It would be symptomatic of a decreasing concern over the "image and goodness" of the group. Ethnic self-consciousness during this period would still be high, but of a much more objective and self-critical kind. Defensiveness may diminish. Finally, there may be a stage where references to the ethnic group depart completely from the conscious stream, to be replaced by the majority group identification. The desirability of this last step remains a value question.

However, because of visibility and the ease of identification, the "identity" of the Japanese American remains vulnerable to general American feelings toward Japan. Their experience during World War II, when even the most acculturated who identified totally with America were

---

[5]Nathan Cohen, private conversation. The writer is indebted to Professor Cohen, of the Graduate School of Social Welfare at UCLA, who served as a springboard and testing source for many ideas.

looked on as "Japanese" and the "enemy," is all too recent and illustrates the dilemma.

Other identifiable groups face a similar situation—blacks have related to us the rather quizzical looks from even among close white friends about their identities and sympathies during the Watts riots.[6] A recent campaign to "save the whales" has centered on Japan as one of the major violators, and young Japanese Americans have had slurs directed against them.

The process of developing an ethnic identity is difficult because the major reinforcers are essentially negative.[7] For a long period of time, being Japanese meant being the "enemy" and identifying with a racial stereotype that restricted membership to a second-class role. Models of personality development generally ignore the psychosocial development of minority children who are constantly reminded of their differences. Heroes, role models, and norms are chosen and represent a dominant group perspective. It will therefore be interesting to analyze the effects of an "instant identity," whereby previously negative images, such as black and yellow, were turned around and made beautiful. There is still little evidence to indicate that such quick identities are less appropriate than other models.

The Issei and Nisei have retained much of their Japanese identification, whereas the Sansei are much more American. The Sansei have few ties with Japan—nor do they retain a broader ethnic identification of being Oriental, nor do they identify with skin color—consequently, many Sansei are insulted if referred to in any other terms but American. But the majority of the Sansei and Yonsei and the majority of Americans still perceive them as different, so that it is still accurate to indicate that they retain a hyphenated identity, but less so than their parents and grandparents. One of the newer changes is the emphasis on an "Asian" identity, which may include a pan-Asian and a Third World perspective.

ASSIMILATION BY AREA OF RESIDENCE

All Nisei-Sansei groups, no matter what the area of residence, have achieved cultural assimilation or acculturation. Structural assimilation as measured by intermarriage is also taking place, so that the experiences of the Japanese American appear isomorphic to that of European immigrants, although less rapid. Interestingly enough, assimilation is taking place while the attitudes of the Japanese remain primarily pluralistic.

[6]Harry H. L. Kitano, *Race Relations* (Englewood Cliffs, N.J.: Prentice-Hall, Inc., 1974), p. 128.
[7]Ibid., pp. 117–30.

Some indication of the feeling of the Japanese in the Los Angeles area can be gathered from a question concerning marital preferences. Ninety-seven percent of a sample of Nisei parents preferred that their children marry only other Japanese, although a high proportion conceded that the idea of marriage to a Caucasian was not so disturbing as it once seemed.[8]

A more recent study indicated that even among those who married out of the group there remained a preference for in-group marriage, although it was not a major issue.[9]

In the occupational area, the opportunities for Japanese to find positions commensurate with their training and experience appear to be better away from California. Once again, numbers play an important role, and it is probable that even in the East there is room at the top for only a small, select group of Japanese. There appears to be an unofficial quota system in operation; it would be unusual to see more than one person of Japanese ancestry in an executive position in the same American business, even on the East Coast. However, positions below the executive level remain plentiful for the Japanese American.

Occupational problems in Hawaii stem more from the type of economy and from overall employment patterns there. Many trained Hawaiians of Japanese descent emigrate to the mainland simply because of the better opportunities on the mainland.

Housing is not a major problem for the Japanese. There are still areas that practice covert discrimination, but, in general, the Nisei and Sansei can buy homes in "desirable" neighborhoods, depending on their income and occupation. The progress in housing can be inferred from the mixed reaction of Nisei and Sansei to Proposition 14, a controversial 1964 California ballot measure on discrimination in housing. Many Japanese took the side of the California Real Estate Association, which opposed fair-housing laws.

The political situation of the Japanese Americans today clearly reflects the power of numbers. The Nisei United States senator and several elected members of the House are from Hawaii, and the successful Japanese-American candidates in California government are from areas, such as Gardena,[10] of heavy ethnic concentration. However, in spite of the few elected and appointed officials, most observers describe the Japanese American as extremely naïve politically. If we use knowledge of political issues, active participation in political organizations, and the like as

[8]Harry H. L. Kitano, "Passive Discrimination: The Normal Person," *The Journal of Social Psychology* 70 (1966).

[9]Akemi Kikumura and Harry H. L. Kitano, "Interracial Marriage: A Picture of the Japanese Americans," *The Journal of Social Issues* 29, 2 (1973): 67–81.

[10]A suburb of Los Angeles.

criteria, the observations are correct. The Japanese American, at least at this stage of his acculturation, is an apolitical population.

SUMMARY BY GENERATIONS

In summarizing the acculturative history of the Japanese in America, we will find it most convenient, as well as most meaningful, to look once more at the differences among the three generations—Issei, Nisei, and Sansei. For it is by generation that progress along most variables is most clearly seen, and it is from the changes, generation by generation, that one may discern the probable direction of future changes, for predictions of social behavior, like any predictions, must rest on past phenomena.

The Issei

The Issei, who in the 1960s were mostly in the over-seventy age bracket, had virtually disappeared by the 1970s. Those survivors have changed but little in certain areas since their arrival in America at the turn of the century, except in those directions inevitable to advancing age. They were, and remain, products of a vanished Japanese era, conforming, hard-working, group- and family-oriented, clinging to old values, customs, and goals. Oddly enough, it is this, the most exotic Japanese group, that has been least studied, in spite of the fact that it possesses the most striking cultural differences. This is in part because its very life style limits the use of quantitative instruments. An investigator, for instance, finds it difficult to receive answers that reflect anything other than what the Issei expects the investigator to want to hear, for this is the customary convention of conversation. There was a day, in Japan, when the great lord would chop off your head if, when he asked you if you could deliver him a million bushels of corn, you said no. You said yes whether you could or not.

The Issei culture itself is still a relatively classless one, even though its members may be economically distinct. Most of them, however, are in comfortable circumstances and have retired both from their businesses and farms and from their positions as leaders of the Japanese community. Their problems are those of any aging group—the problem of leisure time and of finding useful family roles. They are concerned now not with their own children as much as with their grandchildren, and, again, as is typical of all peoples, seem to be mellower, more understanding, and more indulgent of this generation than of the one whose upbringing was their direct responsibility. The American life styles of the Nisei and Sansei family do not allow the grandparent the same honor and responsibility he would have in Japan, but he has a definite and respected place nonetheless. His role may simply be that of guardian of Japanese ways; for many Sansei, a grandparent is his only contact with the land of his ancestors.

The Issei, for themselves, continue to cultivate their Japaneseness. Many retain a degree of nostalgic nationalistic feeling. Most participate in Japanese-oriented group activities through the church, Issei organizations, Japanese movies. The more affluent often take a trip to Japan, seeing for the first time since they left it at the turn of the century the motherland they had idealized for fifty years. This, predictably, is usually something of a nasty shock. The remembered values of politeness, calm, and honesty have been lost in the jostle of a great Westernized city. They admire the physical achievements and fine accommodations in Tokyo, but find themselves unable to understand the people, and are themselves laughed at and treated as quaint country cousins. Among rural Japanese they are able to find some of the mores they remember, but they are by now unable to tolerate the primitive rural living conditions. The author's mother, on returning, much disillusioned, from such a visit, remarked that Japan is a nice place to visit, but one wouldn't want to live there.

Happily, the elderly Issei can usually find within the Japanese community and family here a fairly satisfying way of life. Most continue to live with or near their children, so that the extended family is maintained at least to a token extent. It is common for widows and widowers to live with their children. There are, of course, no elderly spinsters, but there is the small population of old bachelors, previously mentioned, for whom isolation and social interaction remain problems. As the number of their cronies diminishes, they are more apt than any other Japanese group to fall into the care of Japanese social-welfare agencies and medical facilities.

Data based on the 20 percent sample of the 1970 census showed that there were 20,505 males and 26,654 females who were sixty-five years and over. They made up less than 10 percent of the total Japanese-American population.[11]

The 1970 census showed that 7.5 percent of the Japanese in the United States had incomes below the poverty level, and from this group 20.8 percent were those who were sixty-five years or older.[12]

In an interesting document prepared for the Social Security Admin-

---

[11]U.S. Department of Commerce, Bureau of the Census, *Japanese, Chinese, and Filipinos in the United States*. 1970 Census of the Population, PC (2)-1G (Washington, D.C.: Government Printing Office, 1973), p. 24.

[12]Ibid., p. 42.

istration, Owan[13] describes the "benighted neglect" of the Japanese and other Asian elderly. They are ignored in employment, in funding, and in the social services, and receive only a few benefits from federal, state, local, and private agencies.

The problem of aging is exacerbated by differing ethnic and cultural styles. A Japanese placed in a retirement home is apt to miss ethnic foods, familiar language, and compatible forms of recreation and entertainment. The Japanese community is beginning to recognize these problems and is attempting to provide more adequate facilities, so that the entire burden is not placed on families and relatives.

But in general, the remaining Issei population have adapted to their new status in much the same way they had adapted to their other roles. They have done it quietly, without complaint and with a minimum of "trouble." Their complaints—that people pay too little attention to them, that no one really appreciates what they went through, that the younger generation is getting "soft"—are overbalanced by the manifest satisfactions of material well-being and by the pleasure they feel in seeing the success of their children, for whom they had indeed sacrificed much. A comparison of their own circumstances and those of their children with the circumstances of those friends and relatives who stayed in Japan most likely confirms the wisdom of their choice to emigrate, and they have little to regret.

The Nisei

Most Issei, having considered the future of their children more important than the immediate satisfaction of their own wishes, today measure their success in terms of the success of the Nisei, and the Nisei in general have rewarded the sacrifices, in spite of the fact that their transitional position between the Japanese and American cultures has been a difficult one. A Nisei schoolboy found himself similar to Caucasian students on many levels and to his Japanese parents on others, but was considered "Japanese" by his American peers, and incomprehensibly American by his parents. But unlike the situation in some other immigrant cultures, where the transitional generation, most affected by culture conflict, has shown the highest degree of delinquency and mental illness and anomie, the Nisei have functioned successfully, producing what may legitimately be termed a Japanese-American community. Like the Issei, they have constructed an elaborate network of cliques and organizations, but these

[13]Tom Owan, "Asian Americans: A Case of Benighted Neglect and the Urgent Need for Affirmative Action." Paper prepared for the Social Security Administration, October 1974.

organizations are themselves designed according to American models. Family attitudes and concerns are American, yet the sophisticated observer would notice a subtle lack of verbal exchange, a faintly "Japanese" climate there. The college professor, used to giving seminars to Caucasians, would tear his hair at the docile silence of a group of Nisei, yet the cheering and fighting at the Nisei basketball game is as rowdy as at any other American game.

The Nisei have achieved an impressive professional and educational record, comparable to or exceeding that of the majority community. Although this has tended to produce some class distinctions, these are still negligible. The gardener, the CPA, and the doctor may make up a threesome at golf. The fathers of Sansei debutantes are as likely to be nurserymen as lawyers—and very few perceive this as untoward social climbing.

Like any group of established, fairly affluent, middle-aged people, the Nisei find themselves concerned with leisure and community service. Groups in Los Angeles play golf and take Las Vegas weekends. The women often spend a great deal of time in voluntary social work, and many take classes, particularly those that reflect an awakening interest, typical of ethnic groups, in Japanese traditional pursuits, such as flower arranging or Japanese dance. Bridge clubs are popular.

Nisei housing patterns reflect their transitional position. They tend to live at the fringes of the ghetto, in more prosperous circumstances, or to form new contiguous living groups in middle-class subdivisions. Few are to be found randomly scattered in other neighborhoods.

With more leisure and economic success, the Nisei have found time to examine problems of family life, and find there typically American role conflicts and generation conflicts. Some evidence points to an increase in separations and divorce, although this is far from typical. The appearance of several Japanese-American psychiatrists in the Los Angeles community is probably no coincidence. Few Nisei avail themselves of community mental health and guidance facilities, but the group shows good attendance at lectures on child rearing or understanding adolescents.

It is also necessary to consider the atypical but sizable Nisei group who have not achieved economic success and middle-class status. There are, of course, the Nisei gas-station attendants, janitors, and laborers. These individuals probably interact more than their middle-class peers with subgroups outside of the Japanese community, particularly with black and Mexican groups, and in a mild sense can be said to have assimilated, albeit into lower-class society, more than other Nisei. But, as is common with their middle-class Japanese peers, they have retained or modified their culture, so that very few have incorporated the values and behaviors of the lower-class population.

There is a current reaction by many of the younger generations to the Nisei point of view. Many cannot understand their docility, especially during the wartime evacuation, or their overemphasis on hard work, responsibility, and concern about what others think. Or perhaps the adverse reaction may be directed more at the smugness of some Nisei individuals who view their "success" as of such heroic proportions that not only the Sansei or Yonsei are supposed to follow, but also all ethnic minorities and the rest of the world. It has always been the task of older groups to pass on their wisdom to the younger generations, but one predictable outcome is that this sagacity will no doubt be rejected.

The Sansei

What is true for the Nisei is also true of the Sansei generation, although some evidence suggests that deviant behavior is slightly increased in this group. The explanation lies, of course, in the fact that Sansei are, on most measurements of acculturation, almost identical to the Caucasian group. Their test results, achievement and interest preferences, and social values are typically American. They are members of Little League, fraternities, sororities, and other organizations designed on American models, although these are still primarily ethnic in their membership. But even these structural barriers are breaking down. Sansei college students now sometimes join non-Japanese fraternities and sororities, and intermarriage is increasing, although the preference of most remains to marry within the group. In general, however, Sansei thinking and behavior are American.

It is difficult to say, however, that they are not still transitional. The college professor, giving a seminar to Sansei, will notice that, while these students are not so reticent as Nisei, they are still somewhat subdued and conforming. Their education is job-oriented; they enter "secure" professions. The fierce desire for upward mobility is occasionally frightening and is more typical, perhaps, of an aspiring rather than a fully acculturated middle-class American. As has been mentioned, most prefer to marry other Sansei.

But there are built-in structural factors that will literally force a change. The increased differentiation and stratification among the relatively small number of Japanese will inevitably lead to increased interaction with non-Japanese groups on all levels. For example, if we fall back on our eth-gen-class model, the third-generation Japanese Ph.D. social scientist will probably, in looking for a wife, find few Sansei females with comparable background, interests, and values. The old model, "just as long as she is Japanese," will no longer be satisfactory; the same point will hold true for the female Sansei liberal arts major with a strong bent for theater. And the same story will be repeated on all levels of the Japanese-American structure. The social expectations of group members will not be fully satisfied within the ethnic community. We have already seen how this change has operated to affect the ethnic occupational structures, with a generational move from in-community to out-community jobs. We have also seen that outmarriage has changed the picture, and it is the Sansei who are the most involved in this area.

Perhaps the major generalization for the Sansei relates to individual differences. By now the relative homogeneity of the Issei and the Nisei has given way to the Sansei (and the Yonsei, or fourth generation), who are products of a freer and more open world. The boundary maintenance mechanisms entrapping the previous generations in narrow stereotypes are no longer as effective as they once were, nor are the socialization and social-control techniques of parents in shaping their children. Therefore, there has developed a more visible range of individual differences, which has been reflected in a wider span of expectations, life styles, and behavior. It will be interesting to note if the inevitable process of aging will change the younger generations into more predictable patterns as they grow older.

THE RACE QUESTION

This leads to a point of particular significance for study of minorities in America, namely, the question of the assimilation and integration of a racially distinct group. Race is commonly thought to be an almost insurmountable social barrier. Programs for the integration of, say blacks, almost always rest on the tacit assumption that the biological distinction is to be maintained. "Would you want your daughter to marry one?" remains a fundamental, inescapable question.

But evidence, even that collected during the height of wartime passions, shows that a presumably rigid criterion like race is not an absolute one. For example, O'Brien mentions that in the racially segregated city of Memphis, although the Chinese were buried in the black section of Elmwood Cemetery, the Japanese used the same section as whites.[14] We wonder what torturous paths Hitler's Aryan policy must have gone through to include the Japanese nation as a full-fledged ally and partner. And the Japanese businessman, who is an extremely important factor in the current South African economy, is considered as "white," at least for business purposes, in that country. Therefore, historical, political,

[14]Robert O'Brien, "Selective Dispersion as a Factor in the Solution of the Nisei Problem," *Social Forces* (December 1944): 140–47.

and economic factors apparently influence the definition of race in an interesting fashion.

Seventy years has produced a marked change in the attitudes of both the Caucasian majority and the Japanese minority in the United States. Marital preference remains in-group, but the groups themselves are less rigid in their attitudes, and intermarriage brings little opprobrium. The results of the postwar occupation of Japan and the large numbers of Japanese war brides are obvious. As a Caucasian airlines pilot once remarked to this writer, speaking of his Japanese bride, "No one pays much attention to us since there was that movie (*Sayonara*) with Marlon Brando." Perhaps this generalization sounds somewhat too "Hollywoodish," but there is little doubt that the general direction of assimilation, generation by generation, will include biological as well as social integration. An important but often overlooked integration variable also includes the desirability of the Japanese female from American eyes, although such an attraction may be somewhat overexaggerated. Another important point concerning race and acceptance for the Japanese was the factor of differential perception and differential acceptance from the majority group. Although it may have seemed to the Japanese that almost everybody in the United States was always against them (especially during certain periods), this was not so. There were regional differences; there were social-class differences; and there were always a number of influential "Japanophiles"—those who "loved" Japan and the Japanese. Therefore, he was not subjected to the well-nigh universal degree of constant hostility that has been the lot of other racial minorities.

THE MIDDLEMAN MINORITY

But the upward mobility of the Japanese American, especially on the mainland, is not an unlimited one, so that few Japanese can comfortably say that "one can be what one wants to be." Rather, the Japanese American may be in the role of a middleman minority. As we indicate:

> Minority groups often occupy the lower status positions (in a social system), but under certain circumstances they may rise to a higher niche and play . . . the role of a middleman minority. . . . Recent scholarship suggests that the middleman role may result from a wide variety of factors—for example differences in race, nationality, or religion.[15]

[15]Harry H. L. Kitano, "Japanese Americans: The Development of a Middleman Minority," *Pacific Historical Review* (43, 4) (November 1974): 500–19.

Examples of other middleman minorities include the Jew in Europe, the Indian in Africa, and the Chinese in Southeast Asia. High in-group cohesion is one factor that leads to a competitive advantage over some of the more disorganized groups at the bottom, which often leads to a rise in status. However, discrimination imposes a ceiling to their mobility, so that their status is above those of certain groups but inferior to those of the majority. The phrase "caught in the middle" is an appropriate one because middleman minorities often play a buffer role between competing power groups—they must placate the power elite for protection and approval, but they must also contend with the wrath and frustration of those lower in the system. If they are numerically small and lack retaliatory power, they can serve as convenient scapegoats.

A comparison of the Japanese in Hawaii and on the mainland indicates the process leading to different power positions in a social structure. Although both came from the same culture, were of comparative visibility, and faced comparable initial discrimination (e.g., Issei were aliens ineligible for citizenship), the cohesion, numbers, and power of the Japanese in Hawaii was greater. Therefore, it is our observation that the Japanese in Hawaii are much better represented through a wider range of status positions in that system than are the Japanese on the mainland, who exhibit many of the characteristics associated with middleman minorities.

The middleman role is a difficult one, and yet the Japanese often finds himself in such a position—between the blacks and the whites, and between Japan and the United States. Some of the hypothesized middleman qualities include identification with those who are above and an attempt to maintain a distance from those below. The "try harder Avis syndrome" would be another, and questions of identity and status anxiety would be common.

For the Japanese American the important question concerning the middleman is whether the status is a temporary stage in his adaptation or whether it is much more permanent. One factor which tends towards a fixed role is that of legal discrimination, such as "aliens ineligible for citizenship," so that the early Issei faced this barrier. The following generations were not formally excluded from participating in the dominant system, but the internalization of feelings of inferiority, and social psychological perceptions that top positions are reserved for whites may prove to be as effective in limiting upward mobility as discriminatory laws.

Interestingly enough, the adaptation of the Japanese to the United States is similar to that of many European groups—what Park refers to as a natural history cycle.[16] A typical pattern of interaction between groups starts with contact, followed by competition, then by accommodation. Accommodation is usually accompanied by segregated ethnic islands, which eventually leads to the final stage of assimilation. When an observer takes a long-range historical view of the interaction between two cultures, the process as described by Park appears to have high validity.

However, it would be an error to assume that there is an inevitability to the Park cycle and that length of time is the only determinant. For example, Blauner[17] predicts a number of different consequences based on the initial contact. Voluntary immigrants, such as the European and the Japanese, can be differentiated from those groups who were already here and overwhelmed, such as the Indians or from those who were brought over as slaves. Different motivations toward acculturation can be hypothesized for these groups. Then there are the variations in culture and the "cultural fit," so that the Japanese with their community and small-business structures were able to achieve a solid "steppingstone" into American society. Barriers like discrimination and prejudice must also be considered, which in turn depends on visibility, numbers, cohesion, and power, so that predictions must take into account the interaction among numerous variables. However, the Park cycle has high predictive validity under natural conditions—that is, when the social system is open and when such man-made barriers as prejudice, discrimination, and segregation are absent.

The current high rate of outmarriage provides evidence for the validity of the Park cycle, but there is also an interesting development that may decelerate the assimilation process. The reawakening of the issue of an ethnic and pan-Asian identity and the belief that yellow is mellow" are counterforces that may lead to a more pluralistic development. Perhaps the healthiest factor in these newer developments is that *they are voluntary*, and they are realistic options stemming from equal status contact, rather than from the old model of superior to inferior.

It would not be too difficult to foresee the bifurcation of the Japanese community. One-half may follow the Park model to its ultimate conclusion—assimilation, amalgamation, and the melting pot—so that there is a disappearance of the visibility of the Japanese as an ethnic group. But the other half may retain the ethnic structures, the Asian identity, and a pluralistic subculture, so that while one group is "integrating, the other may be segregating." Then, of course, there are the newer Japanese

16Robert E. Park, *Race and Culture*, ed. E. C. Hughes et al. (Glencoe, Ill.: The Free Press, 1950), pp. 138–51.

17Robert Blauner, *Racial Oppression in America* (New York: Harper and Row, 1972).

immigrants, the new Issei who are in the early contact stages of an immigrant group and who may be developing another cycle in race relations.

ACCULTURATION: A NONLINEAR VARIABLE?

One of the common assumptions concerning acculturation is that of linearity, so that the acquistion of one culture is closely linked with the discarding or replacing of the other. For example, in the figure below, each of the Japanese generations is viewed as moving along a continuum from the "Japanese" to the "American," with the reasonable hypothesis that the Nisei suffer from "culture conflict" because they are caught between the two cultures.

Kiefer[18] and Lebra[19] raise an important theoretical issue by questioning the linear assumption. One of the simplest examples is that of food: Does accepting the American cuisine necessarily mean relinquishing the ethnic? We feel that a model emphasizing the additive nature of acculturation is more accurate, so that a person has cultural alternatives, appropriate to time, place, and situation. We have described the bicultural adaptation of ethnic groups[20]—to be ethnic means one style and to be American means another, and most Japanese Americans of our

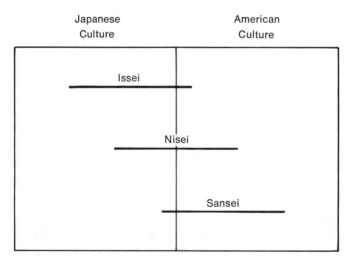

Linear Acculturation by Generation.

18Christie Kiefer, *Changing Cultures, Changing Lives* (San Francisco: Jossey Bass, 1974).

19Takako Lebra, "Acculturation Dilemma: The Function of Japanese Moral Values for Americanization," *Council on Anthropology and Education Newsletter* 3 (1972), pp. 6–13.

20Harry H. L. Kitano, *Race Relations*, p. 210.

acquaintance handle both without any difficulty. It is when acculturation is viewed linearly that we talk of cultural conflict.

CULTURAL PLURALISM

This leads to a pertinent question: What has been the most significant factor in the Japanese acculturative process? The answer seems to be the pluralistic development of a congruent Japanese culture within the framework of the larger American society. If we may be permitted a somewhat elaborate metaphor, this development may be envisioned as two trees, sprung from different seeds but flourishing in the same soil, in identical climatic conditions, the younger of them springing up by the side of the older, so that although the two trunks, rooted in similar values and aspirations, nourished by similar factors of education and industry, are separate, their branches intermingle, and eventually, it may be difficult to distinguish the leaves of one from the leaves of the other. The organic and gradual nature of this metaphor is particularly appropriate to cultural pluralism, yet it must be emphasized that this mode of acculturation seems only to work when two cultures spring from relatively similar seeds. The exotic plant of some cultures seems not to flourish in American soil. For some groups it seems apparent that cultural pluralism hinders acculturation and assimilation simply because the discrepancies between the cultures seem to lead to increased divergence and intergroup tensions. In such cases, assimilation seems to require the dissolution of one of the cultures and its substitution by more "American" patterns of behavior. Such a process inevitably requires more time, more conflict, raises critical questions of value, and creates more difficulties for the individuals and cultures caught in the process. Further, as we have mentioned in our opening chapter, there may be a functional order so that the smoothest method of adaptation follows an acculturation, integration, and assimilation sequence.

A comparison of cultural pluralism with other modes of acculturation immediately involves one in the subtleties of possible modes of selective cultural pluralism. For instance, a purely cultural-pluralistic development might imply the retention of the native language as well as its customs and values. Yet the Japanese have quickly and almost completely discarded the Japanese language, and artificial attempts to preserve it (e.g., Japanese-language school) have largely failed. In other dimensions, too, certain unwieldy Japanese customs were almost immediately supplanted by more efficient American ones. The potential inherent in cultural pluralism for retaining some elements of a distinctive way of life and discarding others is one of its most attractive elements. It is a cliché to say of America that it is a great melting pot, meaning, presumably, that the disparate elements that comprise it are eventually commingled in an amorphous brew labeled "the norm," and that this is desirable. Yet, surely, the distinctive contribution of Asian, of Mexican, of African, and of many other cultures could greatly improve the savour of the bland American brew. The cultural-pluralistic development of the Japanese-American group so far provides another example of how the native and American may coexist.

STRUCTURAL PLURALISM

The problem of structural pluralism is a related issue. Followed to an ultimate extreme, it might describe a society with a vast number of independent groups maintained through restrictions on friendship, dating, and marriage. There is an obvious danger to the proliferation of such structures—the restriction of friendship and marriage to persons within one's own network could very well foster a strong "we" and "they" feeling, leading to less communication, more misunderstanding, more prejudiced attitudes, and higher levels of discrimination.

The development of pluralistic structures for the Japanese was originally based more on necessity than choice—there was little opportunity for Japanese to enter into the social structure of the larger community. Currently, however, the matter of choice appears to be of a more voluntary nature—most Japanese can enter into the social structures of the larger society, although there is always the element of greater risk and possible rejection for those choosing this path. The continued existence of the ethnic structures, however, limits the opportunity for "risk-taking," and many Japanese who might otherwise have ventured into the larger society choose the easy way out through participation in the ethnic structures (even though these groups are as "American" as any). The comment of "being more comfortable and at ease with one's own kind" covers many situations. However, many Japanese still need the ethnic structures and the justification for the cradle-to-grave services (e.g., a Japanese doctor will be on hand at delivery; a Japanese priest will perform over the burial; and in between, one can live a life of friends, dating, and marriage primarily with other Japanese) provided by the ethnic community is important; however, the structures may be playing a negative role when their strength pulls back some who might venture into the larger society. This writer feels that social interaction based primarily on interest and achievement is healthier than one based on ethnicity.

Judged by most standards, the coexistence between the Japanese and the American cultures has been successful. Education, productivity, and "Americanism" have been high, and crime, delinquency, and other forms of social deviance have been low. And if we remember that this has been accomplished by a nonwhite group, the progress appears even more significant.

The unusual part of the Japanese adaptation is that it is being accomplished by a "nonwhite" group and a population heretofore considered to be "unassimilable." In fact, the adaptation has been of such a quality that it has been termed a "model American minority."[21]

But we must also be reminded that the judgment of Japanese Americans as the "model American minority" is made from a strictly majority point of view. Japanese Americans are good because they conform—they don't "make waves"—they work hard and are quiet and docile. As in a colonial situation, there tends to be one set of prescriptions for those in power and another for the subject people. But, ideally, members of the ethnic community should share in any evaluation of the efficacy of their adjustment. For if the goals of the American society include freeing an individual for self-expression and creativity, and if social maturity includes originality, participation, and the opportunity for individuals to function at their highest levels, then certain questions may be asked about the Japanese. It may be a disservice to some of them to continue calling them "good" and reinforcing their present adaptation. The kind of goodness that led them to accept the wartime evacuation can, in the long run, be a drawback as well as a strength. Perhaps this is one group where emphasis on the self—the development of individual self and the satisfaction of ego needs—can be more highly emphasized.

However, it would be tragic if some of the strengths of the Japanese culture were to be forgotten. The ability to look beyond self and to act in relation to others is an admirable quality, and the ethnic identity, whether in terms of a nation and manifested as pride, or in terms of a community, helped the Japanese achieve a degree of cohesion and group loyalty that appears important for a meaningful life. Without an abstraction that leads beyond self, life may regress to self-indulgence and to self-gratification, so that the accumulation of wealth and power—often associated with "success"—may only be an empty victory. Hopefully, the next generation of Japanese Americans will integrate the best of the Japanese and the American cultures, and their lives will reflect the richness of both. But, at the risk of being unduly pessimisitic, the probability that they may draw from the more negative elements of both of the cultures is also a realistic prospect.

However, in spite of different definitions of what constitutes success and of philosophical discussions that may show the Japanese as short of being an "ideal" group, they have achieved a niche in American soci-

21William Peterson, *The New York Times Magazine*, January 9, 1966.

ety. They have been effective in social organization, in socialization, in controlling deviant behavior, and in coming to grips with "success" in American terms. When we look back on the past prejudice and discrimination faced by the Japanese, we find that even their most optimistic dreams have been surpassed. Such a story may give us some optimism for the future of race relations in the American society.

A P P E N D I X

NUMBER OF MALE MARRIAGES AND DIVORCES BY ESTIMATED
GENERATION GROUP OF U.S. JAPANESE*

Male	Ever Married	Divorced	% Divorced
Issei (foreign born Japanese)	28,676	471	1.6
Nisei (ages 20–44)	59,678	941	1.6
Sansei (ages 14–19)	189	3	1.6

*U.S. Department of Commerce, Bureau of the Census, *Nonwhite Population by Race*, 1960 Census of the Population. (Washington, D.C.: Government Printing Office), pp. 55, 90.

TABLE B
GENERATIONAL RESPONSES (BY PER CENT) TO TRUE-FALSE
ATTITUDINAL STATEMENTS*

	Issei N=18	Nisei N=37	Sansei N=48	Caucasian N=82
A. Ethnic Identity				
1. Once a Japanese, always a Japanese (T)	78	63	47	- -
2. I always look forward to going to prefectural (or family) picnics (T)	62	50	17	
3. I would prefer attending an all-Japanese Church (T)	81	44	40	
4. I would prefer being treated by a Japanese doctor when sick (T)	69	50	26	
5. I prefer American movies to Japanese movies (F)	69	14	11	
B. Means-Ends				
6. Even in a minor task a person should put all his energies into it (T)	95	86	86	78
7. It is almost impossible to be a success while strictly abiding by the law (F)	76	94	88	90

C. Masculinity and Responsibility

8. It is only right for a man to marry a girl if he has gotten her into trouble (T)	79	80	48	36
9. My definition of a real man is one who adequately supports his wife and family under all conditions (T)	81	82	63	35
10. It is a natural part of growing up as a man to occasionally "wise-off" at teachers, policemen, and other grown-ups in authority (F)	72	71	67	63

D. Individual-Group Orientation

11. A person who raises too many questions intereferes with the progress of a group (T)	88	43	19	40
12. One can never let himself down without letting the family down at the same time (T)	89	79	59	46

E. Passivity

13. If someone tries to push you around, there is very little that you can do about it (T)	39	29	12	6
14. If you are competing against another fellow for a job, there is not much you can do to push the hiring decision one way or another (T)	53	60	27	16
15. I would not shout or fight in public, even when provoked (T)	70	69	55	51

F. Realistic Expectations

16. Even if one has talent and ability, it does not mean that he will get ahead (T)	67	85	95	91
17. I think I will be a success once I acquire a nice home, a new car, and many modern appliances (T)	50	32	8	6

*Survey of Japanese Americans in San Francisco and Los Angeles, 1963, by the author. Caucasian sample was a Psych 1A class at UCLA.

TABLE C
DIFFERENCES BETWEEN JAPANESE NONPROBATIONERS AND PROBATIONERS
ON THE CALIFORNIA PSYCHOLOGICAL INVENTORY (CPI)*

	Group X (N=30) Japanese Nonprobationer		Group Y (N=30) Japanese Probationer		
	Mean	S.D.	Mean	S.D.	P
Poise, Ascendancy, and Self-Assurance					
Dominance	21.3	6.7	21.3	5.1	
Capacity for Status	15.4	3.4	14.1	3.0	
Sociability (Social Participation)	21.1	5.8	21.5	4.7	
Social Presence	33.2	6.4	32.7	3.5	
Self-Acceptance	18.7	4.4	19.1	3.8	
Sense of Well Being	32.8	5.2	30.7	6.0	
Socialization, Maturity, and Responsibility					
Responsibility	26.4	4.4	20.4	6.1	.01
Socialization (Delinquency)	36.6	6.2	28.3	7.1	.01
Self-Control (Impulsivity)	25.1	9.2	22.1	9.9	
Tolerance	18.8	4.9	15.2	5.0	.01
Good Impression	13.4	6.0	12.7	6.0	
Community (infrequency)	24.8	2.7	24.2	3.1	
Achievement Potential and Intellectual Efficiency					
Achievement via Conformance	23.0	3.4	20.7	5.2	.05
Achievement via Independence	17.4	3.9	14.2	3.6	.01
Intellectual Efficiency	34.8	5.1	30.9	6.3	.05
Intellectual and Interest Modes					
Psychological-mindedness (Psychological Interest)	8.8	3.3	9.3	2.2	
Flexibility	10.7	3.8	8.0	2.9	.01
Femininity	16.8	3.0	14.7	2.7	.01

*Harry H. L. Kitano, "Japanese-American Crime and Delinquency,"
Journal of Psychology 66 (1967): 253–63.

TABLE D
CALIFORNIA MENTAL HOSPITAL RESIDENTS BY ETHNIC
GROUP FOR SELECTED YEARS*

Group (rate per 100,000)†

Year	Japanese	Caucasian	Mexican American	Indian	Chinese	Black
1950	216	300	188	356	535	364
1960	225	242	83	187	376	299
1964	198	213	74	174	361	296

*Adapted from California State Department of Mental Hygiene, Bureau of Biostatistics.
†Rate for 1964 based on 1960 population.
Hospitalization rates among various ethnic groups in California for 1950, 1960, and 1964 provide some interesting comparisons. The trend away from hospitalization in California mental institutions is seen in that all 1964 rates are lower than for 1950. The Chinese hospitalization rates are the highest of all groups; the Mexican figures are a relatively low hospitalized population. However, the proportionate drop in hospitalization rates is very low for the Japanese and may indicate few alternative resources for the Japanese, once he gets to the stage of hospital referral.

TABLE E
DISTRIBUTION OF JAPANESE-AMERICAN POPULATION IN THE CONTINENTAL UNITED STATES, 1880–1970*

State	1880	1890	1900	1910	1920	1930	1940	1950	1960	1970
Alabama	---	3	3	4	18	25	21	88	500	1,043
Arizona	2	1	281	371	550	879	632	780	1,501	2,530
Arkansas	---	---	---	9	5	12	3	113	237	588
California	86	1,147	10,151	41,356	71,952	97,456	93,717	84,956	157,317	213,277
Colorado	---	10	48	2,300	2,464	3,213	2,734	5,412	6,846	7,861
Connecticut	6	18	18	71	102	130	164	254	653	1,571
Delaware	---	---	1	4	8	8	22	14	152	432
District of Columbia	4	9	7	47	103	78	68	353	900	716
Florida	---	14	1	50	106	153	154	238	1,315	3,968
Georgia	---	5	1	4	9	32	31	128	885	1,334
Idaho	---	---	1,291	1,363	1,569	1,421	1,191	1,980	2,254	2,012
Illinois	3	14	80	285	472	564	462	11,646	14,074	17,645
Indiana	---	18	5	38	81	71	29	318	1,093	2,100
Iowa	---	1	7	36	29	19	29	310	599	773
Louisiana	---	39	17	31	57	52	46	127	519	876
Kansas	---	4	4	107	52	37	19	116	1,362	1,566
Kentucky	---	3	---	12	9	9	9	74	774	920
Maine	---	1	4	13	7	3	5	30	343	215
Maryland	---	7	9	24	29	38	36	289	1,842	3,637
Massachusetts	8	18	53	151	191	201	158	384	1,924	4,715
Michigan	1	38	9	49	184	176	139	1,517	3,211	5,464
Minnesota	1	2	51	67	85	69	51	1,049	1,726	2,693
Mississippi	---	7	---	2	---	1	1	62	178	378
Missouri	---	6	9	99	135	94	74	527	1,473	2,320
Montana	---	6	2,441	1,585	1,074	753	508	524	589	613
Nebraska	---	2	3	590	804	674	480	619	905	1,253
Nevada	3	3	228	864	754	608	470	382	544	1,046

TABLE E (cont.)

State										
New Hampshire	---	2	1	1	8	---	5	30	343	252
New Jersey	2	22	52	206	325	439	298	1,784	3,514	6,344
New Mexico	---	2	8	258	251	249	186	251	930	937
New York	17	148	354	1,247	2,686	2,930	2,538	3,893	8,702	19,794
North Carolina	1	1	---	2	24	17	21	98	1,265	2,088
North Dakota	---	1	148	59	72	91	83	61	127	312
Ohio	3	22	27	76	130	187	163	1,986	3,135	5,896
Oklahoma	---	---	48	48	67	104	57	137	749	1,214
Oregon	2	25	2,501	3,418	4,151	4,598	4,071	3,660	5,016	6,213
Pennsylvania	8	32	40	190	255	293	224	1,029	2,348	5,417
Rhode Island	---	5	13	33	35	17	6	25	192	744
South Carolina	---	---	---	8	15	15	33	34	460	675
South Dakota	---	---	1	42	38	19	19	56	188	199
Tennessee	---	6	4	8	8	11	12	104	507	857
Texas	---	3	13	340	449	519	458	957	4,053	6,216
Utah	---	4	417	2,110	2,936	3,269	2,210	4,452	4,371	4,862
Vermont	---	1	---	3	4	1	3	14	79	73
Virginia	---	16	10	14	56	43	74	193	1,733	3,296
Washington	1	360	5,617	12,929	17,387	17,838	14,565	9,694	16,652	20,188
Wisconsin	---	9	5	34	60	24	23	529	1,425	2,449
West Virginia	---	3	---	3	10	9	3	46	176	266
Wyoming	---	---	393	1,596	1,194	1,026	643	450	514	457
Alaska										854
Hawaii										217,175
Total:	148	2,038	24,326	72,157	111,010	138,834	126,948	168,773	260,195	588,324

*Source: U.S. Census of the Population.

211

TABLE F
JAPANESE, WHITE, AND TOTAL POPULATIONS IN HAWAII, 1900–1970*

Year	Japanese	White	Total Population (including other nonwhites)
1900	61,111	28,819	154,001
1910	79,675	44,048	191,909
1920	109,274	54,742	255,912
1930	139,631	80,373	368,336
1940	157,905	103,791	423,330
1950	184,611	114,793	499,794
1960	203,455	202,230	632,772
1970	217,175	298,160	768,561

*U.S. Dept. of Commerce, Bureau of the Census, U.S. Census of the Population, Characteristics of the Population, Hawaii, Vol. 1, Part 13, Table 17, pp. 13–28.

TABLE G
POPULATION CHARACTERISTICS OF THE JAPANESE IN THE UNITED STATES, 1970*

	Total U.S.	Japanese Hawaii	Japanese California	Other
Total Population (000s)	588.3	217.2	213.3	157.9
Percent urban	89	86	94	88
Percent rural	11	14	6	12
Percent native born	79	90	79	64
Percent foreign born	21	10	21	36
Age distribution				
Percent under 18	29	31	30	25
Percent over 65	8	8	7	9
Median age				
Male (years)	29.6	30.5	29.2	28.8
Female (years)	34.3	32.9	32.9	37.8

*Source: Adapted from "A Study of Selected Socio-economic Characteristics of Ethnic Minorities Based on the 1970 Census." Department of Health, Education, and Welfare, HEW Publication No. (US) 75–121 (no date), p. 17.

TABLE H
GEOGRAPHIC DISTRIBUTION OF THE JAPANESE AMERICAN, 1960 AND 1970 (PERCENT)*

	Northeast	North Central	South	West
1960	4	6	4	86
1970	8	7	5	81

*Source: Adapted from "A Study of Selected Socio-economic Characteristics of Ethnic Minorities Based on the 1970 Census." Department of Health, Education and Welfare, HEW Publication No. (US) 75–121, p. 19.

TABLE I
SEX RATIO OF THE JAPANESE-AMERICAN POPULATION
BY CENSUS YEARS, 1900–1970*

Census Years	Total (rounded)	Percent Male	Female
1900	85,700	83	17
1910	152,700	78	22
1920	220,600	61	39
1930	278,700	56	44
1940	285,100	54	46
1950	326,400	52	48
1960	464,300	48	52
1970	591,300	46	54

*Adapted from "A Study of Selected Socio-economic Characteristics of Ethnic Minorities Based on the 1970 Census." Volume II: Asian Americans. Department of Health, Education and Welfare, HEW Publication No. (US) 75–121 (no date), p. 25.

TABLE J
MARRIAGE WITHIN OWN SUBGROUP BY SEX, 1970*

Total 16 years or over	Percent
Male	88
Female	67
16–24 years	
Male	62
Female	54
25–44 years	
Male	84
Female	57
45 years and over	
Male	93
Female	84

*Source: Adapted from "A Study of Selected Socio-economic Characteristics of Ethnic Minorities Based on the 1970 Census." Department of Health, Education and Welfare, HEW Publication No. (US) 75–121, p. 49.

TABLE K
OCCUPATIONS OF JAPANESE BY SEX AND NATIVITY, 1970*

Occupations	Males		Females	
	U.S. Born	Foreign Born	U.S. Born	Foreign Born
Professional, Technical, and Managerial Workers	31	45	21	13
Clerical and Sales Workers	15	13	47	19
Craftsmen and Operatives	33	13	11	31
Laborers, Nonfarm	9	13	1	1
Service Workers, including Domestics	4	9	18	33
Farm-related Managers and Workers	10	7	2	3

*Source: Adapted from "A Study of Selected Socio-economic Characteristics of Ethnic Minorities Based on the 1970 Census." Department of Health, Education and Welfare, HEW Publication No. (US) 75–121, p. 88.

TABLE L
POVERTY CHARACTERISTICS OF THE JAPANESE IN THE UNITED STATES, 1970*

	Percent	
	U.S. Total	U.S. Japanese Total
1. Percent Families Receiving Public Assistance	5.3	2.7
2. Percent Families Defined as "Poverty" by U.S. Census	11	6
3. Percent of Persons 65 and Over in Poverty	26	19

*Source: Adapted from "A Study of Selected Socio-economic Characteristics of Ethnic Minorities Based on the 1970 Census." Department of Health, Education and Welfare, HEW Publication No. (US) 75–121, p. 118.

Bibliography

Allen, Gwen F. *Hawaii's War Years*. Honolulu: University of Hawaii Press, 1950.

Amano, Matsukichi. "Study of Employment Patterns and a Measurement of Employee Attitudes in Japanese Firms in Los Angeles." Ph.D. dissertation, University of California, 1966.

Arkoff, Abe. "Need Patterns in Two Generations of Japanese-Americans in Hawaii." *The Journal of Social Psychology* 50 (1959): 75–79.

————; Meredith, G.; and Iwahara, S. "Dominance-Deference Patterning in Motherland-Japanese, Japanese-American, and Caucasian-American Students." *The Journal of Social Psychology* 58 (1962): 61–66.

Beach, D. C. *Oriental Crime in California*. Stanford, Calif.: Stanford University Press, 1932.

Beardsley, R. K., J. W. Hall, and R. E. Ward. *Village Japan*. Chicago: University of Chicago Press, 1959.

Bell, Richard. *Public School Education of Second-Generation Japanese in California*. Education-Psychology Series, nos. 1, 3. Stanford, Calif.: Stanford University Press, 1935.

Belli, M. M., and D. R. Jones. *Belli Looks at Life and Law in Japan*. New York: Bobbs-Merrill Co., Inc., 1960.

Benedict, Ruth. *The Chrysanthemum and the Sword*. Boston: Houghton Mifflin, 1946.

Bennett, John, Herbert Passin, and Robert McKnight. *In Search of Identity*. Minneapolis: University of Minnesota Press, 1958.

Black and Gold, McKinley High School Yearbook. Honolulu, 1944.

Blauner, Robert. *Racial Oppression in America*. New York: Harper and Row, 1972.

Bloom, Leonard, and Ruth Riemer. "Attitudes of College Students Toward Japanese-Americans." *Sociometry* 8 (May 1945).

————, and Carol Credon. "Marriages of Japanese Americans in Los Angeles County." In *University of California Publications in Culture and Society*, no. 1, pp. 1–24. Berkeley, Calif.: University of California Press, 1945.

Bonacich, Edna. "A Theory of Middleman Minorities." *American Sociological Review* 38 (October 1973): 583–94.

Bosworth, Allan R. *America's Concentration Camps*. New York: W. W. Norton and Co., 1967.

Broom, Leonard, and John Kitsuse. *The Managed Casualty*. Berkeley, Calif.: University of California Press, 1956.

————. "The Validation of Acculturation: A Condition to Ethnic Assimilation." *The American Anthropologist* 57 (February 1955): 44–48.

Burma, John. "Current Leadership Problems Among Japanese-Americans." *Sociological and Social Research* 37 (1953): 157–63.

Burrows, Edwin G. *Hawaiian Americans*. New Haven, Conn.: Yale University Press, 1947, p. 135.

Caudill, William. "Japanese-American Personality and Acculturation." *Genetic Psychology Monographs* (1952).

Cheng, C. K., and Douglas Yamamura. "Interracial Marriage and Divorce in Hawaii. *Social Forces* 36 (Oct.–May, 1957–58) : 77–78.

Cleland, R. G. *A History of California, the American Period*. New York: The Macmillan Co., 1922.

Cohen, Nathan E. Private conversation, June 16, 1967.

Coffman, Tom. *To Catch a Wave*. Honolulu: University of Hawaii Press, 1972.

Conroy, Hilary. *The Japanese Frontier in Hawaii*. Berkeley and Los Angeles: The University of California Press, 1953.

Cressey, Donald. "Crime." In *Contemporary Social Problems*, edited by R. Merton and R. Nisbet, pp. 21–76. New York: Harcourt, Brace and World, Inc., 1961.

Daniels, Roger. *The Politics of Prejudice*. Berkeley, Calif.: University of California Press, 1962.

————. "Westerners From the East: Oriental Immigrants Re-appraised." Paper presented to the Fifth Annual Conference of the Western History Association, October 15, 1965, at Helena, Montana.

Daws, Gavan. *The Shoal of Time*. New York: The Macmillan Co., 1968.

DeMotte, M. "California . . . White or Yellow? *The Annals* 93 (January 1921): 18–23.

DeVos, George. "A Quantitative Rorschach Assessment of Maladjustment and Rigidity in Acculturating Japanese Americans." *Genetic Psychology Monographs* 52 (1955): 51–87.

————, ed. *Socialization for Achievement*. Berkeley and Los Angeles: University of California Press, 1973.

————, and Hiroshi Wagatsuma, eds. *Japan's Invisible Race*. Berkeley, Calif.: University of California Press, 1966.

Didion, Joan. *Slouching Towards Bethlehem*. New York: Dell Publishing Co., 1961.

Doi, L. T. "Amae—A Key Concept for Understanding Japanese Personality Structure." *Psychologia* 5 (1962): 1–7.

Dore, Ronald P. *City Life in Japan*. Berkeley, Calif.: University of California Press, 1958.

"Emotion-based Problems Among Nikkei Males on Mainland High," *Pacific Citizen*, April 4, 1975.

Enright, J., and W. R. Jaeckle. "Ethnic Differences in Psychopathology." Paper presented at the Pacific Science Congress, August 23, 1961, at Honolulu, Hawaii.

Erickson, Al. "L. A.'s Nisei Today." *California Sun Magazine*, Summer 1958.

Erickson, Erik. *Childhood and Society*. New York: W. W. Norton and Co., 1950.

Fenz, W. D., and Arkoff, A. "Comparative Need Patterns of Five Ancestry Groups in Hawaii." *The Journal of Social Psychology* 58 (1962): 67–89.

Fisher, A. R. *Exile of a Race*. Seattle: Ford T. Publ., 1965.

Fuchs, Lawrence. *Hawaii Pono: A Social History*. New York: Harcourt, 1961.

———. *Family Matters*. New York Random House, 1972.

Glazer, Nathan, and D. P. Moynihan. *Beyond the Melting Pot*. Cambridge, Mass.: MIT and Harvard University Press, 1963.

Gordon, Milton M. *Assimilation in American Life*. New York: Oxford University Press, 1964.

Gordzins, M. *Americans Betrayed*. Chicago: University of Chicago Press, 1949.

Gray, Francine du Plessix. *Hawaii: The Sugar-Coated Fortress*. New York: Vintage Books, Random House, 1973.

Greenwood, Leonard. "Brazil's Japanese: Story of Hardship and Success," *Los Angeles Times*, October 20, 1974.

Gulick, S. L. *The American Japanese Problem*. New York: Charles Scribner's Sons, 1914.

Hansen, Arthur A., and David Hacker. "The Manzanar Riot: An Ethnic Perspective." *Amerasia Journal* 2 (Fall 1974): 112–57.

Haring, Douglas G. "Japanese Character in the 20th Century." *The Annals* (March 1967).

Hawaii, Department of Health. Statistics Dealing with Mental Health Division Patients. Print-out sheets. August 12, 1974.

Hechter, H. H., and N. O. Borhani. "Longevity in Racial Groups Differs." *California's Health* 20 (February 1, 1965).

Hokubei Mainichi Yearbook. San Francisco: Hokubei Mainichi Shinbunsha, 1964.

Hunter, Louise H. *Buddhism in Hawaii*. Honolulu: University of Hawaii Press, 1971.

Ichihashi, Y. *Japanese in the United States*. Stanford, Calif.: Stanford University Press, 1932.

Ichioka, Yuji, Yasuo Sakata, Nobuyas Tsuchida, and Eri Yasuhara. *A Buried Past: An Annotated Bibliography of the Japanese American Research Project Collection*. Berkeley and Los Angeles: University of Calfiornia Press, 1974.

Iga, Mamoru. "Changes in Value Orientation of Japanese-Americans." Paper read at the Western Psychological Association Meeting, April 28, 1966, at Long Beach, California.

————. "Cultural Factors in Suicide of Japanese Youth with Focus on Personality." *Sociological and Social Research* 46 (October 1961).

————. "Do Most Japanese-Americans Living in the United States Still Retain Traditional Japanese Personality?" *Kashu Mainichi (California Daily News)*, Los Angeles, California, June 21, 1967.

Inouye, Daniel. *Journey to Washington.* Englewood Cliffs, N.J.: Prentice-Hall, Inc., 1967.

Inouye, Y. "Wadatsumi," translated by Chizuko Lampman. *The East* 2 (1966): 71–75.

Ishizuka, Yoshikazu. "Resentment Continues to Grow in Hawaii Over Japanese Takeover." *Nichi Bei Times*, San Francisco, April 2, 1974, p. 3.

Ito, Hiroshi. "Japan's Outcasts in the United States." In *"Japan's Invisible Race,"* edited by G. DeVos and H. Wagatsuma, pp. 200–21. Berkeley, Calif.: University of California Press, 1966.

Iwata, Masakazu. "The Japanese Immigrants in California Agriculture." *Agricultural History* 36 (1962): 25–37.

Jacobs, Paul, and Saul Landau. *To Serve the Devil.* Vol. 2. New York: Random House, 1971.

Japanese, Chinese and Filipinos in the United States. 1970 Census of the Population, PC (2)-1G. U.S. Department of Commerce, Bureau of the Census, U.S. Government Printing Office, Washington, D.C., 1973.

The Japanese Immigrant in Brazil. Tokyo: Tokyo University Press, 1964.

"Japanese Immigrants in Brazil." *Population Index* 31 (April 1965): 117–38.

The Japan Times, Tokyo, Japan, March 23, 1967.

Johnson, Herbert B. *Discrimination Against Japanese in California.* Berkeley, Calif.: The Courier Publishing Company, 1907.

Kalish, R. A., M. Maloney, and A. Arkoff. "Cross-Cultural Comparisons of Marital Role Expectations." *The Journal of Social Psychology* 68 (1966): 41–47.

Kaser, Tom. "Japanese Americans Largest Group in the DOE." *Honolulu Advertiser*, Honolulu, Hawaii, July 19, 1974, C-2.

Kiefer, Christie. *Changing Cultures, Changing Lives.* San Francisco: Jossey-Bass, 1974.

Kimura, Yukiko. "Psychological Aspects of Japanese Immigration." *Social Process in Hawaii* 6 (1940): 10–20.

————. "Rumor Among the Japanese." In *Community Forces in Hawaii*, ed. by Bernard Hormann, Honolulu: University of Hawaii Press, 1968.

Kitagawa, Daisuke. *Issei and Nisei: The Internment Years.* New York: The Seabury Press, 1967.

Kitano, Harry H. L. "Changing Achievement Patterns of the Japanese in the United States." *The Journal of Social Psychology* 58 (1962): 257–64.

————. "Differential Child-Rearing Attitudes Between First and Second Generation Japanese in the United States." *The Journal of Social Psychology* 53 (1961): 13–19.

————. "Housing of Japanese Americans in the San Francisco Bay Area." In *Housing and Minority Groups*, edited by N. Glazer and D. McEntire, pp. 178–97. Berkeley, Calif.: University of California Press, 1960.

————. "Inter- and Intragenerational Differences in Maternal Attitudes Towards Child-Rearing." *The Journal of Social Psychology* 63 (1964): 215–20.

————. Japanese-American Crime and Delinquency." *The Journal of Psychology* 66 (1967): 253–63.

————. "Japanese-Americans on the Road to Dissent." In *Seasons of Rebellion*, edited by Joe Boskin and R. Rosenstone, pp. 93–113. New York: Holt, Rinehart & Winston, (1972).

————. "The Japanese in America." Faculty Lecture Series: The Many Faces of Integration, UCLA, October 21, 1963.

————. "Mental Illness in Four Cultures." *The Journal of Social Psychology* 80 (1970): 121–34.

————. "Passive Discrimination: The Normal Person." *The Journal of Social Psychology* 70 (1966): 23–31.

————. *Race Relations.* Englewood Cliffs, N.J.: Prentice-Hall, Inc., 1974.

————. Unpublished collection of private intreviews, letters, and looseleaf data, 1962.

Kong, Hester. "Through the Peepsight of a Grocery Story." In *Community Forces in Hawaii*, edited by Bernard Hormann. Honolulu: University of Hawaii Press, 209–13.

Koyama, Takashi. *A Study of Contemporary Families.* Tokyo: Kobundo, 1960.

Kuroda, Alice K., Kuroda Yasumasa, and Gary Martin. *Hawaii's Reaction to Japanese Investment and Tourism*, paper prepared for delivery at seminar on Japanese investments in Hawaii, sponsored by Honolulu Japanese Chamber of Commerce, Honolulu, Nov. 10, 1973.

Kurokawa, Minako. "Proposed Research in the Field of Childhood Accidents." University of California, May 1964.

Kuwahara, Yasuo, and Gordon Allred. *Kamikaze.* New York: Ballantine Books, 1957.

Kuykendall, R. S. *The Hawaiian Kingdom*, Vol. 3, 1874–1893. Honolulu: University of Hawaii Press, 1967.

Lanman, C. *The Japanese in America.* London: Longmans, Green, Reader and Dyer, 1872.

LaViolette, Forest E. "Canada and Its Japanese." In *Race*, edited by E. Thompson and E. C. Hughes, pp. 149–55. New York: The Free Press, 1958.

Lebra, Takako. "Acculturation Dilemma: The Function of Japanese Moral Values for Americanization." *Council on Anthropology and Education Newsletter* 3 (1972): 6–13.

Leighton, Alexander. *The Governing of Men.* Princeton, N.J.: Princeton University Press, 1945.

Levine, Gene, and Darrel Montero. "Socio-Economic Mobility Among Three Generations of Japanese Americans." *Journal of Social Issues* 29 (1973): 33–48.

Light, Ivan. *Ethnic Enterprise in America.* Berkeley and Los Angeles: University of California Press, 1972.

Lind, Andrew. *Hawaii's Japanese: An Experiment in Democracy.* Princeton, N.J.: Princeton University Press, 1946.

———. *Hawaii's People.* Honolulu: University of Hawaii Press, 1967.

Lomax, Louis E. *The Negro Revolt.* New York: Signet Books, 1963.

Lyman, Stanford. "Higher Education and Cultural Diversity." Workshop presentation given at the Annual Program of the Western College Association, March 10, 1967, at San Diego, California.

McClatchy, V. "Japanese in the Melting Pot: Can They Assimilate and Make Good Citizens?" *The Annals* (January 1921): 29–34.

Matsuura, Patsy. "Language Schools on Shaky Grounds." *Honolulu Star Bulletin and Advertiser,* Sept. 12, 1971, Section C, p. 1.

Memmi, Albert. *The Colonizer and the Colonized. New* York: The Orion Press, 1965.

Meredith, Gerald M. "Amae and Acculturation Among Japanese College Students in Hawaii." *The Journal of Social Psychology* 70 (1966): 171–80.

———. "Observations on the Acculturation of Sansei Japanese Americans in Hawaii." *Psychologia* 8 (June 1965).

———, and C. G. W. Meredith. "Acculturation and Personality Among Japanese-American College Students in Hawaii." *The Journal of Social Psychology* 68 (1966): 175–82.

Merton, R. K. *Social Theory and Social Structure.* Glencoe, Ill.: The Free Press, 1961.

Meyer, Dillon S. "The WRA Says 'Thirty,' " *The New Republic,* June 1945.

Miranda, Manuel, and Harry H. L. Kitano. "Barriers to Mental Health Services: A Japanese and Mexican-American Dilemma," in progress.

Misaki, H. K. *Delinquency of Japanese in California.* Education-Psychology Series, vol. 1. Stanford, Calif.: Stanford University Press, 1933.

Miyakawa, T. Scott. Japanese-American Research Project. Private discussion, August 16, 1966.

Miyaki, M. *Outline of Japanese Judiciary.* Tokyo: The Japan Times Mail, 1935.

Miyamoto, Frank. "Social Solidarity Among the Japanese in Seattle." *University of Washington Publications in the Social Sciences* 11 (December 1939): 57–130.

Miyamato, Kazu. *Hawaii, End of the Rainbow.* Rutland, Vermont and Tokyo: Charles E. Tuttle Co., 1964.

Mizushima, Keiichi. "Delinqunecy and Social Change in Modern Japan." In *Socialization for Achievement,* edited by George DeVos, pp. 327–68. Berkeley and Los Angeles: University of California Press, 1973.

Modell, John. *The Kikuchi Diary.* Urbana, Ill.: University of Illinois Press, 1973.

Morimoto, Kiyo. "A Developmental Analysis of the Japanese Community in Pocatello, Idaho." Term paper, May 25, 1956.

Mosley, Leonard. *Hirohito.* Englewood Cliffs, N.J.: Prentice-Hall, Inc., 1966.

Myers, Dillon. *Uprooted Americans.* Tucson, Ariz.: University of Arizona Press, 1971.

Nakane, Chie. *Japanese Society.* Berkeley and Los Angeles: University of California Press, 1970.

Nee, Victor G., and Brett DeBary. *Longtime Californ'.* Boston: Houghton Mifflin, 1974.

Nichi-bei Times. San Francisco, California, April 23, 1959.

———. San Francisco, California, December 3, 1963.

———. San Francisco, California, January 24, 1965.

O'Brien, Robert W. "Selective Dispersion as a Factor in the Solution of the Nisei Problem." *Social Forces* 23 (December 1944): 140–47.

Ogawa, Dennis. *Jan Ken Po.* Honolulu: Japanese Chamber of Commerce, 1973.

Okano, Yukio. "Correlating of Ethnic Identity in Japanese Americans." Masters' thesis, University of Denver, 1970.

Okimoto, Daniel. *Americans in Disguise.* New York: Walker, Weatherhill, 1971.

Okumura, Takie. *Seventy Years of Divine Blessings.* N.P., 1939, 191 pages (autobiography).

Onishi, Katsumi. Lecture in a class of American Studies 620, at the University of Hawaii, Honolulu, on July 17, 1974.

Owan, Tom. "Asian Americans. A Case of Benighted Neglect and the Urgent Need for Affirmative Action." Paper prepared for the Social Security Administration, October 1974.

Peterson, William. "Success Story: Japanese American Style," *The New York Times,* January 9, 1966.

Reynolds, C. N. "Oriental-White Race Relations in Santa Clara County, California." Ph.D. dissertation, Stanford University, 1927.

Sabagh, George, and Dorothy S. Thomas, "Changing Patterns of Fertility and Survival Among the Japanese Americans on the Pacific Coast." *American Sociological Review* 10 (October 1945): 651–58.

Samuels, Frederick. *The Japanese and the Haoles of Honolulu.* New Haven, Conn.: College and University Press, 1970.

San Francisco Chronicle, May 16, 1900.

———, August 2, 1900.

Sasaki, J. K. Private interview, May 19, 1966.

Sherman, Bezalel. *The Jew Within American Society*. Detroit: Wayne State University Press, 1961.

Shibutani, Tamotsu, and Kian Kwan. *Ethnic Stratification*. New York: The Macmillan Co., 1965.

Shimamoto, Gail. "Participant Observation and Interviews with Japanese Families." Class paper, International Christian University, Tokyo, 1973.

Smith, Bradford. *Americans from Japan*. Philadelphia: J. B. Lippincott Co., 1948.

Strong, Edward K., Jr. *The Second Generation Japanese Problem*. Stanford, Calif.: Stanford University Press, 1934.

Tachiki, Amy, Eddie Wong, and Franklin Odo, eds. *Roots: An Asian American Reader*. Los Angeles: UCLA Asian-American Studies Center, 1971.

Tamashiro, John. The Japanese in the United States as Discussed in the Editorial Pages of the *Honolulu Advertiser* and the *Honolulu Star Bulletin* from June 1, 1941 to Dec. 31, 1945 (Dept. of American Studies, University of Hawaii). Unpublished dissertation, draft copy in process, 1972.

ten Broek, Jacobus, E. Barnhart, and F. Matson. *Prejudice, War and the Constitution*. Berkeley, Calif.: University of California Press, 1954.

"The Rainbow," A History of the Japanese Chamber of Commerce. Honolulu: Honolulu Japanese Chamber of Commerce, 1970.

Thomas, Dorothy S. *The Salvage*. Berkeley, Calif.: University of California Press, 1952.

————, and R. Nishimoto. *The Spoilage*. Berkeley Calif.: University of Californ Press, 1946.

Tinker, John N. "Intermarriage and Ethnic Boundaries: The Japanese American Case." *Journal of Social Issues* 29 (1973): 49–66.

Tsutsumi, Chizuko. "World of Mrs. Kiyoko Smith." Japanese-American marriage study report. Mimeographed. San Francisco: International Institute, 1962.

U.S. Department of Commerce, Bureau of the Census. *Japanese, Chinese, and Filipinos in the United States*. 1970 Census of the Population, PC (2)-1G. Washington, D.C.: Government Printing Office, 1973.

U.S. Department of the Interior, War Relocation Authority. *Impounded People*. Washington, D.C.: Government Printing Office, n.d.

U.S. Department of Justice, Federal Bureau of Investigation. *Crime in the United States*. Uniform Crime Reports, 1940, 1950, 1960.

————. *Crime in the United States*. Uniform Crime Reports, 1964–73.

Uyeki, Eugene. "Correlates of Ethnic Identification." *American Journal of Sociology* 65 (March 1960): 468–74.

Vogel, Ezra, *Japan's New Middle Class: The Salary Man and His Family in a Tokyo Suburb*. Berkeley and Los Angeles: University of California Press, 1965.

Wakukawa, Ernest C. *A History of the Japanese People in Hawaii.* Honolulu: The Toyo Shoin, 1938.

Who's Who in Government in Hawaii (1971–72). Honolulu, Hawaii, Chamber of Commerce.

Wong, Harold H. "The Relative Economic Status of Chinese, Japanese, Black, and White Men in California." Ph.D. dissertation, University of California, 1974.

Wood, Ben. "Driftwood." *Honolulu Star Bulletin,* July 7, 1974, Section G-1.

Yomiuri Shimbun. Tokyo, September 15, 1966.

Yoshida, Jim, and Bill Hoslokawa. *The Two Worlds of Jim Yoshida.* New York: William Morrow and Co., 1972.

Index